EDWIN ARLINGTON I

A Critical Stud

EDWIN ARLINGTON ROBINSON

A Critical Study
by ELLSWORTH BARNARD

OCTAGON BOOKS

A DIVISION OF FARRAR, STRAUS AND GIROUX

New York   1977

Copyright, 1952 by The Macmillan Company

Reprinted 1969
by special arrangement with Ellsworth Barnard
Second Octagon printing 1977

OCTAGON BOOKS
A DIVISION OF FARRAR, STRAUS & GIROUX, INC.
19 Union Square West
New York, N.Y. 10003

LIBRARY OF CONGRESS CATALOG CARD NUMBER: 70-88599
ISBN 0-374-90380-8

Manufactured by Braun-Brumfield, Inc.
Ann Arbor, Michigan
Printed in the United States of America

For my mother and father

Acknowledgments

Many of my obligations for permission to quote copyrighted material are indicated on the copyright page. My greatest debt is to The Macmillan Company for permission to quote at length from the indispensable *Collected Poems, Selected Letters,* and Hermann Hagedorn's *Edwin Arlington Robinson;* and more briefly from Robinson's play *Van Zorn,* Charles Cestre's *An Introduction to Edwin Arlington Robinson,* Robert Frost's "Introduction" to *King Jasper,* Daniel Gregory Mason's *Music in My Time,* and Harriet Monroe's *Poets and Their Art.*

The quotations from Robinson's *The Town Down the River* and the quotation from Allen Tate's *Reactionary Essays* are used by permission of the publishers, Charles Scribner's Sons. The passages from *Untriangulated Stars: Letters of Edwin Arlington Robinson to Harry de Forest Smith, 1890–1905,* edited by Denham Sutcliffe, and Laura E. Richards's *E. A. R.* are reprinted by permission of the publishers, the Harvard University Press. The material from Esther Willard Bates's *Edwin Arlington Robinson and His Manuscripts* and *Letters of E. A. Robinson to Howard G. Schmitt,* edited by Carl J. Weber, is quoted by special permission of the Colby College Press (Waterville, Maine). The quotations from Rollo Walter Brown's *Next Door to a Poet,* Laura E. Richards's *Stepping Westward,* and T. K. Whipple's *Spokesmen* are reprinted by permission of Appleton-Century-Crofts, Inc. To all these publishers my thanks are due.

I am especially grateful to William Sloane Associates, Inc., and to New Directions (Norfolk, Connecticut) for their generous permission to quote a number of passages from Emery Neff's *Edwin Arling-*

ton Robinson and Yvor Winters's *Edwin Arlington Robinson,* respectively, two works with which my own may appear to be to some extent in competition. I wish also to record my indebtedness to Curtis Brown, Ltd., for permission to quote from John Drinkwater's *The Muse in Council* (originally published by Houghton Mifflin Company); to Harcourt, Brace and Company for permission to quote from Mabel Dodge Luhan's *Movers and Shakers;* to Harper & Brothers for permission to quote from Aldous Huxley's *Eyeless in Gaza* and Joyce Kilmer's *Literature in the Making;* to Henry Holt and Company, Inc., for permission to quote from Theodore Maynard's *Our Best Poets* and Robert Frost's *The Masque of Reason;* to Houghton Mifflin Company for permission to quote from Amy Lowell's *Tendencies in Modern American Poetry* (originally published by The Macmillan Company); to Medill McBride Company for permission to quote from Ben Ray Redman's *Edwin Arlington Robinson;* and to the Viking Press, Inc., for permission to quote from Carl Van Doren's *Three Worlds* (originally published by Harper & Brothers).

I am also under obligations to the Duke University Press for permission to quote from David Brown's "A note on *Avon's Harvest,*" Louise Dauner's "The Pernicious Rib: E. A. Robinson's Concept of Feminine Character," and Floyd Stovall's "The Optimism Behind Robinson's Tragedies," from *American Literature;* and Frederika Beatty's "Edwin Arlington Robinson As I Knew Him," from the *South Atlantic Quarterly.* I am also indebted to the editors of the following periodical: the *Catholic World,* for permission to quote from William T. Walsh's "Some Recollections of E. A. Robinson"; the *Commonweal,* for permission to quote from Henry Morton Robinson's "No Epitaph"; the *Nation,* for permission to quote from Eda Lou Walton's "Robinson's Women"; the *New England Quarterly,* for permission to quote from Louise Dauner's "Vox Clamantis: Edwin Arlington Robinson As a Critic of American Democracy," and Lewis M. Isaacs's "E. A. Robinson Speaks of Music"; the *New Republic,* for permission to quote from Malcolm Cowley's "Edwin Arlington Robinson: Defeat and Triumph"; *Poetry,* for permission to quote from Hoyt H. Hudson's "Robinson and Praed"; the *Satur-*

day Review of Literature, for permission to quote in full a letter from Robinson to Carl J. Weber concerning *The Whip* and a letter from Earl F. Walbridge offering an interpretation of *En Passant;* the *Virginia Quarterly Review* and Mr. Daniel Gregory Mason for permission to quote from "Early Letters of Edwin Arlington Robinson"; and the *Explicator*, with the authors, for permission to quote from notes on *Luke Havergal* and *For a Dead Lady* by Richard Crowder and Robert H. Super, respectively.

My thanks are also due to the following persons: Mr. H. Bacon Collamore, for permission to quote from a letter by Robinson printed in his *Edwin Arlington Robinson;* Miss Louise Dauner, for permission to quote from an unpublished chapter of her doctoral dissertation, *Studies in Edwin Arlington Robinson;* Mr. Edwin S. Fussell, for permission to quote from his unpublished doctoral dissertation, *The Early Poetry of Edwin Arlington Robinson;* Mr. Alfred Kreymborg, for permission to quote from *Our Singing Strength* (originally published by Coward-McCann, Inc.); Mr. Ludwig Lewisohn, for permission to quote from *The Story of American Literature* (originally published by Harper & Brothers); Mr. Lloyd Morris, for permission to quote from *The Poetry of Edwin Arlington Robinson* (originally published by George H. Doran Company); and above all, Mrs. William Nivison, the poet's niece, for her cordial interest in my undertaking, as well as for permission to quote from Robinson's unpublished letters in Houghton Library at Harvard University. I am also indebted to Professor William A. Jackson, Librarian, for making these letters available to me; and I am grateful to the staffs of Widener, Lamont, and Houghton libraries for their friendly and efficient aid.

To more or less complete my list of obligations for quoted material, I ought to mention reports of three important interviews with Robinson: one by Nancy Evans in the *Bookman*, which has ceased publication; and two in the Boston *Evening Transcript*, by William Stanley Braithwaite and Karl Schriftgiesser, respectively. And I have been helped in many ways, although I have not had occasion to quote from it, by Charles Beecher Hogan's *A Bibliography of Edwin Arlington Robinson*.

Preface

Few twentieth century poets have been more written about than Robinson. Recognized during the twenties, after a quarter-century of relative neglect, as the foremost of America's living poets, he became the subject of many articles and several books. Some of these reached a high critical level, and have permanent value; but all are necessarily tentative. Even Charles Cestre's full-scale study at the end of the decade, which won the warm approval of the poet himself, missed the last six volumes of Robinson's verse and took no account of his life, then almost completely unknown to anyone but a few intimate friends.

The six volumes just mentioned, each except *Nicodemus* devoted to a single long and not always lucid narrative, all even-tempered, farsighted, resolute in following a long-since-charted course through the gathering hurricane of social change, seemed to have little to say to a generation struggling, if not for mere survival, for one sort or another of escape; and neither the tributes evoked by Robinson's death nor the admirable biography by Hermann Hagedorn could check the trend of taste away from a poet whose deepest roots, after all, were in the nineteenth century.

The continuing publication of letters and reminiscences, however, has shown this trend to be far from uniform; and the recent book-length studies by Yvor Winters and Emery Neff testify further to the permanence and force of Robinson's appeal. Yet neither of these two works—partly because of the limitations imposed by the plans of the series to which they respectively belong—has provided the full and systematic treatment of his poetry by which alone this appeal can be adequately defined. There is still room for other critics to try their hand at such a definition.

There will, as a matter of fact, always be room. The present study, despite its length, makes no pretensions to being "definitive." Robinson's life and character, for instance, are treated only as they are directly related to his poetry. Also deliberately excluded, as a primary subject of investigation, is the relation between his work and that of earlier or contemporary writers. And even in the analysis and interpretation of the poetry itself, it is not to be expected that an achievement of such extent, variety, and complexity will be identically viewed by any two critics. Even when there is general agreement, there will be different emphases and illustrations.

On the subject of critical disagreement, a little more should perhaps be said. Where I have quoted and then tried to controvert the opinions of other critics—occasionally in regard to taste but more often in regard to interpretation—I have of course not done so for the sake of controversy; but partly to indicate the elusiveness of much of Robinson's work and the consequent need for searching reflection on the part of the individual reader; and partly, after this, to help establish some measure of general agreement as to what particular poems *mean*—without which, it seems to me, the reader's satisfaction will be incomplete.

This procedure is likely to give the impression of greater disparity than actually exists between my own views and those of other critics; and this is especially true in regard to the work of Mr. Winters and Mr. Neff, simply because they, more than preceding critics, have really come to grips with some of Robinson's obscurer poems and have advanced specific suggestions as to what these pieces are about. I should be sorry to have the reader infer a general disapproval from particular disagreements; and I should like to say that I have read these works, as well as others that I have occasion to mention less frequently or not at all, with both pleasure and profit.

The kind of discussion just referred to is as a rule confined to the notes, where it need not trouble the incurious. It is not intended only for specialists, however; and nothing is included that does not seem to me to have at least an indirect bearing on some important aspect of Robinson's work.

The notes also record the sources of all quotations except those from Robinson's verse. To have given the exact location of each of the latter would have cluttered many pages with references that few readers would have wished to follow up; and those persons who desire to see the passages in context can read the poems in which they occur, which are usually named. The present study, after all, while it assumes no special knowledge of Robinson's poetry on the part of the reader, is not a substitute for the poetry.

Contents

EDWIN ARLINGTON ROBINSON

A Critical Study

ERRATA

p. 41, l. 8 of the quotation for *have* read *had*

p. 294, note 17, l. 10 for *Steal* read *Seal;* so

p. 310, index entry *"Slumber"* and

p. 311, index entry "Wordsworth"

A Foreword on Criticism

"I believe so firmly that poetry that is good for anything speaks for itself that I feel foolish when I try to talk about it."[1] This downright declaration by Robinson would, if taken at face value, leave the critic of poetry no reason for existing. Obviously, however, poetry cannot speak for itself unless it is read; and although Robinson himself was averse to discussing his work in public, he was always gratified to have it discussed intelligently by others. "I am much more than pleased," he wrote to Hermann Hagedorn in 1918, "with your suggestion about a possible article on the Arthurian poems, for I know that they will never be read until people are made to read them." [2]

The second part of this remark applies equally well, or ill, to much of his other poetry; and the present study rests on the assumption that he is partly right. It is true that to *make* people read poetry is an ungrateful if not impossible task. But to make them *want* to read poetry (or other forms of literature), and to enable them to read it with increased understanding and enjoyment, may be reasonably regarded as the sole—and sufficient—aim of the critic. It is true that critics have not always been content with so humble a role; but the best of them have always agreed that the creative power is primary. The creator comes first, and the critic exists to mediate between his creations and the public taste, to extend and refine the appreciation of his work.

In accepting this principle, the critic also accepts certain obligations. One of these is to keep his eye steadily focused on the literature itself of which he is writing; he should not confuse criticism with other forms of intellectual enterprise, such as biography or psychology or cultural history or the study of literary relationships. The New Critics are right in their concern, as critics, with results and not with causes, with the *what* and not with the *why* or the *whence*. The critic simply asks about a poet (for example): "What does he try to do? What is his work *like?*"

Yet (as all good critics, new and old, acknowledge in practice) poems are made by persons, and persons are members of a society. A poet does not exist in a vacuum, and his poetry is not made out of nothing. The more we know about his life and character apart from his work, and the more we know about the society to which he has belonged, the more fully and accurately we shall understand what he is trying to do, the more clearly we shall see what his work is like. To deny this statement is no less unreasonable than to assume that the important thing about a poem is its supposed literary or psychic origins—that it is to be taken as merely the starting point in a detective story, the corpse (and that is what it becomes) whose presence is to be explained. On the other hand, it is hard not to feel that for some of the New Critics, also, a piece of literature is a corpse—the difference being that their interest is in a post-mortem.

Another aim that often diverts the critic's eye from the work itself, and distorts his account of what it is like, is the desire to prove a thesis—to fit the work neatly into some fixed design or theory, leaving no untidy loose ends. This is a normal result of the systematizing tendency of the human mind, strengthened by the false analogy, so long and generally accepted by scholars, between the aim and method governing research in the natural sciences and those appropriate to the study of the humanities. It has been further stimulated by the Darwinian competition for academic advancement, which college and university administrators have made largely dependent on the number of scholarly books and articles to which a teacher's name is attached; for an easy way to practice "productive scholarship" is to evolve a theory which will permit an author's life or character or writings to be explained or interpreted or classified in a fashion hitherto unthought of. If the soundness of the theory is challenged, so much the better; the proponent's name is again called to the attention of at least a little corner of the learned world, and he also gets a chance, by defending his thesis, to add another item to his list of publications. And all this, besides looking to the main chance, gratifies his private vanity.

It does not, however, make for good criticism. No author who is worth writing about can be fitted into a formula, except by the Procrustean stretching and cleaving that Robinson refers to in another connection. Even a generally sound view will have to be modified at many points, for no man of genius is wholly consistent. Of course there is bound to be a general pattern, and the critic has a right and duty to say what he thinks it is. But it is also his duty to do his best (in the words of Arnold, who was not always able to harmonize practice and precept) "to see the object as in itself it really is," and then to report what he sees.

This report may include personal preferences, but it will not attempt absolute evaluations. One obligation that the critic does *not* have is to play God at a literary Last Judgment. Judgment is not for him but for his readers—after they have read the original works. His part is to present the evidence, and to present it honestly, not seeking either to canonize or to condemn—though he may permit himself to rebuke irresponsible disparagement or fulsome eulogy. He plays the judge only in seeing that the evidence is relevant and is presented without prejudice, and in charging the jury concerning the real issues.

This is not to set up the repellent and unattainable aim of complete impersonality. The critic owes it to his readers to make clear his individual response to the literature with which he is dealing, and this response includes the pleasure or displeasure or mixture of both that he feels while reading it; and he will also try to trace the sources of his approval or repugnance. But he will not, if he desires the good opinion of reasonable readers, attempt to elevate a private preference or distaste to the level of ultimate truth.

The pointlessness of authoritarian judgments appears in the estimates of *The Man Against the Sky* that are offered in the two most recent book-length studies of Robinson, written by critics who greatly admire the man and the poet, and who are members in good standing of the fraternity of letters. One declares: "Philosophically, the poem is unimpressive; stylistically, it is all quite as weak as the lines referred to above [the seven lines beginning "But this we know, if we know anything"]; and structurally, it seems to defeat its purpose—for while it purports to be an expression of faith, it is devoted in all save these same few lines to the expression of despair." [3] The other declares: " 'The Man Against the Sky,' bringing to bear upon the supreme problem of human destiny consummate qualities of intellect, human understanding, and art, towers above any other poem written upon American soil." [4]

Twenty-odd years of encountering such contradictory opinions have convinced the present writer, who once held somewhat different views of the critic's function, of the absurdity of pretending that any literary judgment is more than the expression of a personal taste. And if this conviction seems to lead to esthetic nihilism, my answer is that it seems to me to be in accord not only with the facts but with the philosophy that most of us say we believe in. The dictatorship exercised by the Soviet leaders, for example, in the realm of art is detestable not so much because many of its particular judgments seem to most of us to be so egregious, as because of the assumption that in this realm any authority can be absolute.

Yet it would seem that in practice, on the whole and in the long run (in Western civilization, at least), those persons who appear to be the best informed and most sensitive *do* more or less agree in valuing some works of literature more highly than others. And although democracy grants—depends on, in fact, for its very life— the right of anyone to think as he chooses, its justification lies in the faith that this liberty leads individuals eventually to an acquaintance with (borrowing Arnold's words once more) "the best that has been thought and said in the world."

It therefore becomes the critic's duty (defined by such a faith and assumed in all humility) to quicken and to guide this movement of the mind. Thus the argument brings us back to the initial assumption about the critic's function and leads us to place upon him a further obligation; namely, to be intelligible. Men of letters have censured as "jargon" the technical vocabulary developed by social scientists, which the latter defend as a convenience in writing for fellow specialists. But no such defense is valid for the contemporary critics who have developed a vocabulary equally specialized and equally beyond the grasp of the "intelligent layman" if not of the busy teacher of English. Literature is made to be *read*, if not by *the* public, at least by *a* public, and not merely by specialists. The literary artist is "a man speaking to men"; and so, properly, is the literary critic, whose primary function is to awaken in a widening circle of readers the state of mind and the quality of feeling that make possible the enjoyment of "good literature." There are, of course, technical matters, and hence technical terms, with which artist and critic must doubtless be familiar. But these, for the most part, do not concern the public. And if either artist or critic fails to take as his aim the sharing of experience, not only with fellow initiates but with all who wish to share it and who are familiar with the language that the great writers themselves have traditionally been content to use, then he is condemning his work to deserved and not distant oblivion.

A last obligation of the critic is, if possible, to be himself an artist—not merely to make his words intelligible but to give them intensity, not only to clarify his subject but to illuminate it. In an age when the making of books is a process endless beyond what the Preacher ever dreamed of, a critic is scarcely justified in asking anyone to read a book that he has not done his best to make readable.

These remarks are not intended to sound dogmatic or to be unduly challenging, but rather to make clear what is aimed at in this study. The reader will decide how far the stated aims deserve approval and how far they have been adhered to.

ROBINSON'S LIFE: CHIEF EVENTS

December 22, 1869.   Birth at Head Tide, Maine.

September, 1870.   Removal of family to Gardiner, Maine.

June, 1888.   Graduation from Gardiner High School.

1888–1891.   Residence in Gardiner, doing odd jobs and writing verse.

September, 1891.   Matriculation at Harvard as a special student.

July, 1892.   Death of his father.

June, 1893.   Conclusion of study at Harvard.

1893–1897.   Residence in Gardiner, writing poetry, short stories (later destroyed), and a translation, with Harry de Forest Smith, of Sophocles' *Antigone* (fragments published in *Untriangulated Stars*).

November, 1896.   Death of his mother.

December, 1897.   First visit to New York.

1898.   Residence in New York, Cambridge, Gardiner, and Winthrop, Maine.

January–June, 1899.   Employment in administrative office at Harvard.

September, 1899.   Death of his brother Dean.

October, 1899.   Return to New York.

Autumn, 1903–
August, 1904.   Employment on New York subway project.

January–May, 1905.   Employment in drygoods store of his friend William E. Butler in Boston.

6

June, 1905.	Appointment by Theodore Roosevelt to sinecure in the office of the Collector of Customs, New York.
August 12, 1905.	Review of *The Children of the Night* by Theodore Roosevelt in the *Outlook*.
1906–1913.	Attempts at commercial play writing and later at writing novels (which he destroyed).
1909.	Death of his brother Herman.
June, 1909.	Resignation of his position in the Customs Service.
July–October, 1910.	Residence in Chocorua, New Hampshire.
July–September, 1911.	Residence at the MacDowell Colony, Peterborough, New Hampshire (where he spent each succeeding summer until his death).
December 21, 1919.	Fiftieth anniversary tributes by contemporary poets in *The New York Times Book Review*.
1922.	Award of Pulitzer Prize for *Collected Poems*.
April–July, 1923.	Visit to England.
1924.	Award of Pulitzer Prize for *The Man Who Died Twice*.
1927.	Sensational success of *Tristram*. Award of Pulitzer Prize.
April 5, 1935.	Death from cancer.

ROBINSON'S MAJOR PUBLICATIONS

(*The date is that of the first trade edition.*)

The Torrent and The Night Before. November, 1896. Privately printed.
The Children of the Night. December, 1897. Richard J. Badger. Second
    edition, 1905. Scribner's.
Captain Craig. October, 1902. Houghton Mifflin. Revised edition, 1915.
    Macmillan.
The Town Down the River. October, 1910. Scribner's.
Van Zorn (prose play). September, 1914. Macmillan.
The Porcupine (prose play). September, 1915. Macmillan.
The Man Against the Sky. February, 1916. Macmillan.
Merlin. March, 1917. Macmillan.
Lancelot. April, 1920. Thomas Seltzer.
The Three Taverns. September, 1920. Macmillan.
Avon's Harvest. March, 1921. Macmillan.
Collected Poems. October, 1921. Macmillan. Expanded editions in 1927,
    1929, 1937.
Roman Bartholow. March, 1923. Macmillan.
The Man Who Died Twice. March, 1924. Macmillan.
Dionysus in Doubt. April, 1925. Macmillan.
Tristram. May, 1927. Macmillan.
Cavender's House. April, 1929. Macmillan.
The Glory of the Nightingales. September, 1930. Macmillan.
Matthias at the Door. September, 1931. Macmillan.
Nicodemus. September, 1932. Macmillan.
Talifer. October, 1933. Macmillan.
Amaranth. September, 1934. Macmillan.
King Jasper. November, 1935. Macmillan.

chapter i: POETICS

"If I could have done anything else on God's green earth, I never would have written poetry. There was nothing else I could do, and I had to justify my existence." [1] Thus, in characteristically negative fashion, Robinson answers for himself the question, "Why does a poet write poetry?" And his answer comes down to the same thing that all great poets have said who have answered the question at all: "A poet writes because he must."

Robinson is like most of these poets, also, in that the record of his life attests the truth of his assertion. For him no more than for them was the pursuit of poetry pleasant or easy. To him no more quickly than to most of them did fame and security come, nor at a lower cost in pain and struggle. If he was in the end more fortunate than some of his predecessors, it was because he managed to stay alive longer—just how, he himself sometimes wondered. [2] "I knew from the beginning that I was in for it," [3] he said late in life; but the urge to write poetry was unconquerable. "Writing has been my dream ever since I was old enough to lay a plan for an air castle," [4] he told his friend Arthur Gledhill, when he was twenty-four, and still without a vocation, despite the admonitions of a New England conscience that he should be doing something of practical worth. The trouble was, as he remarked in the same letter, "This itch for authorship . . . spoils a man for anything else." But it was more than an itch for authorship; it was an organic and ineradicable need to embody in verse his response to the world of

9

which he found himself a part; though with characteristic self-distrust he sometimes spoke as if it had been the inability to do anything better that drove him into writing poetry; whereas, obviously, it was his passion to write poetry that destroyed any potential leaning toward other occupations.

To his sister-in-law, Emma Robinson, at about the time when he was seeking a publisher for his first volume, he said, "I can't do anything but write poetry, and perhaps I can't do even that, but I'm going to try." [5] Another acceptance of this fate, in the same grim mood, is expressed in a letter to his friend Harry de Forest Smith: "To be born with just one thing to live for, and that thing a relative impossibility, is to be born with certain disadvantages." [6] Many years later, when *The Man Against the Sky* had won enough recognition to make him less morbidly fearful of being accused of vanity, he urged a friend who thought of writing his biography: "Make clear to those people who say I gave up great things to write poetry, that there was only one thing in the world that I could give up, and that was writing poetry, for that was all that meant anything to me." [7]

This is the key to Robinson's dogged adherence, through years and then decades of disappointment, to a life that he knew the world in general would judge to be aimless and worthless. It was this that made impossible the comfortable pattern of life accepted by his boyhood acquaintances in Gardiner, Maine, and made irresistible, after a period of restless drifting, the unclear call of lights and voices from "the Town down the River"—New York. It made him face year after year of loneliness in cramped and desolate attic rooms, forced for mere survival to choose between the dreary, deadening monotony of a job on the subway project and the humiliation of charity, however generously offered, from his friends. It made him refuse Theodore Roosevelt's offers of government sinecures that would have taken him outside New York City, where he felt that his work had to be done, reducing the President to what must have been for him a uniquely plaintive query, "Will you let me know what kind of a place it is that you could accept?" [8] It finally drew him away from the saloons where he

sought to drown in alcohol the bitter taste of life's pervasive wretch-
edness. It called him back, after his excursions into the bypaths of
play writing and fiction, inspired partly by the spiritual need for
recognition and partly by the mundane need for cash, to the nar-
row way and the strait gate that led at last to acknowledged poetic greatness.

Something of this story we find reflected in *Rembrandt to Rembrandt*, in the once honored and now ignored painter's wrestlings
with his two attendant spirits—the evil one bidding him renounce
his vision of how his work should be done, the good one urging
him to hold to it, in the certitude that he is the servant of a Power
that will not betray him, and in whose service is to be found a
richer reward than that of popular acclaim: "You made your picture as your demon willed it;/ That's about all of that." And to this
"wiser spirit" Rembrandt listens:

> for there's a string in me
> Somewhere that answers—which is natural,
> Since I am but a living instrument
> Played on by powers that are invisible.

So Robinson was able to wait, secure in the faith that he was
doing what had been given him to do. But how hard the waiting
was we can read in the ruin of Fernando Nash in *The Man Who
Died Twice*, and in Fargo's darkly destined wanderings among the
infernal threats and temptations and the lost or branded souls in
the "wrong world" of *Amaranth*. For perhaps never was the certitude of power possessed by all great artists alloyed by so complete a
lack of egotism, so strong a constitutional capacity for self-
depreciation, as it was in Robinson. Not only was his published
work ignored by the critics and the public—when it finally *was*
published—but he found his opinion of his own compositions
changing from year to year, as the excitement of creating them
faded into the past.[9]

So his waiting, though calm, had an undercurrent of grimness.
"I know that I can keep on waiting for some time longer in the
dark. It may be worth while, or it may not, but anyhow it seems to
be the only work that I can come within a twelve-inch gun shot of

doing at all. The present day disregard of everything save dynamics and dollars does not worry me in the least. If I happen to be ground to pieces in the hopper, I still have faith in the pieces." [10] Thus he wrote in 1904, when success, as he foresaw, lay far in the future; and it bears witness to the truth of what he told another friend almost thirty years later: "It is good too to know that you have a light, for without one a fellow is either comfortably blind or wretchedly astray. I have always had one to keep me going, though I fear that you and several others have thought at times that it was burning pretty low. Maybe it was, but it never went out." [11]

This peculiar blend of faith and foreboding underlies many of Robinson's comments on poetic "inspiration." It finds a figurative expression in a letter to a poet friend: "I discovered long ago that an artist is just a sort of living whistle through which Something blows." [12] "No one who writes poetry," he observed more cautiously to an interviewer, "can tell why he wrote it." [13] But if poets write because they must, it appears that some who must write are not poets. "I imagine," he told an inquirer, "that the worst poetry in the world has been written in the finest frenzy of inspiration"— adding immediately and characteristically, "and so, probably, has the best." [14] In the same letter he implies that the person who chooses a career as a poet takes an inescapable risk: he must be "ready to gamble his life away for the sake of winning the possible conjunction of a few inevitable words." In a similar mood he speaks in *Caput Mortuum* of "Art's long hazard, where no man may choose/ Whether he play to win or toil to lose."

Perhaps the most tragic among the second group named in this quotation are those who have a vision that would answer a need and command a response from their fellow men, but who have not the power to express it for their own or any future generation; who are, as Captain Craig observes, attuned without their will to

> "the rhythm of God
> That beats unheard through songs of shattered men
> Who dream but cannot sound it."

This conception leads naturally to the analogy in *Many Are Called* between the grace of Apollo and that of the Christian God,

which is vouchsafed (according to one of the strange hard sayings
of the Gospels) inexplicably and irresistibly to but a few of the
many who seek it:

> The Lord Apollo, who has never died,
> Still holds alone his immemorial reign,
> Supreme in an impregnable domain
> That with his magic he has fortified;
> And though melodious multitudes have tried
> In ecstasy, in anguish, and in vain,
> With invocation sacred and profane
> To lure him, even the loudest are outside.
>
> Only at unconjectured intervals,
> By will of him on whom no man may gaze,
> By word of him whose law no man has read,
> A questing light may rift the sullen walls,
> To cling where mostly its infrequent rays
> Fall golden on the patience of the dead.

The last two lines darken the picture still further. For even when
the inspiration is genuine, and even when the achievement is real,
recognition is most often delayed until the poet has died. In the
very nature of things, Robinson would seem to say, artistic excellence must at first encounter resistance or neglect. Only a remnant
realize their dream of assured and acknowledged achievement.

In the long view, perhaps, for Robinson as for Captain Craig,
"The songs all count"—those unsung or out of tune, as well as
those that triumph. But that is another story.

2

So much for the origin of poetry. What of the technique and the
conscious aim? How does a poet actually work, and what does he
work toward?

First, one might safely guess from Robinson's remark about the
source of "the worst poetry in the world" that he does not consider
poetic creation to be merely a matter of "automatic writing."

Apollo may give permission, or even commands, but it is the finite human person that, so far as he is able, executes the design. Of course the essence of poetry remains indefinable and inexplicable; craftsmanship is not enough.[15] But craftsmanship is indispensable.

One may therefore imagine the arduousness of creating poetry when it is done by an artist so analytical and self-conscious as Robinson. "Work with me," he once commented, speaking of the work of writing verse, "means studying the ceiling and my navel for four hours and then writing down perhaps four lines—sometimes as many as seven and again none at all." [16] And this was long after an apprenticeship that had begun as early as his teens, and that was exacting, strenuous, and prolonged. As a youth in high school he translated Cicero's first oration against Catiline and then long passages of Virgil's *Aeneïd* into more than tolerable blank verse. A little later, under the tutelage of Gardiner's eccentric Dr. Schumann, he disciplined himself by the mastery of such demanding forms of poetic artifice as triolets, villanelles, rondeaus, and ballades. "I could never make a rapid writer; I am too fussy. I have fiddled too much over sonnets and ballades." [17] Thus he wrote to Smith in 1893; and two years later he was even more emphatic. "It is hunting for hours after one word and then not getting it that plays the devil with a man's gray matter and makes him half ready to doubt the kindness of the Scheme." [18]

The same attitude is revealed in a letter written many years later: "I thought nothing when I was writing my first book of working for a week over a single line." He "tinkered" some of his sonnets "('The Clerks', for example) for a month"; others, like *On the Night of a Friend's Wedding*, were "begun suddenly, and later worked over for an immoderate length of time":[19]

In those days, time had no special significance for a certain juvenile and incorrigible fisher of words who thought nothing of fishing for two weeks to catch a stanza, or even a line, that he would not throw back into a squirming sea of language where there was every word but the one he wanted. There were strange and iridescent and impossible words that would seize the bait and swallow the hook and all but drag the excited angler in after them, but like that famous catch of Hiawatha's, they were generally not the fish he wanted. He wanted fish that were smooth and shining and subtle, and very much alive, and not too strange; and presently, after long patience and many rejections, they began to bite.[20]

In later years he wrote less slowly, especially in blank verse, to which he turned more and more as age overtook him.[21] Yet in regard to *Merlin*, done in 1916, he speaks of "having written much of the thing twice" and of hoping "to rewrite a good part of it" again.[22] And ten years later, while composing *Tristram*, he comments on his "trouble with the catastrophe part . . . I have already killed them [Tristram and Isolt] three times, but they are like cats with nine lives, and I may have to kill them nine times." [23] And besides this kind of revision of even the longer poems, one must note "the ruthless cutting he often gave his early drafts." [24]

Yet—perhaps surprisingly, after all this—Robinson tells us that the length of time required to write a poem has no necessary connection with its merit. Further, the form, whether easily or arduously achieved, is not the main thing. "As a rule I see the end of a thing before I begin it (if I don't see it then, I am likely never to see it) and the rest of the process is simply a matter of how the thing goes. Sometimes it goes rapidly,[25] sometimes slowly; and so far as I can see, one method produces about the same result as the other, provided I know what I am trying to say. When occasionally I have become disgusted and thrown an unfinished poem away, it has always been because I had really nothing to write about." [26]

Here Robinson seems to be saying that what is primary in poetry is content rather than form, substance rather than style, what the poet has to say rather than how he says it; although this evidently does not mean that the thought must be original or profound, but that it must be genuinely the poet's own. A similar view is implied in a comment made in 1913 on his attempts to write plays and novels. "I see now that my past three years of floundering in prose have been due to nothing more serious than the fact that I had temporarily written myself out." [27]

Other utterances develop this line of thought—always, of course, avoiding overstatement or dogmatism. He asks a friend for an opinion about some lines in *The Return of Morgan and Fingal* that trouble another friend "on account of their directness. If a thing says what I mean it to say, and at the same time has rhythm and music in it, why shouldn't I use it even though I know that now and then a too conscientious critic will find fault with it?" [28] Rhythm and music are naturally essential, but they are not enough; they do not of themselves make a composition come alive, command attention, and compel acceptance from the reader or hearer. Robinson's complaint against the popular versifiers of the time when he was struggling vainly for a hearing is not mainly against the form of their verse but against its emptiness—against its lack of anything new or deep or distinct to *say*. "Oh for a poet," he cries in an early sonnet,

> To put these little sonnet-men to flight
> Who fashion, in a shrewd mechanic way,
> Songs without souls, that flicker for a day,
> To vanish in irrevocable night.

The same essential complaint he brings, interestingly enough, against the *vers libre* and "imagism" championed by Amy Lowell in her own crusade against the "shrewd mechanic way" of the "little sonnet-men" who still, near the middle of the second decade of the twentieth century, dominated America's poetic taste:

what seems to me to be the very best of your *vers libre* is almost exclusively "human" in its subject matter, and therefore substantially old-fashioned. One reason why I haven't more to say on the subject is that I have absolutely no theories. I don't care a pinfeather what form a poem is written in so long as it makes me sit up. "Imagiste" work, *per se*, taken as a theory apart from one special form, seems to me rather too self-conscious and exclusive to stand the test of time. I feel pretty confident that if you had to sacrifice one or the other you would retain that part of your poetry that has in it the good and bad solid old-fashioned human qualities that make us all one crazy family of children, throwing things at each other across the table, and making faces at each other in *saecula saeculorum*.[29]

Further, as one would expect, Robinson is even more severe in his strictures on the obscurities of "modernist" verse, as exemplified in the work of the unfortunate Pink in *Amaranth*:

> "He cuts and sets his words
> With an exotic skill so scintillating
> That no two proselytes who worship them

Are mystified in the same way exactly.
All who believe themselves at one with him
Will have a private and a personal Pink,
And their unshared interpretation of him."

Once more, it is having something to say—some thought that can be understood, some experience that can in imagination be shared —that really matters in poetry.

Yet this is not quite the last word, either. For "solid old-fashioned human qualities" can be dealt with adequately—so as to make one "sit up"—in prose. And poetry does things that prose does not. Robinson even describes it as "a language that tells us, through a more or less emotional reaction, something that cannot be said." [30] And the same conception is implied in a later comment: "Ideas are, of course, inseparable from the medium, but much memorable poetry is not important for what is said." [31] And this unsayable something that poetry adds to the literal meaning of the words it uses—this unanalyzable emotion that poetry communicates along with its rational, fixed, translatable content, that is, its meaning—must be largely a result of form. "Poetry must be music," [32] Robinson insisted; and music, in his view at least, is pure form. Poetry, however, uses words, and not tones; and words, unlike tones, have meaning, in the narrower sense in which that term has just been used. Hence, poetry of necessity—as long as it uses recognizable words—communicates meaning as well as emotion; in it, content and form, the thing said and the way of saying it, are both inseparably present.

All this is perhaps expressed better by Robinson himself in elaborating his definition:

This might be an equally good, or bad, definition of music, but for the fact that the reader would balk instinctively at the qualifying "more or less" before "emotional"—the emotional reaction in the case of music that endures being unquestionably "more." And this, no doubt, is equally true of much of the best poetry, although it seems to me that words, in their very nature, no matter how intense or lyrical their expression, must obviously admit of subtleties of sound and sense that would not be possible in any conceivable combination of tones. As a layman, I cannot resist this opportunity to make myself offensive by setting down my by no means original belief that most of the present-day composers are carefully insuring oblivion for their names and their notes by forcing tones to do the work of words. On the other hand, it is equally true that many poets—Swinburne and Lanier, for example—have gone altogether too far in trying to make words do the work of tones. Generally speaking, I should be inclined to say that the field of poetry is infinitely more various and less definable than that of music, for the simple reason that poetry is language and music at the same time. There is no such thing as "programme" poetry, and some of us are almost willing to wish there might be no more "programme" music.[33]

Beside this admirable prose passage may be aptly set one of Robinson's sonnets, to illustrate as well as state the essence of the poet's inspiration and his craft, the place that his work occupies between intellectually informative prose on the one hand and emotionally stirring music on the other, distinct from either, combining the effects of both:

> The master and the slave go hand in hand,
> Though touch be lost. The poet is a slave,
> And there be kings do sorrowfully crave
> The joyance that a scullion may command.
> But, ah, the sonnet-slave must understand
> The mission of his bondage, or the grave
> May clasp his bones, or ever he shall save
> The perfect word that is the poet's wand.
>
> The sonnet is a crown, whereof the rhymes
> Are for Thought's purest gold the jewel-stones;
> But shapes and echoes that are never done
> Will haunt the workshop, as regret sometimes
> Will bring with human yearning to sad thrones
> The crash of battles that are never won.

3

Concerning the function of poetry, or the purpose which it serves, Robinson has few direct comments, for the self-distrust already noted made him shrink from the bare possibility of being looked on as oracular. "It seems to me that we poor devils who are condemned to write poetry should write it, and not talk about it." [34]

But occasionally, in letters to his friends or in courteous answers to inquirers, he would offer an opinion.

One such statement, remarkable for its unreserve, but characteristic in content, was made to Josephine Preston Peabody, who had apparently incurred his disapproval by confessing, in regard to her book *The Wolf of Gubbio*, a Shelleyan "passion for reforming the world":

> I liked the *Wolf* because I liked it, not because it gave me "bread." The world doesn't want bread from poets, unless it is so completely disguised that they mistake it for cake; and while great poetry has nearly always an ethical value, history would seem to indicate that Apollo doesn't care a d-damn for the Uplift. You have done your best work when you have forgotten what a rotten place this world is.[35]

This unaccustomed warmth continues in his admonition to avoid "more or less nebulous generalizing about a hypothetical human that has never existed and probably never will exist"; to which he adds, by way of softening his severity, "I . . . don't want you to consume yourself in trying to reform the world. I don't mean to be discouraging, but you can't do it." [36] The same conviction underlies his response to a newspaper reporter who was trying to discover his "message." "Poetry should not be propaganda, or, if it is, the propaganda ought to be well concealed, to be, one might say, reprecipitated." [37]

The natural question after reading these pronouncements concerns the precise difference between "ethical value" and "Uplift." Perhaps the latter involves crusading for specific social changes, while the former implies the affirmation of general moral principles—"the merciless old verities" of which Robinson speaks in *Cassandra*, as well as the more merciful and perhaps newer verities at which he hints in *A Christmas Sonnet*. He himself, at any rate, usually stays clear of particular social problems—except for the Dionysus poems attacking Prohibition, in which many readers will feel that he more or less descends to the level of his opponents; although even here it is the danger to human liberty in general with which he is largely concerned. Always it is the broad, basic values that he feels bound to affirm in his poetry, either explicitly or, more often, implicitly. To this extent he is right in calling himself, in the letter to Miss Peabody that has just been partly quoted, "an incurable preacher."

But his "message," so far as he is a poet, is of a special sort. Facts, logic, exhortation—these in the main are matters for the writer of prose. The poet is not neutral, but he is not a partisan, either. His business is with first premises—with the basic beliefs concerning truth and value which are justified by nothing but themselves, and which are the real motive forces in the conflicts which shake human individuals and human societies. And since these, when stated in bare prose, become for the most part mere platitudes, it is for the poet to give them life and passion by clothing them in light and music and by attaching them to human personalities that the reader is made to feel are living and real—the poet's own or those that he has imagined. Thus the "message" becomes poetry and not propaganda.

Of such first premises in Robinson's work we need be here concerned with only one—the spiritual solidarity of mankind. Queried again, by a more sensitive inquirer, about his "message," he answered: "I suppose that a part of it might be described as a faint hope of making a few of us understand our fellow creatures a little better, and to realize what a small difference there is after all between ourselves as we are and ourselves not only as we might have been but would have been if our physical and temperamental make-up and our environment had been a little different." [38]

This sympathy with his fellows, his feeling of sharing with them the painful burden that seemed to him the doom of all humanity, reached at times a point that more robust persons might regard as morbid. His biographer records one episode in particular that gives us a revealing glimpse of this dark region of his soul:

"Do you know?" he said to Torrence one day, "one of the most terrible things is to walk alone and feel that you are receiving deadly wounds."

"What do you mean?"

"It is to go along the street and glance into the eyes of passers-by and catch a glimpse of recognition, and know that you will never see them again." [39]

This demon of frustrated brotherhood lurking beneath the calm surface of everyday existence Robinson was never able to exorcise —though in his verse he rarely surrenders to it so unconditionally as in the somber sonnet called *Alma Mater*:

> He knocked, and I beheld him at the door—
> A vision for the gods to verify.
> "What battered ancientry is this," thought I,
> "And when, if ever, did we meet before?"
> But ask him as I might, I got no more
> For answer than a moaning and a cry:
> Too late to parley, but in time to die,
> He staggered, and lay shapeless on the floor.
>
> When had I known him? And what brought him here?
> Love, warning, malediction, hunger, fear?
> Surely I never thwarted such as he?—
> Again, what soiled obscurity was this:
> Out of what scum, and up from what abyss,
> Had they arrived—these rags of memory?

With such a thought for his constant companion, it does not matter that Robinson forebodes "the probability that there will never be more than one person in a thousand who will know or really care anything about poetry";[40] the bond is there, whether always acknowledged or not, and the poet's office is to make it stronger and closer. While preparing his first volume for publication, he wrote to Smith: "If printed lines are good for anything, they are bound to be picked up some time; and then, if some poor devil of a man or woman feels any better or any stronger for anything that I have said, I shall have no fault to find with the scheme or anything in it." [41] Later, looking toward the dim, far distant future of humanity, Robinson observes (still with a flippant aside to guard himself against any suspicion of sentimentalism), "Meanwhile I shall have brightened the way for a few groping wanderers without lanterns, and shall have comforted them with the assurance that, generally speaking, they haven't a damned thing to say about it." [42]

It remains to consider how, exactly, the poet brightens the way for his groping comrades. In Robinson's poetry we find two approaches to this goal—one direct and explicit, the other oblique and "inferential."

In a relatively small group of poems he simply sets before the reader his own convictions, offers a confession of faith for the consolation or encouragement of those who care to, or can, accept it. The most notable instance is of course *The Man Against the Sky* —which has often been taken, ironically and inexcusably, for a confession not of faith but of despair. "My purpose was to cheer people up," he explained (for once quite without irony) in a letter.[43] And if we properly remember that cheerfulness is relative, we can find such a purpose in almost all his reflective—he would have protested against their being called "philosophical"—poems: in such early sonnets as *Calvary, Dear Friends, The Garden, The Altar, Credo,* and *L'Envoi,* along with the *Octaves;* in the only partly dramatic *Captain Craig,* where the character and faith of the central figure are checkered, but with sunlight; even in poems where he considers with misgivings the pattern of American democracy as it developed during and after the First World War— *Cassandra, Demos, Modernities, Demos and Dionysus,* and especially *Dionysus in Doubt;*[44] and in the elaborate ethical and social allegories, *Amaranth* and *King Jasper,* with which he closed his poetic career.[45]

These poems certainly served Robinson's purpose well enough— some of them, a partisan may think, brilliantly and even splendidly. But perhaps it is in the other group that we find his greatest achievement, his deepest and most enduring appeal. In these poems, which comprise the great majority of both his longer and his shorter pieces, he is content to tell, without insisting on a moral, the simple or complicated, commonplace or strange, sometimes happy but more often sad, stories of all sorts and conditions of men and women—Reuben Bright and Richard Cory and Miniver Cheevy and Lorraine and Jane Wayland and a host of other imagined characters from contemporary life, along with memorable figures from the Arthurian legend, the Bible, and the pages of authentic history, to which the poet attaches freshly conceived and humanly comprehensible—though not always convincingly vital—personalities.

In all these narratives is present, though often unexpressed, the aim which Robinson makes explicit in speaking of his prose play *Van Zorn*, which he says is "supposed to open or partly open all sorts of trap-doors and windows that will give people glimpses into their own cellars and dooryards, and incidentally a fairly good view of the sun, moon and stars." [46] Through such glimpses of the world within and the world outside themselves, the poet clearly hopes to make his readers understand their fellow creatures a little better.

And with this understanding, of course, goes sympathy—more magnanimous judgments where judgment seems called for, less qualified compassion where suffering seems undeserved, more generous sharing of all the shame and splendor of human experience. And this, Robinson would have said, is the main thing—the chief prerequisite for all the social improvement that is possible, the chief alleviation of all the pain that is unavoidable. What he says in *Calverly's* is a theme implicit in all his work—that out of the seeming welter of human frailty and frustration, the blindness and bitterness and ignominy of man's existence,

> something yet survives:
> A record written fair, could we
> But read the book of scattered lives.

It is the poet's work to retrieve and reunite the pages of this book.

chapter ii: BARRIERS

"I just adore your poetry," said the spokesman for three ladies who had cornered Robinson at one of Mrs. MacDowell's teas, and who stood beaming upon him; "in fact, we all do. But it is so hard to understand. I wish you would tell us of some easy way." The poet, always defenseless in such circumstances, fumbled helplessly and apologetically, and inadvertently produced the perfect answer: "I don't know that there is any, except just to read it, one word after another." [1]

It was a perfect answer, that is, to *them*. And it is good advice to any reader—or even to any professional critic. But many serious persons, sensing Robinson's gifts and eager to enjoy his work, find that his obscurity is a genuine obstacle. This is a surprising fact in view of the theories about poetry that have just been set forth and in view of his consistent antipathy to "modernist" art of all kinds, springing from what he regarded as its unintelligibility. Yet it *is* a fact; and the critic had best face it squarely at the beginning and try, at the risk of being tedious, to find the cause of the trouble. Under no circumstances will all of Robinson's poetry be easy to understand. But the obscurity will be less, and less annoying, if we can discover where the difficulty lies.

Robinson himself did not seem to know, although he could not help being aware of his readers' wrestlings with his text, and being deeply disturbed thereby—disturbed and irritated. A friend of his early manhood who asked, concerning a poem that Robinson had just shown him, "What does it mean, Win?" got for an answer,

"That's a hell of a question to ask a poet." [2] And similar questions —asked or implied—throughout his life generally brought forth similar expressions of annoyance and bewilderment. What seems to have been a typical feeling is shown in a comment to a friend with reference to *The Revealer*, his tribute to Theodore Roosevelt. "By the way, did Abbott seem to know what I was driving at in T.R. or did he disagree with it with some degree of intelligence? I have encountered so much rotten imbecility in the way of failure to get my meaning that I am beginning to wonder myself if it may not be vague. But I won't have it anything worse than obscure, which I meant it to be—to a certain extent." [3]

No doubt Robinson is right in his denial of vagueness; no doubt to himself the thought or feeling that he wished to communicate was as clear as Vickery's mountain "Blue in the west." Certainly he never intended serious readers to be as baffled as they sometimes are. Early in his poetic career he wrote to Miss Peabody, "I have come to learn that vagueness is literary damnation (nothing less); and I have determined that whatever I do in the future—excepting now and then an excursion into symbolism, which I cannot wholly throw off—will be tolerably intelligible." [4] And on a later occasion he wrote to another friend: "If ever you find another puzzling place in any poem of mine, I wish you would let me know. Otherwise, it might possibly get by." [5] Both his humility and his self-trust were too profound to let him erect intentional verbal barriers between himself and his readers or to challenge them with puzzles disguised as poetry. "Why don't they *read* me?" he asked.[6] He and they were equally baffled—they by his poetry and he by their inability to find his meaning.

Sometimes this situation exasperated him, as did the reception of *Merlin*. "I was told just the other day that most of the so-called reviewers can make nothing of him and for that reason have dodged him. . . . and I supposed that the thing was as clear as daylight! Well, I still think so—even if I don't know what to think of the human brain." [7] And later he complained: "For the majority of semi-intelligent readers my books might as well be written in Sanskrit. Just why this is, I don't know—but so it is." [8]

To this fact, eventually, he became more or less resigned. On rare occasions he even confessed that he himself might be partly responsible: "I write too much in overtones." [9] And he admitted after finishing *Captain Craig* that it was "too much a matter of 'atmosphere,' I am afraid." [10] But these excellent beginnings of a diagnosis did not lead to a cure. Believing that a genuine poet writes because, and to a certain extent *as*, he must, Robinson probably felt that, having done what seemed good to him, he could do no more.

It may as well be said at once that the substance of Robinson's poems is by its nature difficult to grasp; that he was abnormally sensitive to psychological undercurrents and overtones in the lives of people whom he met or imagined. "I guess . . . I was born with my skin inside out," he confided to a friend. [11] *The Corridor* and *A Song at Shannon's*, written twenty years apart, show how his mind reached out with eager sympathy to the imagined loneliness of a chance-met stranger; only to be foiled by the hesitancy of either to unlock his heart, and to be haunted thereafter by the thought of having lost forever the opportunity to know and perhaps to help a fellow human being. In such feelings he may have been making the mistake, as Mr. Hagedorn suggests, of "measuring others' capacity for pain by his own." [12] But whether what he saw was real or fancied, his record of it is bound to be a dark glass to persons less sensitive.

Moreover, even when the substance of his poetry is not in itself hard to comprehend, Robinson is evidently beset by the fear of making it too obvious—by an apparent dread of insulting his readers, to whom he ascribes as acute a sensitiveness to unspoken overtones of thought or feeling as he himself possessed. And he seems never to have been able to perceive the irony of this attitude.

Not all the fault, to be sure, is the poet's. Sometimes we look in a poem for what is not there and was never intended to be there. We find him protesting to Mrs. Richards, with impatience showing through his jocularity: "Good heavings, no! 'The House on the Hill' is no house that ever was, and least of all a stone house still in good order. I don't know why they assume and say such fool things, but they do, and they will do so for evermore." [13] The poem seems mainly an effort to embody in words a moment of nostalgia, perhaps much like that which finds expression in *On the Night of a Friend's Wedding*, and which was caused by the ringing of church bells "for the wedding of two people in whom I had not the remotest interest." [14] These statements prepare us for the grimness of his comment that *The Gift of God*, where the theme of mother love blind to a son's shortcomings is so trite that it could have been made into poetry only by a union of pathos and irony and irresistible music such as nothing but genius could command, "has been interpreted as a touching tribute to our Saviour." [15]

The reader who sees in *Twilight Song* a like allusion to the Christian story is less censurable. The second stanza almost cries out for such a specific interpretation.

> Long ago, far away,
> Came a sign from the skies;
> And we feared then to pray
> For the new sun to rise:
> With the King there at hand,
> Not a child stepped or stirred—
> Where the light filled the land
> And the light brought the word.

Yet such an interpretation would be wrong, if it is wrong to go beyond the poet's intention, which is "no more than . . . to express in verse—'impressionistic', I fancy—the dim consciousness we have of things going forward"; and he adds, "for that reason I am bothered by the certainty that everyone who reads it will try to read a thousand things into it that I never dreamed of putting there." [16] "It will be hopelessly obscure to the lynx-eyed," he had written earlier;[17] and although the jibe is hardly fair, it is consistent with his later lament, in a seriocomic self-portrait, at "having been born to such an ornery lot as that of an 'intellectual poet'—when, as a matter of fact, anything like a proper comprehension of his product was, and is—so far as it is at all—a matter of feeling, not of cerebration." [18]

Apparently it is a principle with Robinson that a poet should not be too precise, that the effectiveness of his work depends upon his leaving something to the imagination. As a close friend observed, interpreting his attitude in conversation as well as in poetry, "It was as if he liked to leave the enigma undisturbed, when brought face to face with it. Something was lost in the process of elucidation." [19] Or, as he once remarked to an interviewer, "I like to leave a poem with a fringe around it." [20] And to a fellow poet, Joyce Kilmer, after giving his definition of poetry (quoted above) as "a language that tells us . . . something that cannot be said," he continued, "In real poetry you find that something has been said, and yet you find also about it a sort of nimbus of what can't be said." [21]

2

Without wishing to dispel this nimbus, the reader naturally *does* wish to see as clearly as possible what the thing is that "has been said." Among the factors that sometimes thwart this wish are two that at first glance seem incompatible: extreme compression on the one hand, and extreme diffuseness—or what looks like diffuseness—on the other. One subject may be treated in the fourteen lines of a sonnet; another of apparently equal scope may be presented in several thousand lines of blank verse. The result is that, although some works in each group are unchallenged successes, there are some sonnets in which essential points are omitted, and there are some long poems in which the essential points are obscured by the intrusion of what most readers are bound to regard as unessential details.

Of these two traits, the one that is likely to strike the reader first, especially in the early poems, is the compression. Again, this is a tendency of which the poet himself seems to have been aware; for concerning one of the short stories on which he worked before turning definitely to poetry, he remarked to Smith: "I am afraid that there is a little of my old fault of over condensation, but I hope to overcome that someday." [22] Whether he ever succeeded in his prose fiction, we do not know, for he eventually destroyed the manuscripts. But in many of his poems, at any rate, he cuts away every word that might make longer, although perhaps clearer, the pathway to the center of the experience that a poem embodies. In *An Old Story*, for instance, the speaker confesses to having, in baseless resentment against a friend,

> cursed him for the ways he had
> To make me see
> My envy of the praise he had
> For praising me.

The thought here is not difficult, and were it elaborated in prose it would not ask of the reader even a momentary pause; but forced into four lines composed of twenty-four words, all but two monosyllabic, it demands a certain mental effort.

Of the same sort is the well known stanza from *Flammonde*:

> There was a woman in our town
> On whom the fashion was to frown;
> But while our talk renewed the tinge
> Of a long-faded scarlet fringe,
> The man Flammonde saw none of that,
> And what he saw we wondered at—
> That none of us, in her distress,
> Could hide or find our littleness.

Again, the statement of the last line would be clear enough in prose: "We could not conceal the dislike that our meanness of spirit made us feel for her because of a scandal in which she had been involved a long time ago; in fact, we did not even see how petty our attitude was." But when a thought that one would normally express in some forty words is crowded into six, a little "cerebration" is needed.[23]

Other instances come to mind. The disillusioned wife in *Eros Turannos* hides at home from the clamor of gossip,

> While all the town and harbor side
> Vibrate with her seclusion.[24]

"The laugh that love could not forgive" suggests a whole tragic chapter in the zestful life, not untouched but unstained by suffering, that the poet recalls by way of tribute *For a Dead Lady*. A

grim contrast is the story of Clavering in *Calverly's*, "Who died because he couldn't laugh"; but not more grim than the biography
of the friend in *Clavering* to which we are given the key in

> The fiery-frantic indolence
> That made a ghost of Leffingwell.

And still again fate shows its darker side when the once admired—
and envied—and now forgotten woman in *The Poor Relation* finds
mocking compensation in the neglect of the "friends" who "would
have scratched her for her face." In *Bokardo*, on the other hand, a
man fashions his ruin for himself, and his vindictive complaints
against the friends on whom he sponges while deriding religion and
threatening suicide as an escape from his self-created troubles
meet with contempt so concentrated as to be not less than cryptic
in expression:

> But your fervor to be free
> Fled the faith it scorned.

Another aspect of Robinson's verbal economy is the frequent use
of imagery that is something less than obvious. Figures of speech
seem to be a natural part of the language of a poet, whose task it
is to incarnate experience, if only in words—to give it body and
breath, a local habitation and a name. Abstraction, whatever may
be its relation to other arts, is the enemy of poetry. But whereas in
the work of most poets the function of imagery is to clarify and
beautify, to illuminate and adorn, so that it leads often to verbal
opulence and expansiveness, Robinson seems bent on making it
serve first of all the end of economy, in helping to bring together
all essential details within the smallest possible compass.

Thus in *Flammonde*, in the stanza already quoted, there is the
"long-faded scarlet fringe" of a woman's youthful passion that
once led her to transgress the bounds of conventional morality. In
Neighbors we find the desperation of hopeless poverty packed into
the seemingly almost flippant phrase "a wolf-haunted wife"; and
the life that to her was so anguished was to her neighbors so note-
less that when she died, only

> A shadow on the commonplace
> Was for a moment strange.

In *Miniver Cheevy*, where to Miniver's alcohol-eroded mind it is the age and not himself that is out of tune, the terseness of the image is that of a local idiom:

He mourned Romance, now on the town,
And Art, a vagrant.

Finally, to give but one more of many instances, there is the pathetic picture in *Job the Rejected* of the weak and wayward husband who could not hold his high-spirited wife nor yet reconcile himself to her loss.

He fumbled hungrily to readjust
A fallen altar, but the road was clear
By which it was her will to disappear
That evening when Job found him in the dust.

Another of Robinson's devices for loading his verse with more meaning than for many readers it can easily carry is the use of historical or literary or even scientific allusions, without stopping to ask himself whether these may not be too recondite even for well informed readers. The last class, perhaps, may not cause much trouble to a science-minded generation, and we may even smile approvingly when, in *Mortmain*, a man can see "no reason larger than a leucocyte" why something should not happen. The other two groups, however, may give us pause.

It is an admirable economy, doubtless, to use *Maya* and *Karma* as the titles of two sonnets that present respectively a transcendental dialogue between Mind and Soul and an episode wherein a stock-market operator who has ruined a friend salves his conscience by giving a dime to the Salvation Army; and if the reader understands the terms, they act like the prisms of a kaleidoscope, composing all the details of each subject into a pattern of perfect unity and symmetry. But many readers may not have happened to learn the significance of these key words in the timeless religious philosophy of India: to know that "Maya" means, roughly speaking, the whole realm of sensuous and rational experience, which is held to be illusory; and that "Karma" is the term applied to the cosmic law, or process, of cause and effect, which governs impersonally and inflexibly all the workings of the universe. Lacking this key (one does not always have a dictionary at hand in reading poetry, even if dictionary definitions were always adequate), the reader can find only partial satisfaction in either poem.[25]

A large number of Robinson's allusions, to be sure, are to those cultures of which Western civilization is mainly the offspring, and with which, therefore, most of his readers might be presumed to be familiar—that is, the Greek and the Hebrew. Yet though this double heritage is still our strongest defense against the continuing assaults of error, unreason, and deliberate evil, it is one of which we are progressively less conscious.

Schooled by rote, for instance, in unreflective and incessant praise of "democracy," we shall have difficulty in comprehending the first-named character in *Demos and Dionysus*, unless we know the connotation of the name as used by the Greek philosophers, especially Plato; unless we realize that it was this "Demos"—the uninformed, insensitive, arrogant, mass-minded majority—that put to death the best and wisest man of Athens, Plato's great teacher, Socrates.

In the same way, knowing vaguely of Dionysus only as the inspirer of drunken orgiastic revels, and being unaware of his association with the "divine madness" of the poet and the seer, of his identification with the creative urge not only in the physical realm but even more in the realm of imagination, we fail to understand the fitness of his role—in *Dionysus in Doubt* as well as in the poem just mentioned—as the searching critic of the aggressive and muddled materialism that is so large a part of American democracy in practice.

Again, in *For a Dead Lady* we have to grope a bit for the meaning of

> The forehead and the little ears
> Have gone where Saturn keeps the years

until we remember that Saturn's Greek name is Kronos, which the Greeks themselves confused with "chronos," their word for "time"; just as we may have to pause at the "inept, Icarian wings" in *The Master* unless we recall a story told us in childhood or have heard some radio commentator, by way of showing his erudition,

recall man's fabled first attempt to fly; and just as (to give one
final example) we shall miss the whimsical humor of *Momus* unless
we are familiar with the comic figure of the very minor deity who
represents all dull and carping criticism.

Many readers doubtless encounter the same difficulty with Robinson's references to the Bible, of which, like many another skeptic, he was a curious if critical reader, and to which he turned not
infrequently, though not with invariable success, for subjects.[26]
And it is perhaps fair to add that, while he certainly did not go out
of his way to be obscure, he may have smiled a little to reflect that
natural allusions to biblical passages perfectly familiar to him
might be impenetrable to many regular and pious churchgoers.

To be sure, some of these allusions will be clear even to a generation that never hears or reads the Scriptures outside of church.
Most readers will probably understand Old King Cole when he
observes,

> "Or, like One whom you may forget,
> I may have meat you know not of";

and the reference in a neighboring poem, *The Voice of Age*, to
"what Belshazzar couldn't read" is almost proverbial[27]—though for
most persons the details are doubtless a bit hazy. Perhaps even the
"three in Dura" in *The Man Against the Sky* will be identified by
the fact that they

> shared
> The furnace, and were spared
> For glory by that king of Babylon
> Who made himself so great that God, who heard,
> Covered him with long feathers, like a bird.

"The three" are Shadrach, Meshach, and Abednego, and the king,
of course, is Nebuchadnezzar; but how many readers will remember this item in the punishment of his pride? And how many, meeting a little later "Nahum's great grasshoppers," will not be sent—
if they are sufficiently conscientious—to a concordance of the
Bible? Or, as they read in the same poem the lines,

> Or, seizing the swift logic of a woman,
> Curse God and die,

will they receive the full impact of the passage through recognizing that the logic is that of Job's wife in the most powerful spiritual drama of the Old Testament?[28] Or, to take a last characteristic instance, will the reader of *The Revealer*, having been informed by the introductory quotation from Judges that the main theme is a comparison of the achievements of Theodore Roosevelt with those of Samson, recognize and perceive the full implications of the references to other biblical passages in "a small cloud in the skies" and "an Angel with a Sword"?

There is no need to catalogue in this study all the allusions in Robinson's poetry, nor all the imagery.[29] We are concerned here with the question of why his poetry is hard to understand; and clearly one source of the difficulty is his tendency to overload his lines with meaning, to suggest more than is said, to compress as much experience as possible into a given space. And, clearly, two factors contributing to this effect are his imagery and his allusions. It is of course evident from the illustrations given that these images and allusions serve other ends than those of verbal thrift. But these other purposes may for the present be laid aside.

3

So much stress has just been laid on the way in which Robinson's readers are baffled by his brevity that it will seem paradoxical to say that they are sometimes equally confused by his wordiness. And indeed "wordiness" is not exactly the correct term. Yet one can hardly be blamed for applying it to the following lines from *On the Way*, supposed to be spoken by Alexander Hamilton to Aaron Burr concerning Washington:

> I'll beg of you the meed of your indulgence
> If I should say this planet may have done
> A deal of weary whirling when at last,
> If ever, Time shall aggregate again
> A majesty like his that has no name.

Why, the reader may wonder, need five lines of blank verse be used to say, "It will be a long time before there is another man like him"?

Or, again, if a person passing a cemetery happens to reflect ironically that every human being thinks himself uniquely important, why take six lines to say what can be said in seven words? Yet that is what the poet does in a passage from *The Glory of the Nightingales:*

> he thought how each particular
> Few feet and inches of unquiet life
> That was a man or woman was for one
> Or other, respectively, a more germane
> And urgent work of God than was revealed
> In others irremediably unlike it.

Admitting, however, that this sort of writing may sometimes be a defect, we may properly consider whether it is not something more than mere garrulousness; whether these aggregated words do not really serve some purpose. And clearly they do. The first line of Hamilton's statement reveals in its elaborate irony not only his profound distrust of his companion but also his resentment at Burr's sneering reference to "His Western Majesty, King George." And the next two lines not only suggest to the imagination, as a naked prose statement would not, the length of time between the appearances of men like Washington, but also hint that such an appearance is almost a cosmic phenomenon. The fourth line, by a natural thought sequence, impresses on the reader the extraordinary multiplicity of elements and qualities that go into the making of such a character. The last line is again a rebuke to Burr, asserting that to a man like Washington all titles are inadequate and irrelevant. So the question is not whether the passage contains too many words but whether it contains too many ideas; not whether the number of words is disproportionate to the intellectual content but whether that content is essential to the dramatic needs (for the poem *is* dramatic, in intention as well as in form) of the work as a whole.

In the second passage, likewise, the main thought can be briefly stated, but such a statement would omit the ironic contrast between the restless insignificance of an individual human being and the automatic assumption by that same human being of his unparalleled and undiminishing value in the universal economy. The question for reader and critic is whether such a reflection is appropriate and necessary or whether it serves rather to distract attention from the main course of the narrative.

To this question, no absolute answer can be given; and therefore we may proceed to another manifestation of the same reluctance (as to many readers it must seem) to come to the point. This is the poet's habitual use of a negative statement or suggestion, even when his aim is to communicate a positive fact. Instead of saying what a thing *is* or is *like*, or what a person *does* or *says* or *thinks*, he tells what the thing is *not* or is *unlike*, or what a person does *not* do or say or think. The reader must then formulate for himself the affirmative statement that is implied. Instead of saying, for instance, "Half our grief comes from anticipating desired events that never happen," Robinson says, in *Matthias at the Door*:

> "Half the grief
> Of living is our not seeing what's not to be
> Before we see too well."

This passage, however, is childlike in its simplicity compared to that in which Tristram analyzes Isolt's behavior in trying, but somewhat less than wholeheartedly, to pretend that she did not love him, when he had fully recognized already their passion for each other:

> "You had already made yourself in vain
> The loyal counterfeit of someone else
> That never was, and I hope never shall be,
> To make me sure there was no love for me
> To find in you, where love was all I found.
> You had not quite the will or quite the wish,
> Knowing King Mark, not to reveal yourself,
> When revelation was no more the need
> Of my far larger need than revelation."

Equally characteristic and still more complicated is another piece of psychological analysis, this time from *Roman Bartholow*, in which Penn-Raven describes for Bartholow the spiritual predicament of the latter's wife, Gabrielle.

> "Her tragedy
> Is knowing how hard it is to care so little
> For all that is unknown, and heed so little
> Of all that is unseen. She made herself
> Believe she loved the world that wearied her
> Until she left it and saw what it was,
> Unwillingly, that she was not to see.
> She learned of you on your awakening
> What she was not to see, and she saw nothing.
> To-day she will not let herself believe
> She cares whether or not there's anything
> Worth caring for."

All this is to say that Gabrielle's tragedy is that she ceases to value the worldly possessions, indulgences, and achievements with which people are ordinarily more or less satisfied; that on the other hand she believes in the inward vision, the spiritual goals and gains that have come to dominate her husband's life; and that these are nevertheless beyond her reach. The conception is difficult enough for readers unversed in mental subtleties; and they will naturally ask why it should be made still more difficult by being expressed mostly in negatives.

The passage just quoted verges more than once on paradox— that is, the use of statements that taken literally are contradictory, and that make sense only when one term of the contradiction is given an unusual, often figurative, meaning. Such a device seems to suit Robinson's temperament and purposes, for it occurs often in his verse. Turning again to *Roman Bartholow*, we find Penn-Raven "watching, lazily"

> This glimmering scene of all that he had lost
> Before he knew that he had never found it.

Obviously one cannot lose what one has never found; and since it is relatively clear that what Penn-Raven had never found was a

genuine return of his love for Gabrielle, it must be that what he
had lost was the very possibility of winning her love. Had he known
sooner that she did not really love him, he might (the phrasing
may suggest) have acted differently and so have gained from her
the desired response.

There is a similar passage in *Matthias at the Door*, where Matthias says, with reference to Garth's suicide,

> I did not know,
> Until too late, that one who was alive
> Was dead already.

Here "dead" must mean "without the desire to live," or perhaps,
even more definitely, "resolved to kill himself." Again in *Amaranth*
we find "a light/ That was not light" through which Fargo moves
in his curiously coherent dream; and "a young face not young,"
belonging to a woman novelist whose countenance age has left
empty of any mark of the wisdom and the will that are bred by
endurance and achievement.

Sometimes the paradox is complicated by a metaphor, as in
this grimly humorous description of a drunkard in *The Glory of
the Nightingales*—which in this instance, however, is not hard to in-
terpret.

> "He was illuminated for three years
> With light that never revealed him to himself
> As a poor wick that he must saturate
> Unceasingly in order not to see it."

A more elaborate metaphor runs through *The Dark House*, where,
we are told (though not in the poem), the fact behind the figure is
again enslavement to alcohol; but the paradox of the last two lines
ought not to be wholly impenetrable—whether the final word is
taken literally or figuratively—to readers who are Christians:

> And my friend, again outside,
> Will be living, having died.[30]

The paradox in *Luke Havergal*, however, is couched in more complex and less familiar terms:

> But there, where western glooms are gathering,
> The dark will end the dark, if anything . . .

Here we have what might be called a metaphor of the second degree: "the dark" means "death," but the first death is that of the
body (through suicide), which in the disordered mind of the
bereaved lover promises to end his deathlike loneliness.[31]

One more example of Robinson's use of paradox will lead us to
another sort of indirection with which he unintentionally teases
his readers. In *Exit* he admonishes:

> May we who are alive be slow
> To tell what we shall never know.[32]

"What we shall never know" is the truth about the ultimate causes,
and hence about the rights and wrongs of what the dead man did;
what we should be "slow to tell" is what we ignorantly guess.

This quotation differs from those previously given in that their
obscurity may be traced largely to the negative and often seemingly
self-contradictory form of expression. But here the main source of
the difficulty lies elsewhere. Suppose the poet had written "To tell
what we may think we know." The paradox, the negation, would
have been absent, but the essential point—the *what*—would have
been still unrevealed. And this other way of avoiding obviousness
is also characteristic of Robinson. He tells us in effect that *x* equals
y, but he refuses to tell us what *y* equals. Or he says, varying the
formula, that *x* is greater than *y* or less than *y*, but still leaves us in
the dark by failing to assign a value to the second term. That is (to
use grammatical instead of mathematical terminology), such verbs
as "know," "tell," "learn," "see," and "feel" are given objects
which are either noun clauses or nouns compared with other
nouns, and which seem to add nothing to what has already been
said.

Instances of this fault, if it is one, are not far to seek. Levi's
"grim mother" in *The Field of Glory* "told him what she found to
tell," but the poet does not tell *us* what it was. Many a reader of
Old King Cole will sympathize with the man who got only "a dim
reward" for sitting up all night while the King made such remarks as,

> "For I can see what I can see,
> And I'm accordingly alone."

Even more exasperating is the final stanza of *Fragment*, where, having made us intensely curious as to Briony's unhappy but unspecified fate, Robinson remarks almost blandly,

> And who knows all knows everything
> That a patient ghost at last retrieves.

Sometimes, indeed, as in the close of *For a Dead Lady*, the formula is used with admirable effect:

> And we who delve in beauty's lore
> Know all that we have known before
> Of what inexorable cause
> Makes Time so vicious in his reaping.

Few of the many passages in which poets of all ages and nations have protested against the inevitability of beauty's death have clothed the mystery in words more moving. Yet, fine as the passage is, the poet's approach to the thought that he wishes to communicate is still characteristically oblique.

4

This habitual indirection of Robinson's shows itself in his method, as well as in his manner, of presenting his material. Here the first fact to be noted is that sometimes he simply does not give us enough data. An obvious instance is the sonnet *How Annandale Went Out*. We infer clearly enough that the doctor helped what had once been Annandale to a merciful death. He tells us:

> "A wreck, with hell between him and the end,
> Remained of Annandale; and I was there.
>
> I knew the ruin as I knew the man."

Evidently Annandale had once been a man greatly gifted. But what had happened to him? Knowing Robinson's preoccupation with the slow decay of weak or blind or fated men and women, we might reasonably assume that Annandale was one of them, and that a long career of dissipation had brought him to a point where it was a friendly act to help him die. But if we turn now to *The Book of Annandale*, published eight years before, we are bewildered to find Annandale, at the end of the poem, about to enter on what promises to be an idyllically happy marriage. Not until twenty years later, in *Annandale Again*, does Robinson tell us that a merely physical accident—an automobile crash—has in an instant broken body and spirit as well, making intolerable the contrast with the perfect happiness that the earlier poem shows him to have won.

A painstaking scrutiny of Robinson's complete works will doubtless set us right in a similar manner about other difficult pieces, and give us at least a general notion of their meaning. But there are some to which one reader, at least, can find no clue. One of these is *Lost Anchors*:

> Like a dry fish flung inland far from shore,
> There lived a sailor, warped and ocean-browned,
> Who told of an old vessel, harbor-drowned
> And out of mind a century before,
> Where divers, on descending to explore
> A legend that had lived its way around
> The world of ships, in the dark hulk had found
> Anchors, which have been seized and seen no more.
>
> Improving a dry leisure to invest
> Their misadventure with a manifest
> Analogy that he may read who runs,
> The sailor made it old as ocean grass—
> Telling of much that once had come to pass
> With him, whose mother should have had no sons.

The first thing we need to know and are not told is: What *is* the legend? What did they *expect* to find, that made their discovery a "misadventure"? Next, to an unknown legend is added an unexplained fact. Who stole all these anchors? And why should *anybody* want to steal anchors? And then, how can an event of whose significance we are left completely ignorant offer "a manifest analogy" to anything else at all? Finally, to make the puzzle absolutely insoluble, we are left in the dark as to the other member of the alleged analogy. That the sailor's mother "should have had no sons" does inform us with characteristic obliqueness that his life had been misadventurous. But of the only knowledge that would aid us— namely, what his misadventures *were*—we are still deprived.

"Much . . . had come to pass/With him"—but *what?* The poet here gives us, in effect, a single equation with three unknown quantities.[33] He reminds us of the narrator in *Nimmo*, who declares (apparently not trying to be funny):

> Now, mind you, I say nothing of what was,
> Or never was, or could or could not be.

It is true that there are few of Robinson's poems that present to our inquiring eyes so blank a wall. But there are not a few in which the full meaning, at least, eludes us. In *Her Eyes*, for instance, which is unforgettable for its shadowy tones and overtones of imagery and music,[34] we are not sure until the last stanza that it is a real rather than an imagined, ideal woman for love of whom the painter has forsaken the world and whose portrait he has painted with magical skill; and even then we do not understand the nature of the "strife so grim" that—apparently—separated them, nor what "it all" is that "comes back to him."

Another half-told story is the tantalizing *Fragment.* The "faint white pillars" far back among the trees suggest what the phrase "the Briony gold" confirms—wealth and exclusiveness. And perhaps Briony ought to have used his wealth better than he did; for "many a man" in like circumstances

> Would have said, "There are still some gods to please,
> And houses are built without hands, we're told."

But merely being one more of the idle rich would hardly seem to call for a fate so sinister as that at which Briony darkly hints:

> "Sooner or later they strike," said he,
> And he never got that from the books he read.
> Others are flourishing, worse than he,
> But he knew too much for the life he led.

There are parallels here with *Tasker Norcross*, another of Robinson's many "slow tragedies of haunted men," where there are also a house and trees and a lonely man who knows too much of his own inadequacy and unimportance to be happy. But Briony's tragedy seems to be of a different sort. We infer from the final stanza that "they" did strike, sometime, somehow. But who *are* "they"? Are they human, like the never known murderer—or murderers—of Stafford in *Stafford's Cabin*, of "old Ham Amory" in *The Tavern*, of the unnamed woman in *Haunted House?* Are they faces or voices called back from the past by a mind that has brooded too long over some hidden grief or guilt, such as seem to appear in *Luke Havergal, Her Eyes,* and *Cavender's House?* Or is Briony done to death causelessly by apparently inscrutable powers of darkness, like the "grave-diggers" in *Amaranth* or the unseen destroyer of Avon in *Avon's Harvest?* And if so, does he, like the character last named, die of fright, or by his own hand? And finally, what does the title mean, since the poem is obviously complete—at least in the poet's intention? Is it meant to suggest that Briony's life is in some way and for some reason a "fragment" of what it might have been?[35]

These are not idle questions. We are entitled to be told at least enough to make a plausible guess. Yet all Robinson tells us—and again it should be stressed that he never intentionally plays tricks on his readers—is contained in the cryptic lines quoted above. And at this point annoyance tempts us to give up the struggle and forget the whole piece. But, like the previous poems, it refuses to be forgotten. The somber music rings on in our ears, the somber pictures flash unbidden upon our inward eye—the warped and ocean-browned sailor with his harbor-drowned and anchor-laden ship; the "same still room" where the painter worships his portrait that has

> the eyes of a deathless woman,—
> With a gleam of heaven to make them pure,
> And a glimmer of hell to make them human;

the pillars of Briony's house "all gone gray" and its fountain dry. And we keep asking, with Robinson's friend, "What does it *mean?*"

5

The "inferential" method just considered, of which Robinson is so fond, leads naturally to symbolism and allegory—that is, the use of a specific object, situation, story, or group of characters to express a general, abstract idea. This tendency in the poet grew stronger as he grew older, and his last two poems, *Amaranth* and *King Jasper*, are obviously and elaborately allegorical—though in both works the meaning of the allegory is far from obvious.

But even among Robinson's earlier and shorter pieces there are some that almost compel us to look beneath the surface or behind the scenes. Theodore Roosevelt, reviewing the second edition of *The Children of the Night*, wrote: "I am not sure that I understand 'Luke Havergal', but I am entirely sure that I like it."³⁶ Readers less extroverted and less occupied than Roosevelt may agree with the latter part of this presidential proclamation and yet feel less than satisfied until they *do* understand the poem—until they know who or what the speaker is, who "she" is, and what "the western gate" is to which Luke Havergal is bidden go. And even if, after long reflection, we decide tentatively that "she" is the woman, now dead, whom Luke has loved; that the voice is that of his own grief and longing; and that "the western gate" is self-inflicted death, we still do not *quite* know. Robinson's own references to the poem—once as "my uncomfortable abstraction" ³⁷ and again as "a piece of deliberate degeneration"—³⁸ still leave the picture far from clear.

Some of his comments about other poems *do* help us; and the admirable selection of his letters edited by Ridgely Torrence now gives much aid that was not available during the poet's life. His comment on *Twilight Song* has already been quoted. His revelation that *Merlin* and *Lancelot* have "a certain amount" of "symbolic significance"—that they "were suggested by the world war— Camelot representing in a way the going of a world that is now pretty much gone"—³⁹ illuminates and intensifies the stories that they tell. *The Flying Dutchman*, whose protagonist is forever finding and abandoning "one fog-walled island more," can readily be interpreted, in the light of a statement in the *Letters*, as a parable of "science" and its limitations.⁴⁰ Also helpful is his comment that *Amaranth* is "a sort of nightmare about people who are living in the wrong world";⁴¹ although it hardly goes far enough to prevent struggling readers from feeling that it is perhaps true of them as well as of the characters in the poem. Even Mr. Hagedorn's expansion leaves many details unclear. And the same biographer evidently thinks that the comparable *King Jasper* (described by the poet as his "treatise on economics")[42] demands an even fuller elucidation, for which most readers will be duly grateful, although areas of uncertainty remain. And there will be readers who will ask whether, after all, a poem ought not to be self-explanatory.

Not always, of course, even without footnotes, is Robinson's symbolism impenetrable. "The False Gods," for example, are quite clearly those of modernist art. "The Man Against the Sky" is Everyman, and the ways he may have taken are those along one or another of which all humanity moves; we hardly need to be told that "his way was even as ours." And these ways all lead to "The Town Down the River," which on one level is New York, but whose more inclusive identity is Destiny, or Fate, on whose inscrutable face all come to look with joy, indifference, or despair, answering eagerly or reluctantly her irresistible command. The same meaning is manifest in a symbol in a later poem—the "Door" through which Matthias's friend and his wife are permitted to pass, but from which he himself is turned away; but here Destiny is presented in its ultimate but still ambiguous form of death.

Yet rarely, with or without footnotes, do we feel confident that we have exhausted the meaning of Robinson's symbols. Although in the course of this study further explorations of the poet's symbolism will be undertaken, those readers who are "hot for certainties" are doomed to get from many of his poems only "a dusty answer." [43]

6

One final source of obscurity in Robinson's method of handling his materials is his refusal in his dramatic poems to take sides for or against his characters. Readers who have been taught to expect that the poet himself will give them all the answers are bound to be confused or even annoyed at having to decide for themselves where their sympathies ought to lie.

A poem in point is *John Gorham*, which the dancing verse and sparkling imagery make irresistible to the reader's ear and his mind's eye. But is it John Gorham or Jane Wayland who is to blame for opening the gulf that separates the lovers with a finality like that of death? Is the man a devoted and patient suitor who still has enough integrity to break away from the woman who has only been playing with his affections?

> "You are what it is that over rose-blown gardens
> Makes a pretty flutter for a season in the sun;
> You are what it is that with a mouse, Jane Wayland,
> Catches him and lets him go and eats him up for fun."

Or is he a humorless egotist who cannot understand that a woman can possess sincerity without sentimentality, can cloak affection in "foolishness," can laugh at him and still love him?

> "Won't you ever see me as I am, John Gorham,
> Leaving out the foolishness and all I never meant?
> Somewhere in me there's a woman, if you know the way to find her.
> Will you like me any better if I prove it and repent?"

Here we realize the force of Robinson's remark about "feeling" and "cerebration." If most readers choose the second interpretation, it is because they *feel* in the words of the speakers the qualities of character that call for such a choice. To be sure, "cerebration" has its place, especially when backed by familiarity with the poet's other works; for we recall Robinson's pervasive chivalry and his frequent portraits of women bruised in spirit by masculine egotism or imperceptiveness—*Eros Turannos*, *The Woman and the Wife*, *Tact*, *An Evangelist's Wife*, *Matthias at the Door*. Perhaps we find in *John Gorham* a telling in more detail of the tragedy compressed into one magical line of *For a Dead Lady*—"The laugh that love could not forgive." Yet, on the other hand, we are reminded by *The Unforgiven, Llewellyn and the Tree*, and *The Whip* that the bitterness of a broken love or marriage may also be caused by feminine cruelty—which in these poems one feels to be more envenomed than any harshness to be found in men.

So it will be hard for one reader of *John Gorham* to prove to another reader who has a different "feeling" for the poem that the man is or is not at fault. And so in regard to other poems of Robinson's, such as *London Bridge* and *The Clinging Vine*, the doctors of letters may disagree. Professor Cestre says of the former: "There is a period in a woman's life when, if her nerves are not steady, wild imaginations will rush into her mind, with such power of impact that her life and that of her husband and children may be shattered,—unless her husband keeps cool and, with mixed argument and authority, brings her back to her senses." [44] But Mr. Hagedorn considers both poems to be examples of "the struggle of the lonely woman against the self-centered or disloyal male," [45] and speaks elsewhere of "the outburst of the wronged wife" [46] in *The Clinging Vine*. Concerning *London Bridge* it would seem that Mr. Hagedorn is right—that at least the last speech of the wife rings true. But concerning *The Clinging Vine*, though this time Professor Cestre agrees that it is a portrait of a "jilted wife" and her "anger against her fickle husband," [47] other readers may still find it hard to decide whether the woman's torrential denunciation of her husband springs from righteous anger or hysterical delusions.

There is always, of course, a third possibility—that the blame belongs wholly to neither, partly to each. This would be perhaps less satisfying as drama but, it might be argued, more satisfying as a record of day-to-day reality. And such seems to be Robinson's own view, for in a letter to a friend who had evidently had difficulty with *The Clinging Vine*, he remarked: "The husband is there, of course, or she wouldn't repeat, as question, what little the poor devil finds to say. Probably he deserves all that he is getting." [48] Apparently the husband *has* been unfaithful; but perhaps the wife, in turn, has not been quite a model of marital affection, and the philandering for which she now flays him so mercilessly may have been indirectly her own fault.

Finally, the poet's use of "Probably" brings up a fourth possibility—that we do not know the "true" interpretation because the poet himself does not know. We recall Robinson's remark that the man in *Doctor of Billiards* "*seems* to be throwing away a life which, *for some reason known only to himself,* is no longer worth living." [49] Such a statement, of course, raises profound esthetic issues. Is it not the duty of a dramatic artist to know his characters, to have in mind their portraits clear in each detail, to have defined for himself their every thought, emotion, and motive? Are they not, after all, his own creations, having no existence but in his mind, experiencing nothing but what he wills? Is it not affectation, as well as a shirking of one's task, to attribute to them an independent, unknown life?

Perhaps. Yet the poet draws his material from the "real world"; and what we know of it outside ourselves is only its surface. We hear words, and infer feelings; we see actions, and guess at motives. In real-life dramas of marital discord, which the poems just mentioned reflect so faithfully, one may have as close and clear a vantage point as is ever possible for a third person, may hear both sides of the story, told in each instance with what seems passionate sincerity, and yet at last know no more than at first what the true story is—what has actually happened or who is to blame —except as "feeling" may dictate.

This is not to say that Robinson does not have a clear general conception of the situations and the persons that he puts before his readers. It is only to suggest that he sometimes leaves to those persons a certain area of privacy, a certain measure of escape from the fallible judgment of other persons. Something like this, perhaps, is the final touch of the great dramatist in perfecting the illusion of reality at which he aims. [50]

7

And here, finally, is the great source of the obstacles to understanding that the reader meets in Robinson's poetry. The stripped, compressed, metaphorical or allusive intensity of certain passages; the seeming diffuseness of others, where what ought seemingly to be obvious facts are almost lost in a maze of subtle and but distantly relevant details; the frequent lack, on the other hand, of what the reader can only regard as essential data; the inferential,

tentative, oblique, contingent, often negative, ironic, or paradoxical manner of expression; the resort to symbolism and allegory;
the dramatic, unannotated presentation of story and character—all
these reflect the quality of Robinson's vision, his sense of the unconquerable elusiveness of the ultimate fact, his acceptance of the
equivocal nature of all that we apprehend outside ourselves.

> And who's of this or that estate
> We do not wholly calculate,
> When baffling shades that shift and cling
> Are not without their glimmering.

These words do not apply only to the unheroic Levi in *The Field of
Glory*. Their application is universal; just as what the poet says of
the death of Leffingwell might be said of all deaths—and of most
events in life: "We do not know/ How much is ended or how much
begun." Concerning a person's inward life, especially, where the
motives and emotions are perhaps unconfessed even to himself, our
most searching questions must often go unanswered.

> But when were thoughts or wonderings
> To ferret out the man within?

the poet asks as he muses on the fate of Clavering, one of the
many engaging ne'er-do-wells who people his pages. Even Flammonde, admired by all, escapes from any sure analysis, is free even
from his creator.

> How much it was of him we met
> We cannot ever know; nor yet
> Shall all he gave us quite atone
> For what was his, and his alone.[51]

Even those of us who risk the fateful look into the eyes of Amaranth see only the truth about ourselves. The truth about our fellows we can only guess at, on evidence that is always fragmentary,
often contradictory. The world is a vast jigsaw puzzle, and even in
the small section that we have looked at closest and longest, some
of the crucial pieces are missing, and some that we have do not
fit. And it is not the poet's function, according to Robinson
(changing the metaphor), to tell "the story as it should be," but
to tell it as it seems to him. "I may not see life as it is," says Van

Zorn, "but I see it as I see it"[52]—not as someone else may tell him he ought to see it; not, perhaps, as he himself would like to see it; but as he *does* see it.

And so Robinson himself might have spoken. Granted that a poet's work is the creation of his own mind and imagination, still, it is in some sort a mirror of life, or it is nothing. And to leave out the elusiveness, Robinson would have felt, is to leave out an essential quality of life itself.

chapter iii: WORDS AND MUSIC

The obscurity just analyzed at such length, however, is not the only trait of Robinson's style that calls for comment. Nor was it the only trait that in the beginning made the acceptance of his poetry so slow and grudging. Not only were editors and critics inclined to magnify what are perhaps genuine defects in his poetry, but they were blind to many of its merits, and especially its merits of style.

To understand this attitude we must recall the time. The great Victorians—and they *were* great—were dead, except Thomas Hardy, who was turning from prose to poetry. So were their American counterparts, except Mark Twain, symptomatically sounding the depths of disillusionment, and Henry James, writing for a steadily narrowing circle of readers.[1] The great creative impulse of the nineteenth century was spent, and no comparable source of energy had made itself felt. Poetry, especially, was derivative, and completely satisfied a reading public that still admired Tennyson and Longfellow for their faults. A. E. Housman caustically described the age just past as one "flowing with milk and water," and in poetry these were still flowing. Housman's own poetic response was honest and admirable, but opened no new vistas.[2] William Butler Yeats was still clothing lovely fantasies in liquid syllables. Again the magic was authentic, but the beauty was of the twilight and not the dawn. Kipling, indeed, had struck a new note, and excited Robinson's enthusiasm by his concern for commor

men and by his daring use of common speech, as well as by the
finer rhythms of his less popular poems; but the journalistic quality from which his writing was only rarely free did not wholly appeal to the mature taste of his American contemporary; and the
strain of "imperialism" in his work, grossly magnified and vin-
dictively misconstrued, alienated most of such serious literary
leaders as there were.

As for America, it is hard to recall any poetry of permanent significance in addition to Robinson's (except Emily Dickinson's,
posthumously published and soon to be forgotten for almost a
generation) that appeared during the last decade of the nineteenth century or the first decade of the twentieth. What writers
wrote and readers read was verse that was smooth, pretty, sentimental, trite, making none but the easiest demands upon the ear,
the emotions, or the intellect. And this taste prevailed not only
among the "general public," but among the editors and critics
who were the established arbiters of taste.

So when Robinson's work made its appearance, marked by the
"plain excellence and stubborn skill" in style that one of his
sonnets commends in George Crabbe, and by a depth of feeling
often masked by irony or understatement, it naturally inspired
few paeans of praise. On the other hand, it had no eccentricities
to provoke attacks that might have brought attention, or to provide a rallying point for the forces of revolt that were to burst forth
a few years later. And even when this revolt arrived, he still had
to wait for the fame that came so quickly to poets whose work was
more obviously novel. Even near the end of his life, he remembered with painful intensity the heartbreaking refusal of recognition. "If only they had said something about me! It would not
have mattered what. They could have called me stupid or crazy if
they liked. But they said nothing. Nobody devoted as much as an
inch to me. I did not exist." [3]

2

"Isaac and Archibald were two old men," he begins; and this casual, conversational opening, without romance, without drama, without obvious musical allure, moved the turn-of-the-century critic only to a bored "so what?" Even his friends were shocked by his use, further along, of such a phrase as "sweat blood." [4] Nor could most readers get excited about Reuben Bright "Because he was a butcher and thereby/ Did earn an honest living," or because

> when they told him that his wife must die,
> He stared at them, and shook with grief and fright,
> And cried like a great baby half that night.

And who would wonder more than idly why such a simple-minded fellow afterward "tore down the slaughter-house"? Perhaps, also, *Captain Craig's* weary travels in search of a publisher would have been shorter if it had had a more arresting introduction than,

> I doubt if ten men in all Tilbury Town
> Had ever shaken hands with Captain Craig.

One reviewer complained that the blank verse was "little more than inverted prose chopped into lines," and spoke of "a seemingly perverse carelessness"—itself a judgment almost perversely imperceptive. Another, Frank Dempster Sherman, was likewise critical of "the rough, crude, and altogether prosaic character of the blank verse." [5]

It is true that when "Richard Cory, one calm summer night,/ Went home and put a bullet through his head," even careless readers could feel the impact of so quiet a statement of such an unexpected catastrophe; and accordingly (and because it was short) the poem was soon in the anthologies. But most readers would doubtless have said, if asked, that they responded not because but in spite of the simple language.

Not always, to be sure, even at the beginning, did Robinson insist on such naked brevity of statement. There is siren music in the slow refrain of *Luke Havergal*, heavy with the echoes of lost lives.[6] "The broken flutes of Arcady" are clear and mellow in *Ballade of Broken Flutes*. In such sonnets as *The Garden, The Altar,* and *Credo*, we hear more than once "a bar/ Of lost, imperial music." The quiet late afternoon of life, toward twilight, where Isaac and Archibald follow what might seem a monotonous round of trivial pleasures, is consecrated for the half-comprehending boy by "The flame beyond the boundary, the music,/ The foam and the white ships . . ." Nevertheless, the first impression is dominant, and remains so throughout Robinson's works. [7] Our quarrel with his early adverse critics is not mainly as to fact but as to taste—about which, in spite of the classical dictum, literary criticism is mostly a dispute.

This quality of style has two sources, one a matter of temperament, the other of principle. First, there is the poet's native reserve, his shyness, his fear of even the suspicion of affectation or display; a trait apparent in his hatred of large social gatherings in private life and in his resolute refusal to have any public life outside his poems. Second, there is the impersonal motive of the artist for whom the world of men is illumined clearly but not with brilliance or glitter, and in subdued and often even somber colors; and who finds no alternative except to "draw the thing as he sees it." "I am what I am; and therefore I have my own paint-pots to dabble with. Blacks and grays and browns and blues for the most part—but also a trick, I hope, of letting the white come through in places." [8]

Moreover, as was shown above, language was always a medium, never an end in itself; and to falsify the substance for the sake of stylistic charm was as unthinkable as to falsify it for the pleasure of those readers who prefer to see reality through a mist of sentiment. In Robinson's work words serve no ultimate purpose except to embody experience, and experience is often grim. The poet, he felt, must make no concession to the large portion of the reading public who, in the words of the British philosopher, "so dislike the nude that they find something indecent in the naked truth"; nor to those who assume that clothes and cosmetics are the essential part of human beauty. "I like the romance of the commonplace," he wrote to Smith, "without any guns or swords or cavaliers to speak of." [9] And again: "There is poetry in all types of humanity—even in lawyers and horse-jockeys—if we are willing to search it out." [10] There is even poetry in their speech, as perhaps he first noted in Kipling.[11] He was, in fact, deliberately seeking, as he said long afterward, a "poetic idiom" that would "preserve the rhythms of ordinary speech within the traditional forms." [12] To reveal to the world the worth and significance that he discerned in the everyday lives of plain men and women was an aim hardly to be achieved by the use of "hifalutin diction." [13]

3

Robinson's language, however, is always the result of taste and temper, not of conscious theorizing; and therefore in each poem it adapts itself without' difficulty to the materials and the mood. Hence, the range of his interests and sympathies, the sweep and intensity of his vision, give birth to more various forms of expression than are to be found in the work of most of his contemporaries. The words are not always those of simple men, nor the music always the steady elemental rhythm of the outward movement of daily life. Beneath the surface of even normal existence are unsounded depths of endurance, unsuspected surgings of desire. To deal justly with these is a task to which the poet must devote the. full resources of language, however long and often some of them may have been used before. To reject the old because it is not new is mere affectation.

So it is without hesitation that Robinson resorts at times to the grand style and to the rhetorical devices that have been for centuries an accepted part of the poetic craft of the Western world. The sober and serviceable words that fit the unreflective Reuben Bright, gripped suddenly by dumb grief, yield in the portrait of Eben Flood, for whom derelict years have not dimmed the remembrance of other days when stately doors stood wide to receive him and a world of achievement lay all before him, to a rich and resonant music only a little thinned by distance.

> Alone, as if enduring to the end
> A valiant armor of scarred hopes outworn,

He stood there in the middle of the road
Like Roland's ghost winding a silent horn.
Below him, in the town among the trees,
Where friends of other days had honored him,
A phantom salutation of the dead
Rang thinly till old Eben's eyes were dim.

On this passage we may pause for a brief analysis of sound effects and the devices by which they are secured. Of these, two are dominant, assonance and alliteration: the placing near each other of stressed syllables in which the same or similar vowel sounds occur in conjunction with different consonant sounds; and the spacing at close intervals of stressed syllables beginning with the same or similar consonant sounds followed by different vowel sounds. Something halfway between these two is the use of differing vowel sounds at the beginning of stressed syllables. Further, the use of the same consonant sound at the end or in the middle, as well as at the beginning, of adjacent words is not without effect.

Thus, in the stanza quoted, we find instances of assonance in such combinations as "valiant," "armor," and "scarred"; "road," "Roland's," "ghost," "below," and "town"; "winding" and "silent"; and "phantom," "salutation," and "rang." Alliteration occurs unobtrusively in "scarred," "stood," and "silent"; and more obviously in "town" and "trees." Different vowels at the beginning of stressed syllables are found in "end," "armor," and "outworn"; in "other" and "honored"; and in "old" and "eyes." The most obvious repetition of a consonant, leaving aside alliteration and rhyme, is that of d in "end," "scarred," "stood," "middle," "road," "had," "honored," "dead," and "old"; but the repetition of l and n also contributes to the total effect.

There seems no point in carrying such analysis further. If the reader chooses, he may note in the quotations throughout this study the constant presence of the devices just described. The main concern of the critic is not with the process but with the result: with how the sound supports the meaning, how it clarifies or intensifies the character, the mood, or the philosophic conception that the poet is striving to incarnate in words.

4

The character delineation that fills so many pages of Robinson's books is in most cases highly intellectual, and the figures take shape largely as a result of conscious observation and analysis by the reader. But even here, especially in the shorter sketches, there is an appeal to the ear as well as to the intellect.

Even the names of Robinson's people, it may be noted, often suggest by their sound what their possessors are like. "Flammonde" could be the name of no ordinary mortal; it strikes the ear with overtones of the remote and heroic, irreconcilably alien to the life of Main Street—or Tilbury Town—yet undisturbedly superior to any material environment. "Miniver Cheevy," on the other hand, could only belong to a man whom fate had sentenced never to be taken seriously. Aaron Stark, we scarcely need to be told, is a "meagre man" and a miser. Bewick Finzer and Tasker Norcross can only come from aristocratic families; yet we are not surprised to find their lives marked for futility. Roman Bartholow, however, coming as one would expect from similar surroundings, is clearly destined for a higher fate.

The poet here faces a problem, however, in the fact that a name will affect each reader not only according to its sound but according to the particular associations that it has for him, and that the effect will therefore be unique and unpredictable. Recognition of this fact perhaps accounts for Robinson's consistent use of uncommon names, which are unlikely to have fixed associations for most readers.[14]

Passing from the names of the characters to the words in which they are described, we find again that our picture of a character is created not only indirectly, through the meaning of the words, but directly, by their sound. The "firm address and foreign air" of Flammonde have made an impression on us before we become fully aware of what the separate words denote, and so has the "glint of iron in his eyes." When we are told that Aaron Stark was "cursed and unkempt, shrewd, shrivelled, and morose," the words

fall like "sullen blows," even as do Aaron's own. Again, we perhaps pause to admire the sharp and bright detail with which the
poet pictures Bewick Finzer; but even before we pause, we have
felt the impact:

> The broken voice, the withered neck,
>   The coat worn out with care,
> The cleanliness of indigence,
>   The brilliance of despair,
> The fond imponderable dreams
>   Of affluence,—all were there.

So in Ben Jonson's worshipful portrait of his beloved master,
Shakespeare's daring and unquestioning genius forces itself upon
the reader ahead of the sense of the words:

> He treads along through Time's old wilderness
> As if the tramp of all the centuries
> Had left no roads—

So likewise when Merlin plucks the "flower of wonder" that is Vivian, and that holds "the wayward fragrance of a rose/ Made
woman by delirious alchemy," we need not weigh and measure the
words to be aware that they describe a magic older and stronger
than Merlin's. And why she yields we partly understand without
analysis when told that she is like "a queen a little weary/ Of in-
land stillness and immortal trees."

One might expect that in dialogue even more than in description the characters would come alive through the sound as well as
the sense of what they say; but Robinson apparently lacks the
power to stamp the utterance of a character with a distinctive,
unique accent and rhythm. His people do not all talk the same, to
be sure, for the poems vary greatly in form and tone. But within
each poem, no matter how many speakers may appear, all the
spoken passages seem much alike in vocabulary, imagery, and sentence structure. Isaac and Archibald are indistinguishable in speech
except by what they say; so are John Gorham and Jane Wayland;
so are Tristram and Isolt—both Isolts, in fact, as well as Mark and
Morgan and the rest; and so, it seems to me, are the different characters in every poem where dialogue occurs.[15]

When we turn to a consideration of the use of sound to communicate directly to the reader an emotion, mood, or mental atmosphere, we are of course dealing with a basic element in all poetry; and wherever we look in Robinson's work, we find illustrations of his mastery of this aspect of the poet's art. Through every line of *Luke Havergal* echoes the old desperate urge of a bereaved lover to gamble on self-inflicted death as a way to reunion with his lost love.

> There is the western gate, Luke Havergal,
> There are the crimson leaves upon the wall.
> Go, for the winds are tearing them away,—
> Nor think to riddle the dead words they say,
> Nor any more to feel them as they fall;
> But go, and if you trust her she will call.
> There is the western gate, Luke Havergal—
> Luke Havergal.

Another, clearer study of a suicidal mood is *The Mill*, where the final note is not of tormented conflict between doubt and desire but rather of yearning for release and oblivion.

> Black water, smooth above the weir
>   Like starry velvet in the night,
> Though ruffled once, would soon appear
>   The same as ever to the sight.

Different in tone but similar in technique are the early poems *Cortège*, *The House on the Hill*, and *Villanelle of Change*, all laden with a faintly bitter but unprotesting acknowledgement that the past is irretrievable.[16] But of all Robinson's triumphs in this kind of writing, perhaps the most signal is *The Dark Hills*, understandably a favorite with anthologists, in which the poet arrests forever the peculiar poignancy of a fading sunset.

> Dark hills at evening in the west,
> Where sunset hovers like a sound
> Of golden horns that sang to rest
> Old bones of warriors under ground,
> Far now from all the bannered ways
> Where flash the legions of the sun,
> You fade—as if the last of days
> Were fading, and all wars were done.

Passing from such sharply defined, self-contained moments of emotion to the varied and shifting moods of the longer poems, we find endless additional examples of the poet's power to make feeling come alive by the magic of sound. One is the "white birds/ Flying and always flying and still flying" about Isolt of Brittany as, at the beginning of *Tristram*, she waits, with a trust as steady as their flight, for fate to bring her beloved back; and as, at the end, she waits to see how her life can go on when Tristram's death has made it as directionless as seems the endless circling of the gulls and as empty as "the white sunlight flashing on the sea."

Another memorable instance is the re-creation of the four movements of the great symphony that Fernando Nash, "the man who died twice," hears in the dream that comes to save him, for a while, from death; in which, like Moses, he is given by Divine Grace a vision of the promised land that for his sin he may not enter. The poet's words build first a

> quivering miracle of architecture
> . . . .
> . . . a gay temple where the Queen of Life
> And her most loyal minions were protracting
> Melodious and incessant festival,

which is destroyed by the intrusion of "a singing horde of demons." The second movement gives a voice to

> that passionate regret
> And searching lamentation of the banished,
> Who in abandoned exile saw below them
> The desecrated lights of a domain
> Where they should walk no more.

To this succeeds a "frantic bacchanale of those usurpers," in which

> They soiled with earthy feet the shining floor
> Flinging the dregs of their debaucheries
> From crystal cups against the gleaming walls
> Of Life's immortal house. Too ignorant
> Of where they were to be afraid to know,
> They shrieked and sang in shrill delirium
> With vicious ecstasy for louder drums.

And when finally these are silenced,

> Far off there was a murmur and a stirring
> Of liberation, and a marching hymn
> Sang of a host returning

to be challenged for a last time by the drums of Death,

> till once more
> There were those golden trumpets, and at last
> There was that choral golden overflow
> Of sound and fire, which he had always heard—
> And had not heard before.

No doubt a mood or emotion almost naturally finds for itself, in the work of any sensitive poet, the right word-music. In presenting more abstract, rational, "philosophic" statements, however, the artist has a harder task. Even great poets, when offering an explicit "criticism of life," have not always avoided prosiness, bombast, or bathos. In Book III of *Paradise Lost*, for instance, the Almighty wins few friends by the self-defense that Milton puts into his mouth; and Wordsworth's Happy Warrior, in comparison with his Highland Girl, is a stodgy character.

It is, of course, always difficult to draw the line between feeling and thought, mood and meditation. "Ideas" are themselves the source of emotion—perhaps even of the most intense and enduring emotion. The Sermon on the Mount *is* a sermon, and its precepts are expressed sometimes with almost naked simplicity. Yet centuries of repetition have not succeeded in destroying its emotional power. What is important, apparently, is that in the exposition of ideas (given their intrinsic appeal), the language, whether direct or figurative, must fit the thought; the sound, again, must be appropriate to the sense.

This requisite, in reflective passages, Robinson seldom fails to meet. When, with a rare surrender to severity, he denounces in *Cassandra* the smug materialism of America, the words crack like a whip:

> "Your Dollar, Dove and Eagle make
> A Trinity that even you
> Rate higher than you rate yourselves;
> It pays, it flatters, and it's new."

But when in *Hillcrest*, instead of arraigning a nation's greed and pride, he is describing, in the same stanzaic form, what is apparently a fated and blameless but lamentable blindness to pervasive and oppressive wrong, the music of the words is muted by pathos and resignation.

> Who sees unchastened here the soul
> Triumphant has no other sight
> Than has a child who sees the whole
> World radiant with his own delight.

But it is not always human frailty that is mirrored and echoed in Robinson's verse. *The Man Against the Sky* makes of human existence nothing less than a cosmic drama, and the mystery and magnitude of the adventure find a voice in organ tones reverberant with awe and splendor:

> Dark, marvelous, and inscrutable he moved on
> Till down the fiery distance he was gone . . .

5

All this is perhaps part of what underlies Robinson's definition of poetry, already twice quoted. But by "language," of course, he means more than what has been analyzed in the preceding pages. It is not only the words but the meter, not only the sound but the rhythm, and in some poems rhyme and a stanza form as well, that tell us what the writer of prose cannot say. And here again we shall see how perfectly and inextricably, in Robinson's poetry, the form is fitted to the substance.

To appreciate this result, it is necessary to consider briefly what constitutes the essence of poetic form. The source of the pleasure that poetry gives, as a distinct form of literature, is repetition accompanied by variation. A pattern—for a foot, a line, a stanza—having been once established, the reader anticipates its recurrence and is pleased to have his anticipation fulfilled. But the pattern must not be repeated exactly and mechanically, or it becomes first monotonous and then repellent. Most English blank verse before

Marlowe is almost literally unreadable; the unvarying iambic beat becomes a source of torture. And accordingly, the reader of poetry anticipates variety as well as sameness. He cannot, however, predict when or how the basic plan will be modified; and the unexpectedness with which the changes are introduced by a skilled craftsman in verse is a source of never ceasing delight to the sensitive reader. Such a craftsman Robinson unquestionably is. His technical virtuosity, matching his imaginative power, is partly revealed in the sheer variety of metrical and stanzaic forms that he employs. During his youth, as already noted, he experimented both with numerous stanza forms and with blank verse. On the whole, it is the former that he seems to have found more congenial during the first half of his literary career. In *The Torrent and The Night Before* there is no blank verse except the lines to Walt Whitman, and none is added in *The Children of the Night* except the *Octaves*. In the *Captain Craig* volume, on the other hand, Robinson deserts rhyme not only in the title poem but in three others—*Isaac and Archibald, Aunt Imogen,* and *The Book of Annandale*—and some readers will question whether any of his later blank verse surpasses his achievement in some parts of these poems. Among the few reviewers, however, there were some who offered harsh comments on the style of the title poem; and for this or some other reason the poet includes no blank verse at all in *The Town Down the River* and only one poem in that form in *The Man Against the Sky*, two volumes which contain the poetical output of fourteen years. From this point on, however, rhyme fights a losing battle. The blank-verse poems from *Merlin* to *King Jasper* occupy about twelve hundred pages in the *Collected Poems*, whereas rhymed verse written during the same period fills less than one hundred. This is doubtless a natural change, for the lyric impulse, and perhaps also the dramatic power, yield almost inevitably, as age advances, to reflection and analysis, which can find freer and fuller expression in blank verse.[17]

The seeming need for freedom and fullness, however, is one to which the poet yields at his peril. Let his inspiration fail, and he becomes rambling and garrulous—a fate which the greatest poets have not invariably escaped. Shelley is right in declaring that in blank verse "there is no shelter for mediocrity." Rhyme may be a benevolent despot, compelling brevity and relevance; and Robinson sometimes packs more drama into the fourteen lines of a sonnet than into forty pages of blank verse.

One need only call to mind the cherished though broken dream of *The Story of the Ashes and the Flame*, the ironic tangle of desire and destiny in *Job the Rejected*, the betrayal and moral abyss of *Karma*, the triumph of forgiveness in *Ben Trovato*, the tranquillity qualified by recollection in *Firelight*. These and other sonnets tell precisely the same sort of story, with the same possibilities for extended treatment, that is told in *Roman Bartholow*, *Cavender's House*, *The Glory of the Nightingales*, *Matthias at the Door*, *Talifer*, and others of the long narratives in blank verse. And if the former are not necessarily superior as works of literary art, they are certainly more likely to be read. The theme of *Shadrach O'Leary*, for instance, is identical with that of *Amaranth*—the escape of a man from the "wrong world" of romantic endeavor in an art for which he has no capacity into a world of more prosaic but useful work that he can do well. But the intellectual and even poetic wealth of *Amaranth* will remain unknown to many readers who are willing to ponder and approve the wisdom tersely expressed in *Shadrach O'Leary*.

The sonnet, of course, like any other elaborate and somewhat rigid form, has its own dangers. A poet's pleasure in meeting its challenge to his technical skill may lead him to repeat too often the small triumph of turning out a formally impeccable sonnet that never comes to life. One recalls the Elizabethan sonneteers, among whom even Shakespeare not infrequently nods, while his hand goes on fashioning the neat rhymes and the well measured rhetoric. And there is the even more ominous example of Wordsworth's five hundred-odd sonnets, of which at least nine-tenths are never read outside of graduate-school seminars.

But although some might argue that Robinson's blank verse suffers from a similar overproduction, the poet was able in his sonnets to exercise greater restraint, permitting only eighty-nine to survive in the *Collected Poems*—hardly an excessive number for a career of forty years. Yet in this limited number, the variety of theme and treatment is far wider than in the work of either the Elizabethans, conventionally preoccupied with one or another aspect of love, and always in relation—at least theoretically—to their own lives, or Wordsworth, who is almost always reflective and moral. His nearest ancestor is Milton, in the great half dozen sonnets of the middle years; though neither Milton nor any other predecessor in the use of this form had divined the dramatic possibilities that Robinson compelled it to reveal.

From Milton, however, as from the others, he is separated by his twentieth century self-consciousness. His sonnets are most often, especially in his later years, verbally unadorned, psychologically subtle, and emotionally restrained, securing their effects through irony and understatement. At the same time they have a unity of tone and temper, a steadiness of outlook, that set them apart from the restless excursiveness, the dallyings with disillusionment and sentimentality, that mark the sonnets of such gifted young contemporaries as Rupert Brooke and Edna St. Vincent Millay.

The sonnet form best suited to such a temper is obviously the Italian, or Petrarchian, with its relatively slow movement and its adaptability to the expression of complex emotions and thoughts. Whereas the English, or Shakespearean, form marches steadily forward through the first twelve lines and ends with a climactic couplet (which may easily become anticlimactic), the Italian, with its backward-looking rhymes, moves deliberately through the first eight lines and then pauses while the poet considers the general truth that he has stated or the particular situation that he has described; and then proceeds at the same measured pace to a particular application of the general truth, a general comment on the particular facts, or a continuation of the narrative to a logical if not always expected outcome.

In only one sonnet, *An Evangelist's Wife*, does Robinson follow the Shakespearean pattern. In only two, *Horace to Leuconoë* ·(a translation) and *The Torrent*, does he fail to come to a full stop after the eighth line. Furthermore, in only nine of the eighty-

nine sonnets does the sestet have the *c d c d c d* rhyme scheme
which produces the most rapid and climactic movement of all the
combinations possible to this form. And in fifty-six, the last line is
removed by at least two lines from the line with which it rhymes; so
that these sonnets end with neither a bang nor a whimper, but with
a finality that is quieted and qualified by reminiscence.[18]

These matters, though technical, are not irrelevant to an understanding of Robinson's mind as well as of his art. They suggest
once more his rejection of dogmatism in philosophy and melodrama in narrative, his indirect and inferential method, his tentative and contingent vision of life in general, his belief that the
mysteries of the universe have "Too vast an answer for the time-
born words/ We spell."

Some sense of the quality of Robinson's writing in the sonnet
form can be gained even from the few quotations that space permits: illustrating the three main purposes—simple character portrayal, dramatic narrative, and philosophic comment—which his
sonnets usually serve; and drawn in each instance from the sestet,
where the movement can be most highly individualized.

Among the sonnet portraits there is none more sharply etched
than that of the miser Aaron Stark. He is a lost soul if there ever
was one, and, as already noted, the words in the octave that describe him are as hard as the money he worships. The movement
of the sestet emphasizes his slow descent into the Inferno, and the
last line stamps upon him the mark and seal of his damnation—
that the only motive to mirth that he acknowledges is the thought
that anyone pities *him:*

> Glad for the murmur of his hard renown,
> Year after year he shambled through the town,
> A loveless exile moving with a staff;
> And oftentimes there crept into his ears
> A sound of alien pity, touched with tears,—
> And then (and only then) did Aaron laugh.

The dramatic narratives are of course more various in the
rhythms to which the stories march, and not all of these can be illustrated. One characteristic ending, however, is that of the second

sonnet in *The Growth of "Lorraine"*. Unlike the ill starred husband in *The Unforgiven*, Lorraine *does* have red lights behind her and the "fumes of many-colored sins"; yet her last words have something of the quality of Hamlet's "the rest is silence"—something of relief that the tempestuous voyage across a sea of troubles at last is ending, and something of certitude that in the undiscovered country beyond there will at least be peace. Chastened but unbroken in spirit, she pens a final confession to the lover whom she once rejected:

> "You do not frown because I call you friend,
> For I would have you glad that I still keep
> Your memory, and even at the end—
> Impenitent, sick, shattered—cannot curse
> The love that flings, for better or for worse,
> This worn-out, cast-out flesh of mine to sleep."

Less impetuous but not less masterful is the love of the wife revealed in *Ben Trovato*, already mentioned. The broken rhythm here suggests an almost intolerable though concealed tension, which in the last line lingers toward release:

> "Though blind, with but a wandering hour to live,
> He felt the other woman in the fur
> That now the wife had on. Could she forgive
> All that? Apparently. Her rings were gone,
> Of course; and when he found that she had none,
> He smiled—as he had never smiled at her."

Finally, we come to the sonnets into which the poet puts his own feelings and thoughts. Here for the first time we find a difference between the early and the late work. The former, as already suggested, shows less restraint, greater readiness to reveal personal antipathies and enthusiasms, and less reluctance to admonish or exhort. Hence there is a more confident sweep in the forward movement of the poem, a steady rise through the sestet to a reverberant climax. Such is the case in *Calvary*, where the poet, moved by the exalted and terrifying simplicity of youth's vision, recreates the agony of Christ, and protests against the continuing betrayal of the Saviour by those for whom He died:

But after nineteen hundred years the shame
Still clings, and we have not made good the loss
That outraged faith has entered in his name.
Ah, when shall come love's courage to be strong!
Tell me, O Lord—tell me, O Lord, how long
Are we to keep Christ writhing on the cross!

But in *A Christmas Sonnet*, "for one in doubt," time has subdued
the passion of the protest, and the remoteness of the goal is acknowledged and accepted. In the final line, as so often, we hear
echoes of "the crash of battles that are never won"—and never
lost.

Though other saviors have in older lore
A Legend, and for older gods have died—
Though death may wear the crown it always wore
And ignorance be still the sword of pride—
Something is here that was not here before,
And strangely has not yet been crucified.[19]

6

The variety of rhythmic effects possible to the sonnet, however,
even when it is used by a master, is limited. To appreciate fully
Robinson's skill in this direction, we must turn to his other lyrics,
portraits, and narratives in rhyme.[20] Yet, rather oddly, the thing
that strikes the reader first is their surface simplicity. The meter is
regular, and usually the simple iambic; the lines are generally short
and often of uniform length, tetrameter being most frequently
used; and the typical stanza is a simple one of four or eight lines.
That the poems do not degenerate into jingles is—as in the still
simpler verses of A. E. Housman—a sort of metrical miracle.

Nor is there any consistent adaptation of meter and rhyme, as
there is of language, to varying themes or even moods. *Cassandra*, a jeremiad against American materialism, has the same stanza
form—four lines of iambic tetrameter rhyming *a b a b*—as *Llewellyn and the Tree*, a high-comedy narrative of the worm that
turned; and the same as *Hillcrest*, a meditation in the vein of the

ancient Stoics concerning the winning of wisdom through humility and endurance. A similar stanza—identical except that the first and third lines do not rhyme—is found in *Sainte-Nitouche*, a somewhat cryptic story of a clergyman who seems to make the best of a hand dealt out to him by an ungenerous fate; in *Clavering*, a brief portrait of a man who "clung to phantoms and to friends,/ And never came to anything"; in *Annandale Again*, a common enough story, as far as the story goes, of a happy marriage ended by a tragic accident; and in the whimsical *Two Men*, which verges on nonsense verse.

Making from the first of these patterns an eight-line stanza rhyming *a b a b c d c d*, we have the form used in *The Gift of God*, a matchless study of the irony and pathos mingled in the mirages wrought by a mother's love; in *The Mill*, a somber story of a double suicide; and in *Old King Cole* (with a feminine ending in the sixth and eighth lines), a tragicomic picture of an upright father acknowledging the worthlessness of his two sons and refusing to be crushed thereby.[21] Turning the second pattern into an eight-line stanza rhyming *a b c b d e f e*, we have the form of the nostalgic *Calverly's* and of a penetrating analysis of a universal human type in *The Wandering Jew*. And it is not easy to see how Robinson's many other triumphs in poems having a stanza of eight tetrameter lines—*Flammonde, The Field of Glory, The Poor Relation, For a Dead Lady, The Master,* and *The White Lights,* among others—are dependent for their success on the meter or on the varying rhyme schemes that the poet employs.

Nor is it clear that this meter and one or another of these rhyme schemes would not have done as well as pentameter quatrains for such events and reflections as are recorded in the humorous *Theophilus*, the brief, bitter drama of *Richard Cory*, the serenely meditative *Archibald's Example*, or the tangled motives and unclear lights of *Nimmo*—as well as *Old Trails, Veteran Sirens, Siege Perilous, The Corridor,* and *Three Quatrains*. Even *Mr. Flood's Party*, in which each stanza is formed by combining two of the stanzas just referred to, and in which it is hard not to feel that the substance has been given an absolute and inevitable form, is not strikingly different in theme and tone from some of the pieces mentioned in the preceding paragraph.

Finally, the long, tripping lines (heptameter and octameter, some iambic and some trochaic) of *John Gorham, Stafford's Cabin, London Bridge, The Valley of the Shadow,* and *Leonora* would seem, abstractly considered, to be singularly unsuited to the chill moonlight of the first-named poem, the bloodshot flame or gloom of the next three, and the doubtful illumination of the last. Only in *The False Gods,* a cheerful satire on modernist art, does the swinging rhythm seem appropriate. No doubt the contrast between form and theme is sometimes intentional and ironic, but it is not clear how the varying degree of success achieved in these poems is related to such an arrangement.[22]

It therefore seems fair to conclude that in each of these poems—all in their different ways characteristic of the writer—the success is not due to the metrical and stanzaic form in general, but must be due (as far as it is not the result of language alone) to the way in which the form is adapted to the particular, unique experience that each piece is an attempt to recreate.

There are, however, other poems in which the contribution of form to effect is more obvious; and some analysis of these will throw light on the compositions that are more subtly contrived. In *Miniver Cheevy,* for instance, the short last line with its feminine ending provides precisely the anticlimax that is appropriate to the ironic contrast between Miniver's gilded dream and the tarnished actuality:[23]

> Miniver loved the Medici,
>   Albeit he had never seen one;
> He would have sinned incessantly
>   Could he have been one.
>
> Miniver cursed the commonplace
>   And eyed a khaki suit with loathing;
> He missed the mediæval grace
>   Of iron clothing.

With this poem may be contrasted *Eros·Turannos,* another study of self-delusion and its cost, though one at which the reader does not smile. In this, also, the last line of each stanza is shorter than the others and has a feminine ending. But here, by using a single rhyme in the three preceding lines, the poet achieves each time a climax of action or emotion. The last stanza moves to its conclusion with the finality of fate itself. The catastrophe has occurred, the heartbroken wife has shut her door against the eyes and tongues of her neighbors, and the narrator comments:

> Meanwhile we do no harm; for they
> That with a god have striven,
> Not hearing much of what we say,
> Take what the god has given;
> Though like waves breaking it may be,
> Or like a changed familiar tree,
> Or like a stairway to the sea
> Where down the blind are driven.

The last four lines are worth further analysis, which brings to light not only the tremendously effective use of assonance in the long-*a* sound, and the hammering recurrence of *d* in the last line, but also a steady acceleration. Line 5 must be read slowly, for all but two of the syllables contain long vowels, and the consonant combinations in "like waves breaking" compel deliberation; line 6 moves faster because of the short vowels, but "changed" still slows the pace; whereas in line 7 there is nothing to stop the rush of words, until in the last line they pause to measure the heavy footfalls of Fate.

If, however, we now glance back to the first stanza, we may be surprised to find exactly the opposite effect—a steady slowing up of the movement through the corresponding lines:

> But what she meets and what she fears
> Are less than are the downward years,
> Drawn slowly to the foamless weirs
> Of age, were she to lose him.

But on reflection we see that the poet by this device is emphasizing the intolerable distances that the future presents to the lover who fears that he or she must measure them alone.

The same painstaking craftsmanship went into the making of all of Robinson's shorter poems, although not always with unqualified

success; for in particular works, as well as in the poetic calling itself, "no man may choose/ Whether he play to win or toil to lose."
But the ratio of success in this part of his work is high, and the
quality of the success is sometimes unsurpassable.

Such success, as hinted above, is perhaps most frequent in poems
written in iambic tetrameter, despite the fact that the light quick
cadence of the lines seems an odd medium for the close psychological analysis, the irony, the pathos, the passion that comprise the content of so much of Robinson's work. Yet the sheer music compels
us to abandon our preconceptions and surrender unconditionally
to the poet's judgment. If we *do* resist and pause for analysis, the
range of effects achieved within this simple form is astonishing.
Eros Turannos has already furnished instances, but other poems
are thronged with passages that weave the same enchantment.

One is *The Unforgiven*, another of Robinson's many studies of
unhappiness in marriage. This time it is the husband whose suffering is deepest and least deserved:

> He stares in vain for what awaits him,
> And sees in Love a coin to toss;
> He smiles, and her cold hush berates him
> Beneath his hard half of the cross.
> They wonder why it ever was;
> And she, the unforgiving, hates him
> More for her lack than for her loss.

Another is *The Gift of God*, wherein the adoring mother of a somewhat less than heroic son

> Transmutes him with her faith and praise,
> And has him shining where she will.

And so, however commonplace may be the reality,

> His fame, though vague, will not be small,
> As upward through her dream he fares,
> Half clouded with a crimson fall
> Of roses thrown on marble stairs.

There is also the heartbreaking poignancy of *The Poor Relation*,
for whom a blameless life has been no charm against the irretrievable defeat of beauty, wealth, and joyousness by illness, poverty, and
solitude, and who now waits only for release through death:[24]

And like a giant harp that hums
On always, and is always blending
The coming of what never comes
With what has past and had an ending,
The City trembles, throbs, and pounds
Outside, and through a thousand sounds
The small intolerable drums
Of Time are like slow drops descending.

And finally, among other unforgettable pictures is that of Lincoln
in *The Master*:

For he, to whom we had applied
Our shopman's test of age and worth,
Was elemental when he died,
As he was ancient at his birth:
The saddest among kings of earth,
Bowed with a galling crown, this man
Met rancor with a cryptic mirth,
Laconic—and Olympian.

Every poem about Lincoln takes us back inevitably to Walt
Whitman and *When Lilacs Last in the Dooryard Bloomed*. Com-
parisons are no doubt particularly odious in poetry, but only when
the purpose is partisan acclamation or disparagement. And placing these poems of Robinson and Whitman side by side illuminates
two facts not irrelevant to the present study. One is the power of
poetic genius to vitalize and transfigure any poetic form, however
fluid or however fixed. The other is Robinson's gift, unshared by
Whitman, or indeed by many poets, of fusing the lyric and the dramatic.[25] Whitman's mood in this poem—as always in his finest verse
—is wholly lyric; the emotion is personal, immediate, elemental.
Robinson is detached, objective, analytical, presenting his subject
as seen through other eyes than his; and yet by some miracle infus-
ing it with warmth, radiance, and the ring of truth. Whereas the intense feeling and infallible music that mark the finest lyrics are
born most often of Sidney's precept, "Look in thine heart, and
write," Robinson looks first at the world around him and into
the hearts of other human beings; and the depth of his own emotion
is only to be inferred.[26]

Even in the poems (some among his most perfect) that his biographers believe to have had reference to personal experiences or relationships, Robinson does not obviously unlock his heart.[27] The treasures there revealed seem not particularly his. In a different way than Shelley's poet, "he is moved not, but moves." This the reader feels, whether in the rare jubilation of *The White Lights,*

> Here, where the white lights have begun
> To seethe a way for something fair;

or the nostalgia of *Calverly's,*

> We go no more to Calverly's,
> For there the lights are few and low;
> And who are there to see by them,
> Or what they see, we do not know;

or the tender valediction of *For a Dead Lady,*

> The grace, divine, definitive,
> Clings only as a faint forestalling;
> The laugh that love could not forgive
> Is hushed, and answers to no calling;
> The forehead and the little ears
> Have gone where Saturn keeps the years;
> The breast where roses could not live
> Has done with rising and with falling.

7

Turning from those poems in which the rhyme and meter clarify or strengthen a moment of drama, a portrait, or a particular mood, to those in which they illuminate and reinforce the poet's vision of human life as a whole, we find some of Robinson's most brilliant achievements in the adaptation of form to substance.

In *Twilight Song* we encounter an unexpectedly buoyant representation ("'impressionistic,' I fancy," Robinson said) of humanity's march across the ages:

> Through the shine, through the rain
> We have shared the day's load;
> To the old march again
> We have tramped the long road . . .

No reader can miss the onward impulse of the verse; nor is the source difficult to find. Each line has six syllables, with a definite break between the first three and the last three. The pattern of the first three is always the same: the first syllable moderately stressed, the second unstressed, the third strongly stressed; but in the second half, two of the syllables always have a strong stress, and it is this heavier emphasis in the latter part of each line that creates the lift and drive. Ordinarily the stresses fall on the first and third syllables, but this pattern could easily become monotonous and mechanical, and therefore on occasion the stress is moved from the first to the second syllable.

The march of the human spirit is also the theme of *The Town Down the River*.[28] But in this poem the mood is not that of a participant, committed and confident, but of a dispassionate and far-sighted "Watcher by the Way," who sees no fruition of the dreams and desires whose voices the marchers hear as the sound of the River, "calling always, night and day"; but who, as he joins the age-smitten stragglers at the end, admits having known

> That the Town would have its own,
> And the call be for the fated.

And so the movement is not of marching feet but of flowing waters —a complex movement where many surface eddies partly hide the steady, irresistible current below.

To show in detail the metrical arrangements by which this movement is secured would be an undertaking almost without an end. Here there is space only for a general outline of such an analysis. It is to be noted first that the unit of organization is not the eight-line stanza but the section of four stanzas and thirty-two lines, and that in each of the sections there is the same elaborate pattern of meter and rhyme, adhered to with almost mathematical precision. Hence, only the first section need be quoted:

> Said the Watcher by the Way
> To the young and the unladen,
> To the boy and to the maiden,
> "God be with you both to-day.
> First your song came ringing,

Now you come, you two,—
Knowing naught of what you do,
Or of what your dreams are bringing.

"O you children who go singing
To the Town down the River,
Where the millions cringe and shiver,
Tell me what you know to-day;
Tell me how far you are going,
Tell me how you find your way.
O you children who go dreaming,
Tell me what you dream to-day."

"He is old and we have heard him,"
Said the boy then to the maiden;
"He is old and heavy laden
With a load we throw away.
Care may come to find us,
Age may lay us low;
Still, we seek the light we know,
And the dead we leave behind us.

"Did he think that he would blind us
Into such a small believing
As to live without achieving,
When the lights have led so far?
Let him watch or let him wither,—
Shall he tell us where we are?
We know best who go together,
Downward, onward, and so far."

In analyzing this verse, we note first, in contrast to *Twilight Song*, the metrical variety of the lines. These vary from five to eight syllables, and may begin or end with either a stressed or unstressed syllable. All we can be sure of in advance is that each line will have at least two strong stresses; we cannot predict exactly where these will fall, nor whether others will be added. But although such variations are unpredictable, they are not unplanned; and by means of these calculated changes the poet not only avoids monotony but mirrors the surface movement of the river with all its hesitations and retreats. At the same time the two or more strong beats in every line mark the steady forward movement of the whole, and a sense of swiftness and fluidity is added by the frequent feminine endings and consequent double rhymes, in contrast to the strong concluding stress of each line in *Twilight Song*. The continuity is emphasized further by the rhymes that link successive stanzas (and to some extent the poem as a whole).

Finally, taking an over-all view, we find the author's scrupulous workmanship apparent not only in his adherence to the pattern established in the first section, but in the fact that, without departing from this pattern, he varies the tempo of the first stanza of each section, keeping pace with the various travelers toward the Town. The Watcher by the Way speaks first

> To the young and the unladen,
> To the boy and to the maiden;

then

> To the fiery folk that hastened,
> To the loud and the unchastened;

next

> To the slower folk who stumbled,
> To the weak and the world-humbled,

and finally

> To some aged ones who lingered,
> To the shrunken, the claw-fingered.

But it is only the people and not the River whose progress becomes slower; and therefore after each of these beginnings the verse quickly resumes its usual pace to show the inexorable onward movement of the stream.

The title poem of Robinson's next volume, *The Man Against the Sky*, treats a similar theme but is dominated by a different mood and is written in a different form—one used in English poetry with a rarity that is surprising in view of the advantages that it seems to offer. *Lycidas* and *Dover Beach* are the only really famous examples.[29] The meter is iambic, but the lines vary in length (although pentameter predominates), and there is rhyme but no regular rhyme scheme. Like blank verse, it is easy to write, hard to write well. It invites to freedom, and betrays the poet who has no strong feeling for form, who cannot discipline himself.

But in the hands of a master, as *Lycidas* proves, it is capable of unsurpassable richness and variety. And Robinson is also a master. *The Man Against the Sky*, like *Twilight Song* and *The Town Down the River*, presents a pageant of human life. But its mood is one neither of eagerness nor of endurance, but rather of reflection —a weighing and balancing of appearance and reality, of materialism and idealism, of the odds on extinction and on survival. The lines therefore neither march nor flow, but advance, pause, recede, pause, and advance, like waves upon a shore. One is reminded of *Dover Beach*, with its finely calculated wavelike rhythm; but in Robinson's poem the movement is swifter and stronger. Long lines slide down to a trough of doubt or despair, sweep up to a crest of defiance or confidence. Then comes a break in the rhythm, as a shorter line drives home the point of what has just preceded or, more often, marks an ironic reversal of thought or feeling.

This quality of the verse is revealed in the following lines, where the affirmation of faith underlying the urgent irony rises through repeated sweeping questions to a climax of intensity, and then subsides, though only for a moment, to the "pondering repose of 'If.'" If, says the poet, man abandons belief not only in what he may regard as the outworn superstitions called "Heaven" and "Hell" but also in any kind of purpose or continuity beyond this life,

> If, robbed of two fond old enormities,
> Our being had no onward auguries,
> What then were this great love of ours to say
> For launching other lives to voyage again
> A little farther into time and pain,
> A little faster in a futile chase
> For a kingdom and a power and a Race
> That would have still in sight
> A manifest end of ashes and eternal night?
> Is this the music of the toys we shake
> So loud,—as if there might be no mistake
> Somewhere in our indomitable will?
> Are we no greater than the noise we make
> Along one blind atomic pilgrimage
> Whereon by crass chance billeted we go

Because our brains and bones and cartilage
Will have it so?
If this we say, then let us all be still
About our share in it, and live and die
More quietly thereby.

Robinson uses this form in two other poems: *An Island*, a study
of Napoleon dying on Saint Helena, alone, half mad, and haunted
by the past—a piece which, despite some fine passages, gives us
neither the traditional picture nor a new one that is entirely clear,
coherent, and persuasive; and *Dionysus in Doubt*, a searching but
not ill humored or unhopeful criticism of American democracy and
its threat to the liberty of the individual. The first poem is purely
dramatic, and there seems no particular fitness in the form. But the
second is again a statement of one aspect of Robinson's philosophy,
put into the mouth of the mythical Dionysus. This assumption of
objectivity, of an analytical rather than a confessional approach,
finds expression not only in more colloquial language but also in
shorter lines, that have a quicker, lighter, more varied and casual
movement; as when Dionysus reminds doctrinaire reformers

"That when a sphere is hammered square
All that was hammered is still there;
Also that Humbug is no less
Himself in his best dress."

8

Before passing to Robinson's blank verse, we may consider
briefly the poems written in other meters without rhyme. Such imi-
tations of the Greek and Roman poets always give the impression
of being *tours de force*, and this Robinson naturally recognized.
Apparently, however, he was interested in the technical problems
that these verse forms involved; and he considered five experiments
in this sort of writing to be worthy of inclusion in the *Collected
Poems*: *The Chorus of Old Men in "Ægeus," The Wilderness, The
Klondike, Pasa Thalassa Thalassa*, and *Late Summer*.[30] The last of
these, written in alcaics, treats the familiar Robinsonian theme of

disappointment in love, and the form, although handled with apparent ease,[31] seems not particularly appropriate. In the other four, however, the poet shows his usual deftness in fitting form to thought, rhythm to sense and feeling.

The Chorus, composed for a projected drama on the Greek model which was never written, is made up of unrhymed lines of various length, with frequent departures from the basic iambic meter; and it has something of the almost unique union of somber dignity and delicate lyricism with which (even in translation) the Choruses in the tragedies of Sophocles pronounce man's physical, but not his moral, subservience to fate:

> And thou, the saddest wind
> That ever blew from Crete,
> Sing the fell tidings back to that thrice unhappy ship!—
> Sing to the western flame,
> Sing to the dying foam,
> A dirge for the sundered years and a dirge for the years to be!

The Klondike, like *The Town Down the River,* has a movement suggestive of a river's flow; intended here to represent the lure of gold that so many men have found irresistible, and that through the ages has come to be looked on as a sort of epitome of man's everlasting discontent with present possessions.[32] Thus the dying adventurer apostrophizes "the golden river":

> "Twelve," he says, "who sold their shame for a lure you call
>   too fair for them—
> You that laugh and flow to the same word that urges them:
> Twelve who left the old town shining in the sunset,
> Left the weary street and the small safe days:
> Twelve who knew but one way out, wide the way or narrow:
> Twelve who took the frozen chance and laid their lives on
>   yellow."

The converse of this poetic coin is *The Wilderness,* in which the call of far places and unknown experiences yields in the end to the longing for home with its familiar ties now made dear by distance; and the triumph of this backward pull is faithfully reflected in the verse:

Come away! come away! there is nothing now to cheer us—
Nothing now to comfort us, but love's road home:—
Over there beyond the darkness there's a window gleams to
    greet us,
And a warm hearth waits for us within.

Perhaps the most finely wrought of the poems in this group is
Pasa Thalassa Thalassa, a memorial to the sea captain Israel Jor-
dan, a neighbor (when not at sea) of the Robinson family and a
romantic figure in the childhood world of the poet-to-be: [33]

Gone—faded out of the story, the sea-faring friend I remember?
Gone for a decade, they say: never a word or a sign.
Gone with his hard red face that only his laughter could wrinkle,
Down where men go to be still, by the old way of the sea.

There is, of course, one form of unrhymed verse that has adapted
itself to the English language as to no other, and in that language
has provided a vehicle for the loftiest ascents of the imagination.
And it might seem that blank verse, which Robinson also used in
some of his greatest triumphs, and in which the bulk of his poetry
is written, should receive the most detailed analysis. But, once
begun, a minute examination of the poet's blank verse arrangement of syllable and stress, and the relation of this arrangement to
the substance of particular passages, could not readily be brought
to a logical end; and one may doubt whether it would reveal any
prosodic principles or devices not already noted. Only a few general comments therefore seem needful.

It has been stated already that after the *Captain Craig* volume
in 1902, Robinson published (and presumably wrote) no more
blank verse until *Ben Jonson Entertains a Man from Stratford*,
which was written in 1915. It is not surprising that after so long an
interval there should be evident a striking change in the structure
and consequent rhythm of the lines. The early verse, though composed with skill and never monotonous or mechanical, is relatively
regular; that of the later years is marked by greater fluidity and variety. On the formal side, this change appears to be due mainly
to two factors: the more frequent use of feminine endings (one
main source of the distinctive quality of Robinson's blank verse)

and the freer substitution of trochaic or anapestic for iambic feet. The expansive Captain, himself, indeed, breaks all metrical rules; and *Isaac and Archibald* has something of the same informality. But in *Aunt Imogen* and *The Book of Annandale* only an occasional line ends in an unstressed syllable; whereas in *Ben Jonson* roughly a third of the lines (in one passage, seven in succession) are so constructed. The other change—the shifting of the stress or the addition of an unstressed syllable at the beginning or in the middle of a line—is perhaps less noticeable but nevertheless important.[34]

There appears to be no profound significance in these changes, which are by no means unexampled. Most masters of blank verse have used the form with more freedom as they grew older; and this freedom, it may be noted, usually marks an advance in technique. As far as metrical skill is concerned, Robinson's powers are probably at their peak in his late long poems. One critic goes so far as to declare that in these poems "Robinson has created a style of writing in blank verse that is far more continuously interesting as style, as verse, than that of his lyrical measures." [35]

This fact has been obscured by the tendency of most other critics to lump together all the poems following *Tristram* and to declare that in these the blank verse grows steadily more involved, more obscure, more remote from actual speech. This notion, however, does not fit the facts. In the last three poems, at least, the blank verse seems to me to be more straightforward, less mannered, closer both in language and rhythm to everyday usage than any that Robinson had written since *Isaac and Archibald*. *Talifer* is not at all difficult reading—though, as always, there are gaps in the story that the reader who is not constantly on the alert for clues will find hard to bridge; and to this difficulty, in *Amaranth* and *King Jasper*, is added that of an allegory whose true interpretation is not immediately clear. But there is little trouble with the style. The language is relatively simple, the sentences are not hard to understand.[36]

What this verse lacks—so that all the poems after *Tristram* are

less appealing to many readers than are those that have gone before—is energy, eagerness, intensity. The poet's eye is as sharp, the
mind as searching, the judgment as shrewd, the humor as tolerant,
the hope as constant, as ever; but the "choral golden overflow" of
life into music is not heard.

Yet there is no mystery here. "In Broceliande," Merlin says,
"Time overtook me as I knew he must"; and in Peterborough
Time overtook a man who had done longer service to a more exacting mistress. He too, if only in imagination, had created kings
and kingdoms "to be a mirror wherein men/ May see themselves,
and pause"; and in real life had watched with no indifferent eyes
the death of "a played-out world." And it was not merely a malignant physical growth that sapped his energy in the last years, and
left him at the end of each successive summer of creative effort
closer to complete exhaustion. What Ben Jonson is made to say
about Shakespeare is the utterance of a man who knows the cost of
poetic creation:

> For such as he, the thing that is to do
> Will do itself,—but there's a reckoning;
> The sessions that are now too much his own,
> The roiling inward of a stilled outside,
> The churning out of all those blood-fed lines,
> The nights of many schemes and little sleep,
> The full brain hammered hot with too much thinking,
> The vexed heart over-worn with too much aching,—
> This weary jangling of conjoined affairs
> Made out of elements that have no end,
> And all confused at once, I understand,
> Is not what makes a man to live forever.

The poems following *Tristram* are the work of an old man, and
the proper charge to be brought against the style is not obscurity
but—by those who want the exuberance of *Captain Craig*, the
lyricism of *Merlin*, the power of *The Man Who Died Twice*—
monotony. Yet the critic who denounces the verse as simply and
invariably dull is revealing nothing but his own ignorance or
dullness. There is still something here that could not be said in

prose; as perhaps one may find, if he will, in the lines in *Amaranth*
in which the clear-eyed and compassionate Evensong bids farewell
to the fellow-failure who would not be reconciled to Truth:

> "So then, to Pink—and to an easy voyage
> Over a lonely sea that shall be ours
> In turn to cross. If when our voyage begins
> There may not be much weeping on the wharves,
> We shall not care; and those we leave behind
> Will suffer less than if they needed us."

Or one may find it in *King Jasper*, in the words of the equally
clear-eyed Zoë, whose mission forbids her to be equally compassionate, as she reveals the rotten foundations of industrial king-
ship. "It is your chemistry," she tells King Jasper (meaning the
ways by which he rose to power),

> "That shows me clearer than it has shown those
> Who wrought it, the long monstrousness of life
> That most have suffered and a few been crowned for."

But though all the late works contain passages that only the perverse will refuse to admit are poetry, by any definition, it is in the
earlier poems that we find the blank verse to be most obviously expressive of the event, the thought, the mood, that is recorded. It is
perhaps nowhere more so than in *Captain Craig*, Robinson's first
successful essay in this form. In this poem, which combines a brilliant and objective character study with the poet's own spirited and
resonant reading of life, the verse has a variety and a vitality that
are astonishing. Whatever may be the experience that is to be recorded, the right rhythm is confidently summoned. It may be the
impression made on a lonely child by a friendly word,

> "a faint forest wind
> That once had made the loneliest of all
> Sad sounds on earth, now made the rarest music;
> And water that had called him once to death
> Now seemed a flowing glory";

or an unrepentant and even humorous inspection, by a dying man,
of a life that people in general would call wasted, would judge to
have been

> "As unproductive and as unconvinced
> Of living bread and the soul's eternal draught
> As a frog on a Passover-cake in a streamless desert";

or, again, the serenity, the brightness, the savor of a world experienced to the full and found good, which is the keynote of the poem and which Robinson in his later volumes never quite recaptured:

> So, now and then,
> That evening of the day the Captain died
> Returns to us; and there comes always with it
> The storm, the warm restraint, the fellowship,
> The friendship and the firelight, and the fiddle.

The presence of such a distinctive note, or tone, giving to the whole work a unity of style, is perhaps one of the things that contribute most to the effectiveness of Robinson's most successful blank-verse poems. So much depends on "feeling," to be sure, that such a proposition is scarcely capable of proof, and the reader will wish to test it for himself. Yet one may suggest that it is illustrated at least in the three Arthurian poems. Through *Merlin* from the beginning, in the rhythm of the verse, there echoes a premonition of the end of every love and every kingdom born or built in Time; and also, though heard but faintly in the distance, the faith that after every ending will come a new and better beginning:

> "All this that was to be is what I saw
> Before there was an Arthur to be king,
> And so to be a mirror wherein men
> May see themselves, and pause. If they see not,
> Or if they do see and they ponder not,—
> I saw; but I was neither Fate nor God.
> I saw too much; and this would be the end,
> Were there to be an end."

In *Lancelot*, on the other hand, the note is one of finality. The world of romantic love and romantic royalty is passing, not for a time but—as far as Lancelot and Guinevere are concerned—forever. For them the wars and passions of men and women are destined to give place to the peace of God. And as this destiny closes irresistibly upon them, its approach is proclaimed and measured by the movement of the lines. The last two lines of each of the last four sections will make clear the contrast with *Merlin*:

> He carried her away. The word of Rome
> Was in the rain. There was no other sound.

> The King, and the King's army followed them,
> For longer sorrow and for longer war.

> "Peace to your soul, Gawaine," Lancelot said,
> And would have closed his eyes. But they were closed.

> But always in the darkness he rode on,
> Alone; and in the darkness came the Light.

In *Tristram* the verses move to still a different music. Though Robinson rejected violently the magic potion as a motivating force, and attempted to rationalize the lovers and their story, he does not altogether exorcise the fairy-tale atmosphere that pervades the legend in its earliest surviving forms—the remoteness, the brightness, the innocence of sin, the uncomprehending welcome, submission, or opposition accorded to life's irrational events. This changefulness and irrationality are at every turn symbolized by the sea—unpredictable, uncontrollable, calm or frenzied on its surface, mysterious in its depths. And these qualities find their way inevitably and perhaps unconsciously into the movement of the verse. It lingers as if in benediction over the last meeting of the lovers:

> Never before
> Had such a stillness fallen on land or sea
> That he remembered. Only one silent ship
> Was moving, if it moved.

The sunlit stillness is stirred but briefly by the flash of Andred's knife and Tristram's cry. The sunlight goes, the sea darkens, but the stillness stays—as it always will—for Mark as he watches

> The sea and its one ship, until the sea
> Became a lonely darkness and the ship
> Was gone, as a friend goes. The silent water
> Was like another sky where silent stars
> Might sleep for ever, and everywhere was peace.

But on the shores of Brittany the restless waves beat for the living Isolt a ceaseless unanswerable "Why?" as she gazes out upon a world that seems empty of all but

> waves and foam
> And white birds everywhere, flying and flying . . .
> And the white sunlight flashing on the sea.

Two other poems, at least, may be mentioned in which a dominant tone seems clearly evident. *Tasker Norcross* is the portrait of a man whose appeal to the reader's interest and sympathy lies, paradoxically, in the fact that he is consciously but helplessly destitute of every trait or talent through which interest and sympathy would normally be aroused. And accordingly the style, while never becoming really dull and so ceasing to be poetry, is subdued almost to dullness:

> "He could see stars,
> On a clear night, but he had not an eye
> To see beyond them. He could hear spoken words,
> But had no ear for silence when alone.
> He could eat food of which he knew the savor,
> But had no palate for the Bread of Life,
> That human desperation, to his thinking,
> Made famous long ago, having no other."

Beside these level lines may be put for contrast a few that in their turbulent forward surge strike the keynote of *The Man Who Died Twice*—the note of boundless powers thrown away, yet leaving

> in him always,
> Unqualified by guile and unsubdued
> By failure and remorse, or by redemption,
> The grim nostalgic passion of the great
> For glory all but theirs.

These lines may serve as a last example of what this chapter tries to say: that in Robinson's poetry there is a constant and often brilliantly successful effort to make the language and meter fit the thought—to fuse the means and the end, the form and the substance, as in art they must be fused.

chapter iv: ORGANIC FORM

A poem, according to Coleridge's famous definition in *Biographia Literaria,* is distinguished from other types of literature whose primary aim is to give pleasure in that the pleasure is derived both from the separate parts and from the whole. That is, separate stanzas, lines, and images are pleasurable in themselves; and at the end the reader finds added pleasure in having experienced the work as a whole—its unity, its harmony of proportion, the arrangement of the parts in a pleasing order.

It is with the first of these sources of poetic pleasure—the effects produced by separate parts, which might be referred to generally as "style"—that the preceding chapter has been mainly concerned. We have now to consider the second—the way in which the work as a whole is put together so as to produce added pleasure. Here we are concerned with two principles. One is unity—the simple adhesion of the parts to each other around some central nucleus, as scrap iron adheres to an electromagnet. But of course this mere gathering together of materials that all have some connection with a central concept or theme is not enough to make a poem. There must be some kind of order, or organization, such as (to continue the analogy with magnetism) the lines into which iron filings on a sheet of paper are drawn when a magnet is passed beneath them.

This might be called "structure," except that the term suggests a mechanical and completed arrangement of inert materials; whereas the analogy of the magnet must now be dropped. For the order, the pattern, in a poem has to be produced in time. This does not mean that a poem must tell a story, or that the controlling and ordering principle may not be logical (in some sense) rather than chronological, but that what the poem has to say to the reader becomes clear only by a gradual process as he goes through it from beginning to end. There must, that is, be a *development*, not a mere casual accretion of details, even though these may all be related to the central theme. Perhaps an appropriate term to apply to the combined principles of unity and development is "organic form."

2

Form, of course, is not wholly separable from style. We have seen already how Robinson varies the rhythm of his lines so as to make them contribute in a certain way to the total effect. From these techniques it is only a short step to another device by which Robinson gives unity to a work, makes it hang together in the reader's mind so as to be remembered as a single experience. This is the repetition at carefully calculated intervals of some key word or phrase. In speaking repeatedly of "the man Flammonde," Robinson gradually builds up the impression of his hero's uniqueness; of Flammonde's isolation from his fellows not because of any eccentricity but because of so much more humanity, so much more of what men ought to be, than they have. In *The Gift of God* the recurrence of "shining" or "shine" suggests both the brightness and the insubstantiality of the mother's mirage. In *The Clinging Vine* the mounting hysteria of the wife is reflected in the way she keeps throwing back at her husband (in the first, sixth, and eighth stanzas) his apparent advice "Be calm"; and the phrase "moon and stars and ocean" is used in the second and last stanzas to drive home the fact that no human warmth remains in her feeling for the husband who has been false.

These happen to be the first three pieces in the *Collected Poems*, all published with *The Man Against the Sky* in 1916. But the same device is used in the early and in the late poems. It may, in fact, have been suggested to Robinson by the repetition of lines in the French forms which he so studiously emulated during his apprentice years, although only four examples are preserved in the *Collected Poems*: *Ballade by the Fire, Ballade of Broken Flutes, Villanelle of Change*, and *The House on the Hill*.

Allied to these are the poems (also early, for the most part) in which Robinson introduces a refrain. In *John Evereldown* the repeated questions and answers build for the reader an image of the treadmill of desire on which the man is doomed to wear out his life. "Where are you going, John Evereldown?" and "Why are you going, John Evereldown?" are given answers that end with "There's where I'm going, to Tilbury Town" and "That's why I'm going to Tilbury Town." Likewise, Luke Havergal's doom reverberates in the repeated cadence of the words spoken by his ghostly tempter: ". . . the western gate, Luke Havergal." In *The Wilderness* and *The Klondike* opposite impulses are expressed in the repeated call of home—"Come away! come away!"—and in the urgent phrase, reiterated until the words fail on frozen lips, "to find the golden river." A more buoyant spirit in the treatment of a similar theme finds a voice in "Through the shine, through the rain" of *Twilight Song*. But in *The Town Down the River*, again, the strife is darker, the outcome more equivocal. The title phrase, occurring twice in the poem, suggests the attraction of the River's call; while the forces—of stability or inertia, according to one's point of view—which resist the call so long but at last in vain, are hinted at in the cadence of the line which opens each section: "Said the Watcher by the Way . . ." Finally, the tragic pageantry of *The Valley of the Shadow* is punctuated by the repetition of the title phrase in the first line of the first stanza and in the next to the last line of each of the eight succeeding stanzas.

This use of a regular refrain Robinson gradually abandoned, although a similar purpose is sometimes served by people's names: Jane Wayland and John Gorham in alternate stanzas of *John Gorham*, at the end of the first line; the full name of the central figure in *Miniver Cheevy* at the beginning of the first and last stanzas, the first name at the beginning of the others; Vickery in ten of the fourteen stanzas of *Vickery's Mountain;* Eileen in five of the nine stanzas of *Lisette and Eileen;* Oakes and Oliver at brief intervals in *Two Gardens in Linndale;* Priscilla and Llewellyn likewise in *Llewellyn and the Tree.*

A more frequent form of verbal tie in the later poems, however, is the one mentioned at the beginning: the reiteration of key words and phrases, but only at irregular intervals, with a casualness intended to conceal the art. There are Llewellyn and his "roses"; Vickery and his "golden" dream; Mr. Flood "alone" with his "jug." There are roses, also (only here they are a symbol not of romance but of change and death), and "shadows and echoes" in the first part of *Pasa Thalassa Thalassa;* and in the second part the theme "shrouded in silence he lies" is repeated at the end in a variant form, "down where he lies tonight, silent . . ."

The same kind of repetition, like that of a theme in music, also helps to give unity to the longer poems. In *Toussaint L'Ouverture,* one of Robinson's medium-length blank-verse pieces, the word "black" occurs eleven times in 271 lines; five times in the phrase "a black man," which is contrasted with "black earth," and "a black commodity" in an implied assertion of the equal humanity of black and white, which will triumph over the hate that now, in the person of Napoleon, denies it. In *The Three Taverns,* a recreation of the Apostle Paul that perhaps comes as near to translating the essence of the Epistles into modern idiom as will ever be possible, the speaker refers ten times to "Rome," and in its resonance we seem to hear a sentence of death for Paul himself, but at the same time a prophecy of lasting and widening life for the religion that he preaches.

In the verse-novels, beginning with *Merlin,* the repetition is naturally less frequent, so that it may not become monotonous or obtrusive. Merlin's recurrent "I saw," or sometimes "I saw too much," may be scarcely noticed by the reader. Yet gradually he receives the impression which the poet is striving to convey—of Merlin's superiority to other men in his power to foresee the future and of his equality with them in his lack of power to alter it. In the same poem the reader will remember, also, Merlin's twice-seen vision of a "town of many towers,/ All swayed and shaken," that presently crumbles away into black and crimson clouds. Its first appearance seems to symbolize the consummation of his love for Vivian; its second, the overthrow of Arthur's kingdom. But since Merlin, even by foregoing his love and staying in Camelot, could not have saved the King, perhaps the connection is that both visions reflect the power of "the torch of woman," which is even more dominant in Arthur's life than in Merlin's: first in the person of his sister, who becomes Modred's mother, and then in the person of Guinevere.

This power, Merlin prophesies, "together with the light/ That Galahad found, is yet to light the world"; and Galahad's is "the Light" that is alluded to so often in *Lancelot*, although it may seem so remote as to be almost unnoticed amid the thickening gloom that shrouds the story. But it registers none the less, helping us to realize the strength of what is drawing Lancelot away from Guinevere, and preparing us for the mystic vision that comes to him at last as he emerges from the maze in which men and women lose themselves in pursuing worldly ends.

In *Tristram*, also, there are painful mazes in which the people wander; and again Robinson suggests their various plights by the repetition of distinctive phrases, which in this poem, especially, derive added force from their appeal to the senses. The destined loneliness of Isolt of Brittany is always framed by "white birds flying," while the passion of Tristram and Isolt of Ireland moves to the somber music of "the moaning wash of Cornish water,/ Cold upon Cornish rocks." [1]

In the same way, in *Matthias at the Door*, the mood of the poem is established by the ever returning image of "a dark Egyptian door"—a door that men and women open to let themselves out of life. And in *King Jasper* there is constant reference to the "chimneys" which symbolize the industrial empire over which Jasper rules; and to the "unseen hands" by which the Queen is haunted, which are perhaps only a symbol of inevitable change.

The most elaborate use of such leitmotifs, as they may be called, occurs appropriately in *The Man Who Died Twice*. Fernando Nash's asseverated "I had it—once" is compounded half of lingering pride and half of admitted guilt, and suggests the duality that has been the key to his genius and his ruin. "The drums of death" that were forever sounding in his ears eventually overwhelmed the certitude that it was in his power sometime to receive the "celestial messengers" that were to bring the "choral gold" and the "singing fire" of a music such as hardly one man in a century may compose. He "did not wait," therefore, for their coming; and the "drums of life" that he now beats for a revivalist sect are only an ironic symbol of all that he has had and lost.

The same kind of suggestiveness can occur where the verbal repetition is not exact or not important. Here the unifying power lies not in the words themselves but solely in the image that is called to the reader's mind—some sight or sound or thought, some feature of the physical or psychic landscape. Such a use of suggestion is obvious in *The Book of Annandale,* where the book is a symbol of the new life that Annandale has subconsciously been waiting to build with another wife, and that Damaris has been waiting to build with another husband.[2] A like symbolism is in *The March of the Cameron Men* (published thirty years later). The song that comes uncalled into the man's mind, the words of which he repeats to the woman, with a reluctance that belies his assertion that he does not know their meaning, is a symbol of the distance that has already been placed between them by the death, not of the woman's husband, but of what they thought was love.

Perhaps a more natural use of symbolism is the house in Stratford that so exasperates Ben Jonson by its incongruity with what Shakespeare's greatness ought to desire. His irritation grows as he thinks on the one hand of the splendid worlds created by his friend's imagination and on the other of his assertion, "It's all Nothing"; both hopelessly inconsistent with the poet's apparent desire to impress the little world of Stratford. There is a climactic progression in the speaker's references to "that House," "that prodigious grand new House," "that damned House," and "O Lord, that House in Stratford!"

Another significant house is the ancestral home of Roman Bartholow, apparently representing a world of false values (the "custom" that Penn-Raven speaks of so frequently) which led him and Gabrielle into a marriage that in turn drove him to the verge of madness, and that drives her, after his recovery, to death; for she knows that the house of a new life that he talks of building with her would rest on as infirm a foundation as the old.[3] Nor is this the only recurrent image in which is darkly reflected the somber story in which Gabrielle is destined to be the victim. The moths that keep beating their wings against the screen, "Still angry at their freedom" and "Torn by their own salvation," appear to symbolize in general the helplessness of human beings to achieve by their own efforts what they most desire; and in particular, perhaps, the wish of both Gabrielle and Penn-Raven to escape from the loneliness which for them is the other face of freedom into an existence that is limited but also warmed by love.

Such use of symbolism appears to have been congenial to Robinson, and perhaps we may trace a more or less definite line in its development. The simple refrain used in the early poems as a means of securing unity gradually gives way to a less frequent and less formal repetition of words, phrases, or images, and these tend to be laden with more and more symbolic significance. Without insisting on any sharp lines of demarkation, and without being dogmatic about definitions, we may view this change as a progressive movement from mechanical to organic form.

3

Unity properly begins, however, with subject matter. If in a narrative or dramatic poem episodes or persons are introduced that have no clear connection with the main characters or the main line of action, then the most skillful technique can at best impose only a specious unity upon the work.

One cannot help feeling that this is what happens in some of Robinson's poems. It is perhaps not a coincidence that in each of the two poems that are by far the longest that he ever wrote, *Roman Bartholow* and *Tristram*, considerable space is given to a character who seems in no way essential to the story. If in the former the thirty-odd pages of talk between Bartholow and Umfraville were omitted, the poem would certainly be easier to get through, and it is hard to see that much would be lost that could not be spared. It may be said that Bartholow needs a confidant who can look with an impartial eye on Gabrielle and Penn-Raven, and to whom he can turn when both have been lost to him. But his need is not profound, for his spiritual crisis has been surmounted, with Penn-Raven's aid, before the poem begins; and, as both Penn-Raven and Umfraville tell him, nothing can deprive him of the salvation that he has gained. Nor does Umfraville seem to have any independent function in the poem. His character and situation, the hermit's life that has been his solution to the problem posed by his grotesque appearance, is not clearly related to the situations and problems of the other characters, although such a relation may well have been intended. His story seems to ask for a separate telling, and no doubt deserves it. As it stands, it aggravates the weaknesses of a poem that even without it would be too long and too analytical.

A similar criticism can be leveled at the role assigned to Morgan in *Tristram*. Although she occupies only some ten of 133 pages, she is a more troublesome intruder than Umfraville in *Roman Bartholow*. The story is already almost impossibly complicated by the two Isolts, who are bound to compete for the reader's interest, and by Tristram's improbable marriage to the one of them that he does not love. Robinson makes this infidelity perhaps as plausible as it ever can be made to modern readers, but he creates new difficulties by introducing a rather unpleasant and seemingly pointless liaison with Morgan. Her only apparent function in the plot is to motivate, very obscurely, Andred's murder of Tristram, which is already sufficiently motivated by his half-mad devotion to Mark. She does, it is true, engage our interest if not our affection; and Robinson's letters indicate that he enjoyed writing about her. But she seems not to belong in *Tristram*.

In these two poems, then, the unity is impaired by the presence of material that is not made clearly relevant to the main plot. But lack of unity may also result when two related parts of a story enter into competition instead of contributing harmoniously to a single effect. To return to *Tristram*, Isolt of Ireland and Isolt of Brittany vie for the reader's sympathy as they vie for possession of the hero; and while this situation in itself need not destroy the unity, nevertheless, as Robinson tells the tale (following the tradition), the stories of the heroines run parallel, with the hero zigzagging between them. Thus the work has two beginnings and two endings; and when the story of Isolt of Ireland has been told to the end, and the reader is prepared to pause for meditation, to review the events and estimate the significance of her life and Tristram's, there is still Isolt of Brittany waiting to receive a farewell and to bequeath new materials for reflection, while the impact of the earlier ending is diffused and weakened.

Here again *Roman Bartholow* is similar to *Tristram*, in that the reader's attention and sympathy are divided. One would expect the main theme to be the spiritual salvation of the character for whom the poem is named. The work begins and ends with him; the part played by each of the other characters is determined by that character's relation to him; and the plot (such as it is) has its origin in the eclipse and re-emergence of some guiding light and power within him. But this crisis of the soul has already been passed, and our sympathies turn to Gabrielle and her failing fight against despair. When, at the end of Section V, she takes her way to the only refuge she knows of, much of our interest goes with her, and there seems little point to the irony of the ensuing conflict—briefly physical and lengthily verbal—between Bartholow and Penn-Raven over a woman who is dead; in which, besides, Bartholow's furious jealousy of the friend to whom he owes so much, inspired by the latter's love for the wife whom he himself has never really loved, and whom he has just almost callously dismissed, shows him in no agreeable light.[4]

A superficially similar situation occurs in *Matthias at the Door*, in which Matthias survives and finds a new life, while the much more lovable Natalie does not. But the poem succeeds because Matthias's character is initially so much clearer and more credible than Bartholow's, his transformation so much more natural and convincing. Still more important, Natalie's death is not futile, like Gabrielle's, but leads eventually, by a way not wearisome nor too circuitous, to Matthias's redemption. In this redemption, also, Garth and Timberlake have had their share: Garth by his initial planting of the seed of self-distrust in Matthias's mind, Timberlake by the healing friendship that he briefly brings after Natalie's death. Thus all the characters live and die in order to bring about one end; and the only question the reader has reason to raise is whether the result is worth the cost. But to ask such a question here, Robinson would say, is to ask it concerning life as a whole in the "real" world.[5]

Merlin, also, among the long poems, poses the question of unity, but for the present may be passed over. In general, in spite of the exceptions noted, Robinson sticks to his story. He may take too long in telling it, but as a rule he does not wander—a fact that suggests that when he seems to wander, he has probably merely failed to provide a map. *The Man Who Died Twice* contains no detail that does not bear directly on the character and fate of Fernando Nash. *Avon's Harvest* is almost oppressive in its concentration upon Avon's obsession; the reader is grateful for the entrance of Asher and the Admiral, restoring him briefly to the world of substance and sanity. *Cavender's House* will weary some readers by the relentless and unrelieved analysis of the main character. *Talifer* is as well plotted as *Matthias at the Door*, although the characters are weaker. In *Amaranth* the theme of Fargo's redemption from life in the wrong world is never lost sight of. In Robinson's last work, King Jasper holds the center of the stage from beginning to end, except for the brief final conflict between young Hebron and Zoë.

In the shorter poems there is little temptation—one might almost say little opportunity—to bring in material that is not immediately related to the main theme. The space that the poet allows himself is usually so limited in proportion to what he has to say, that the problem is not how to exclude what is irrelevant but how to get in what is essential. This is most obviously true of the sonnets, where the limitation is absolute, except in three instances where Robinson takes two sonnets instead of one to tell his story. And the poet's awareness of the value of brevity seems also to be at work in all the poems not in blank verse. Only ten of these contain as many as one hundred lines; only three—*An Island, The Man Against the Sky*, and *Dionysus in Doubt*, all written in rhyme but without stanzas—contain more than two hundred. None has more than four hundred. The two longest—*The Man* and *Dionysus*—are philosophical and not narrative or dramatic. No doubt some of these poems could be still shorter without loss of effect. But in general it may be said that when Robinson is telling a story in rhyme, he uses no more space than he needs.

4

Form in poetry, however, as has been said, involves not only adherence to a central story or theme, but some kind of progress or development toward a final effect to which each particular part has made its particular contribution.

A simple and famous illustration is *Richard Cory:*

Whenever Richard Cory went down town,
We people on the pavement looked at him:
He was a gentleman from sole to crown,
Clean-favored, and imperially slim.

And he was always quietly arrayed,
And he was always human when he talked;
But still he fluttered pulses when he said,
"Good-morning," and he glittered when he walked.

And he was rich—yes, richer than a king—
And admirably schooled in every grace:
In fine, we thought that he was everything
To make us wish that we were in his place.

So on we worked, and waited for the light,
And went without the meat and cursed the bread;
And Richard Cory, one calm summer night,
Went home and put a bullet through his head.

We need not crush this little piece under a massive analysis; a few more or less obvious comments will suffice to show how carefully the poem is put together. The first two lines suggest Richard Cory's distinction, his separation from ordinary folk. The second two tell what it is in his natural appearance that sets him off. The next two mention the habitual demeanor that elevates him still more in men's regard: his apparent lack of vanity, his rejection of the eminence that his fellows would accord him. At the beginning of the third stanza, "rich" might seem to be an anticlimax—but not in the eyes of ordinary Americans; though, as the second line indicates, they would not like to have it thought that in their eyes wealth is everything. The last two lines of the stanza record a total impression of a life that perfectly realizes the dream that most men have of an ideal existence; while the first two lines of the last stanza bring us back with bitter emphasis to the poem's beginning, and the impassable gulf, for most people—but not, they think, for Richard Cory—between dream and fact. Thus the first fourteen lines are a painstaking preparation for the last two, with their stunning overturn of the popular belief.

To repeat this sort of analysis for each of Robinson's poems would be as profitless as tedious to most readers, who will want to do it themselves if they want it done at all. We may, however, dwell a little on some of the patterns that the poet likes to follow. And first of all, it is to be observed that the structure of *Richard Cory*— the steady build-up to the surprise ending in the last line, is not characteristic.[6] This fact fits in with what was said in the preceding chapter about Robinson's handling of the sonnet, and the quiet, unhurried close that he most often gives it; as well as with what has been all along implied concerning his distaste for every sort of sensationalism. But sometimes, as in *Richard Cory*, a different turn of mind reveals itself, perhaps sprung from the perception that life *does* have surprises, that sometimes only at the very last do we find the key piece that makes the hitherto puzzling picture all at once intelligible. *Bon Voyage* ends like *Richard Cory*, although the blow falls less heavily. *The Whip*, on the other hand, closes with an even more jarring shock. *Haunted House* also comes to a sudden shuddering climax with its revelation of murder. *How Annandale Went Out* follows the same pattern, though here it is not a murder but a "mercy killing" that comes to light in the last line. *Aaron Stark* and *Karma* likewise make the reader wait for a last lurid illumination (though the words are simple) of man's capacity for hardened misanthropy or infirm self-deception. *Reuben Bright* and *Ben Trovato* are two other sonnets that save the climax for the close; but in these it is a more gracious light that breaks through the overcast above the human scene. And a final sonnet on the same pattern is *Fleming Helphenstine*, which almost uniquely among Robinson's poems ends in a burst of merry laughter.

In all these poems, reflecting many moods, though mostly dark, there is, despite the careful preparation, some element of the unexpected in the close. But sometimes, although the tension rises to the very end, the progress is steady, and the climax is foreseen with increasing clarity and certainty. Such are *The Clinging Vine*, in which the advances of the wayward husband are repulsed with unwavering determination by the wife; and *John Gorham*, in which the more and more earnest pleas of Jane Wayland to be understood by the man she loves are rejected with unrelenting sullenness by the man whose vanity she has unwittingly injured.

The climax is also delayed but foreseen in *Avon's Harvest*, where Avon's harrowing though restrained account of his unequal contest with the specter by which he is being hunted down, and the confirmation given to this tale of horror by his altered appearance and manner and by the suppressed but obvious terror of his wife, prepare us for no long delay in the fatal consummation of his ordeal. Nor is there need afterward for more than the few remarks that the doctor makes.[7]

In this poem the reader is perhaps surprised to note that the steady rise in tension is not the result of an uninterrupted chronological narrative. Here, as in many of the other long poems, notably *Merlin*, *The Man Who Died Twice*, *Cavender's House*, and *The Glory of the Nightingales*, the poet plunges into his story not far (in time) from the end, and then returns and gradually reveals what has gone before. This revelation, moreover, is often not con-

secutive and direct, but is offered here and there by hints and suggestions, sometimes contained in apparently casual conversations.
There are also frequent shifts from present to past and back again;
and many of these involve an ironic contrast, the point and force
of which are not immediately clear.

This method makes demands upon the reader that he may
consider unreasonable, and therefore may not care to meet. One
critic, indeed, calls it "a technique of systematic exasperation." [8]
It may be defended, however, on two grounds. One is that it
reflects the quality of life as we know it—the necessity, in actual
life, if we wish a story to be intelligible, of bringing together non-
consecutive, asymmetrical, and shadowed fragments of experience
and trying to make them fit.[9] The other is that the method is in-
trinsically effective: that, skillfully used, it excites the reader's
curiosity, sustains his interest, makes him eager to find the key to
the mystery with which he is confronted. "Holding his subject in
solution, as it were, the poet gains the more powerful effect when
he finally permits its precipitation." [10]

But, however he tells the story, Robinson does not usually,
despite the examples given, end a poem abruptly when the narrative is concluded or the picture is complete. Rather, he pauses to
survey the spectacle that his words have summoned, and to meditate, as if he were a mere observer instead of the creator of it, upon
the significance of what he sees. Many of the sonnets, even, compressed as the drama in them has to be, end on a quiet note. *The
Story of the Ashes and the Flame, The Clerks, A Song at Shannon's,
Firelight, Vain Gratuities, Caput Mortuum, Reunion,* and others,
move gravely to their close. Even when the ending is happy, the
mood is often one of mingled acceptance and reluctance, of finality and suspense, of certitude and mystery. And the tone is the
same whether the conclusion to which the poet's meditation leads
him is stated directly, as in *The Clerks,* or only implied, as in
A Song at Shannon's.

> Two men came out of Shannon's, having known
> The faces of each other for as long
> As they had listened there to an old song,

Sung thinly in a wastrel monotone
By some unhappy night-bird, who had flown
Too many times and with a wing too strong
To save himself, and so done heavy wrong
To more frail elements than his alone.

Slowly away they went, leaving behind
More light than was before them. Neither met
The other's eyes again or said a word.
Each to his loneliness or to his kind,
Went his own way, and with his own regret,
Not knowing what the other may have heard.

The same pattern is followed in many of Robinson's other short dramatic pieces. In *Flammonde* the first three stanzas introduce and describe the hero; the next five tell of the perfect judgment and generous acts that gave aid and comfort to so many townspeople. But then:

So much for them. But what of him—
So firm in every look and limb?
What small satanic sort of kink
Was in his brain? What broken link
Withheld him from the destinies
That came so near to being his?

Then comes another stanza of questions, and a stanza and a half to stress the futility of asking them, and then the conclusion:

We've each a darkening hill to climb;
And this is why, from time to time
In Tilbury Town, we look beyond
Horizons for the man Flammonde.

Old King Cole has a similar structure, with King Cole himself pointing the moral; and then, lest he seem too pontifical, the poet puts an end to his discourse by having him note with good-humored surprise that his hearer is asleep. *Llewellyn and the Tree, Sainte-Nitouche,* and *Nimmo,* among other pieces, have the same three sections: a careful setting of the stage, a little action somewhat obliquely presented, an appropriate comment.[11] In some of the still shorter dramatic studies, however, such as *The Field of Glory, Eros Turannos, Atherton's Gambit, Clavering, Leffingwell,* and

Peace on Earth, the introduction is omitted, and the first line plunges us into the middle of whatever story there is. Typical are the beginnings of the two poems first mentioned:

> War shook the land where Levi dwelt.

> She fears him, and will always ask
> What fated her to choose him.

But the quiet statement at the end is still there, as the first half of the last stanza of each poem will show:

> And who's of this or that estate
> We do not wholly calculate,
> When baffling shades that shift and cling
> Are not without their glimmering.

> Meanwhile we do no harm; for they
> That with a god have striven,
> Not hearing much of what we say,
> Take what the god has given.

Reading these lines, we begin to see why Robinson spoke of himself as "an incurable preacher." After all, Emerson and Thoreau, even Longfellow and Whittier, are not far behind him. Only, an age of doubt has intervened, and his most common moral is that moralizing is dangerous.

From this attitude springs the practice, already noted in the sonnets, and followed also in some of the finest of his other short poems, of simply telling his story and leaving the application to the reader, only attaching at the end a summary or restatement that may give rise to reflection. Here we find *The Gift of God, The Poor Relation, Miniver Cheevy, Vickery's Mountain,* and *Mr. Flood's Party.* The last of these will show the poet's gift for compressing into a few seemingly effortless concluding lines the mood and theme of the whole. Mr. Flood's party—attended by his two selves, his jug, and two moons—is ended, and the hard reality presses in upon him once more:

> There was not much that was ahead of him,
> And there was nothing in the town below—
> Where strangers would have shut the many doors
> That many friends had opened long ago.

Sometimes this plan is followed with equal felicity in the long poems and those of medium length. In *Isaac and Archibald* the boy's sunset vision of a transfigured world, and his succeeding dream—"a shining one,/ With two old angels in it"—provide a faultless summation of the long day's experiences: whimsical, tender, familiar, and exalted. So in *Captain Craig* the warm fellowship enjoyed by the Captain's young friends on the evening following his unreluctant death, and the "large humor" of the brass band in his funeral procession, make an ending that few readers would wish to change. Again, Fernando Nash's story of sordid failure obvious to all and supreme triumph known only to himself leaves one in need of the narrator's matter-of-fact closing statement of faith in the composer's tale.

In the Arthurian poems, likewise, the brooding sense of doom beneath which all the characters move calls for some sort of final reconciliation of human hopes and purposes with a world in which these hopes and purposes apparently count for nothing. Merlin and Dagonet take a melancholy departure from Arthur's tottering kingdom; but Merlin foresees, as Bedivere prophesies (in *Lancelot*), "Another Camelot and another King." And while all the ties of the old knightly order seem to be dissolving, the new tie of affection between the two whom the old order accounted the wisest and most foolish is a pledge of continuing human loyalties. In *Lancelot*, at the end, the unreasoning egoistic passions that have prevailed so long pass from the scene with the deaths of Modred and Arthur; and Lancelot, leaving Guinevere with the peace that she has found in her convent, rides alone to find the Light that human sin and folly may veil but never extinguish. And in *Tristram* the death of the lovers brings release not only to them but also—in a way—to Mark and Isolt of Brittany from the thorny maze in which they have been compelled to wander so wearily for so long.

Occasionally, it is true, the reconciliation is lengthened to the point of tedium, as in the interminable dialogue which continues in *Roman Bartholow* after all the drama is over—first between Bartholow and Penn-Raven and then between Bartholow and

Umfraville; or in the uninspired admonitions of Garth's too talkative ghost toward the close of *Matthias at the Door*. But as a rule, given the general plan, the ending fits.

There is one group of character poems that calls for special treatment in regard to structure. These are the medium-length dramatic monologues, including *Ben Jonson Entertains a Man from Stratford*, *Rahel to Varnhagen*, *The Three Taverns*, *Toussaint L'Ouverture*, *An Island*, *John Brown*, and *Rembrandt to Rembrandt*. In these, perhaps for the sake of verisimilitude, there seems usually to be no logical progression. Different moods and ideas make their appearance as they might in a real-life discourse growing out of the circumstances that are described. Ben Jonson would not have been likely to give a formal analysis of Shakespeare's character to his friend's Stratford acquaintance, but would have delivered precisely such an unplanned account as the poem turns out to be; in which Shakespeare comes to life almost before the reader is aware, as Ben's facile tongue reveals his great contemporary's tastes and views with reference to wine and women, spiders and flies, imagined worlds and actual houses. Likewise, the aging Rahel's account of her early loves by way of testing the devotion of her young admirer; the words with which the body-weary Paul on his last mission seeks to infuse with his own burning faith the converts whose fortitude he perhaps doubts; the imprisoned Negro patriot's defiance, in spite of failing faculties, of the assaults of pain and despair; his conqueror's involuntary confession of moral collapse in the face of a situation in some ways similar; John Brown's *apologia* on the night before his execution; all these, instead of proceeding directly toward a predetermined conclusion, seem rather to revolve asymmetrically around one or two central themes.

Only in the self-analysis of Rembrandt, when he stands at the very summit of his powers, is found a clear and logical development of the thought: the initial estimate of his situation; his discovery of a sort of consolation in the fact that the wife whose death has been his greatest loss will not have to bear the lifelong obscurity and poverty that he foresees; his decisive rejection of any doubt about the rightness and greatness of the qualities in his painting for which the world condemns it; his longer struggle with the devil of doubt about the worth of any human effort; and his final affirmation of faith in a spiritual Power whose service is a sufficient motive for continued life.

These pieces, however, are like those previously discussed in that all except *An Island* and *Toussaint L'Ouverture* close on a note of serenity and acceptance. And this characteristic close, of course, reflects Robinson's view of how life really goes on. "Life is struggle"—prolonged, arduous, ambiguous. For many individuals the outcome appears tragic. And triumph, when it comes, is costly. But seen as a whole, under the aspect of eternity, life is not tragic. For the defeated there is at least peace, in the end, whatever else there may be. And among those who survive, the wounds heal, the ranks close, the struggle continues. After each valiant effort, "Something is here that was not here before."

5

There remains yet unmentioned one possible element of organic form in a narrative or dramatic poem; namely, the development of character in itself, the portrayal of a person who changes in some significant way. This, in most of Robinson's verse novels, helps to compensate for the lack of action and occasional longwindedness. In the shorter poems, of course, such an achievement is nearly—although not quite—impossible. The distinction here is not unlike that between still and moving pictures. Robinson's short character studies might be called "stills," his long ones "movies."

There is no question but that in many ways the former are better. All the details, as a rule, are deftly managed: the crucial moment, the right angle, the proper background, the most effective lighting. And the result is often brilliant, balanced, profoundly stirring or suggestive. But it is static. The person is what he is; and (as the poet says of the painful situation in the *Unforgiven*) "there will be no change to-day." *John Evereldown, Aaron Stark, Miniver*

Cheevy, The Gift of God, The Poor Relation, Mr. Flood's Party—
all these and many more present a picture that is final and finished.
It is even hard to imagine any change. Many pieces, indeed, like
*Inferential, The Rat, The Whip, Bon Voyage, Charles Carville's
Eyes, For a Dead Lady, Clavering,* and *Leffingwell,* are elegiac.
All change is ended for the people about whom these poems are
written. From their dead faces, or from what he guesses or remembers, the poet gathers and fixes in words the essence of their characters.

The *effect,* of course, is dynamic. The progressive addition of
details, the repetition of key items, produce a cumulative impression, of which the full force is manifest only at the end. But this
process of change, leading to a clarified conception, a completed
awareness, is in the reader and not in the person he is reading
about. As far as we know, nothing new has entered Richard Cory's
life to make him kill himself. Only at last the quiet desperation
that he has been living with so long reaches the point where it
becomes unbearable. The change that the poem dramatizes is not
in him, but in his fellow townsmen's conception of him.

It is true, of course, that in each instance there is a story behind
the picture—the story of how the person came to be what he is or
do what he does. In *Flammonde,* indeed, the shadowy past of the
hero becomes almost the main point. He came "from God knows
where," "He never told us what he was"; and the townspeople,
watching his successful undertakings in the difficult field of human
relations, keep asking, "What was he . . . ? What was he, and what
was he not?" The Poor Relation also has her story. Once she had
"friends who clamored for her place,/ And would have scratched
her for her face." But what events have taken place between then
and now we are never told. Again, in *Mr. Flood's Party* we are
reminded that in the town below his lonely hilltop, "friends of
other days had honored him"; but this is only background. The
happy husband and wife in *Firelight* are "Wiser for silence" about
past disappointments. The deacon in *Ben Trovato* asks and answers
the natural question inspired by the wife's generous action toward
the blind and dying husband who

> "felt the other woman in the fur
> That now the wife had on. Could she forgive
> All that? Apparently."

And her forgiveness must have a history. But its history is not here. The decisive choices of both husband and wife have been made long before, and are to be accepted for the sake of the momentary present drama.

In all these poems the controlling principle of structure lies not in the action or situation itself, but in the procedure whereby that action or situation is made clear to the reader. But in the long poems, as a rule, the structure is dictated by the development of one or more of the characters themselves. The interest is not so much dramatic as psychological. The characters call not only for our sympathy—or, in some instances, antipathy—but also for our understanding, as far as that is ever possible, of why human beings change or fail to change.

Even in the short poems, however, Robinson makes attempts—by no means unsuccessful—in this direction. Three times he takes two sonnets to tell the story of a changed relation, sprung from a change of character in one or both, between a man and a woman. *Not Always* and *The Woman and the Wife* are both somewhat obscure, but it is at any rate clear that both partners in the first story and the wife in the second acquire at least a capacity for endurance and a stoic wisdom. One may perhaps even find a hint of further changes that may make less bitter the cup that life has placed before them. However this may be, there is in *The Growth of "Lorraine"* no doubt whatever that the title is accurate—that between the initial and final episodes of her story Lorraine has come to possess an immeasurably greater share of the qualities by which human existence is justified and ennobled.

Two others, at least, among the shorter poems record a similar change, although in each the stages of the change are left more or less to be imagined. In *Llewellyn and the Tree,* whatever we may think of Llewellyn's estimate of what his rebellion has brought him, there can be no question that he is a profoundly different person at the end than he was at the beginning. Likewise, in *Sainte-*

Nitouche Vanderberg's long years of inward struggle following the death of the woman he loved leave him at the end of his life a changed man, although the change may be variously appraised, according to the observer's insight and charity.

Turning to the verse novels, and to those first in which Robinson retells the Arthurian legend, we find that the feature that differentiates them most decisively from the medieval versions of the same stories is that the characters change. Merlin passes from the role of prophet and kingmaker to that of romantic lover, and finally, as an old and tired man, bids farewell to both statecraft and romance, and retires from the world. And each change in his external status is accompanied by an alteration of character. As Vivian's lover he enters a new realm of experience, and new qualities make their appearance—a youthful bent toward poetry, an unprophetic humor, a courtier's tact. But with this venture into ordinary human life come penalties of which he had no prevision—conflict between his love for Vivian and his loyalty to Arthur, the bitter knowledge that all human ties are ultimately broken, the discovery that when he abandoned his godlike isolation and descended into the world of human desire and effort, he became subject to Time and Change, age and disillusionment. It is with a humanized wisdom and a chastened hope that he takes his final departure.

In *Lancelot*, likewise, the main theme—the thing that holds the story together and guides its course—is the development of the hero's character: the slow conquest of his old passion for Guinevere by his new devotion to the Grail, as the ruinous results of the former make themselves evident and as the call of the latter becomes stronger. Guinevere, although her role is more passive, has a similar lesson to learn. Even Gawaine, who has so long ordered his existence on the theory that all is vanity except the pleasure of the passing moment, finds a new motive in the hate for Lancelot that his brothers' death inspires; only to learn at last that this too is vanity. Arthur alone fails to recognize that change is inevitable. It is his tragedy that he cannot alter his old perspective, and that his disillusionment is therefore final.

Tristram also draws its significance and derives its appeal from the changes in the characters. The lovers learn humility; Mark learns the hollowness of hatred; Isolt of Brittany changes from a child whose dreams are touched by an unchildlike solemnity to a woman whose vision of reality has the tragic simplicity of childhood.

In most of the other verse novels, likewise, the story involves a change in the central character. *Avon's Harvest* is the record of a man's loss of nerve, at first gradually and then with catastrophic rapidity, under the subtle assaults of his hated enemy. *The Man Who Died Twice* tells of a man's self-impelled degeneration of mind and will, and his belated, uninvited spiritual salvation. *Matthias at the Door* relates the events by which an imperceptive and egocentric businessman is humanized and regenerated. *The Glory of the Nightingales* is built around a like change in Nightingale, and the consequent release of Malory, his one-time friend and long-time enemy, from the incubus of his desire for revenge. *Talifer* tells the story of the recovery of a not unintelligent man from a stupid delusion that leads him to marry the wrong woman, and of his escape and subsequent marriage to the right one, of whom he is now less unworthy; all which leaves him a happier and wiser man. *Cavender's House* and *Amaranth*, although each deals only with the climax of a long period of inner change, are both adventures in self-discovery. The decisive fact in *King Jasper*, which leads to the destruction of Jasper's kingdom, is that he, like King Arthur, cannot change.[12]

6

The subject of this chapter has been so far treated only in relation to Robinson's narrative poems and his studies of character. The ways in which the poet seeks to achieve over-all unity in a composition, as well as to give the content an order that will compel the reader's attention and approval, have been analyzed mainly with reference to works in which the primary materials are particular actions, events, and situations. But there is also a poetry of ideas, in which the author's purpose is to state more or less directly his beliefs concerning the world of which he is a part. And in such poems also, of course, there must be one ruling idea and a definite line of progress toward the completed expression that the poet intends to give it.

Robinson's pieces of this kind are all relatively short (the longest is *Dionysus in Doubt*, which has 374 lines), and, as in the other short poems, he usually sticks to his point; he may sometimes labor it a little, but he does not leave it. Furthermore, the line that he follows in developing it is, as a rule, relatively straight and clear. And the singleness of effect is enhanced, as already noted, by the distinctive tone that the poet is often able to impart by making the style appropriate to the subject.

Perhaps enough has already been said about the structure of the sonnets, among which are to be found the majority of his direct statements of opinion and belief. Among his other reflective poems perhaps the most scrupulously ordered is *The White Lights*, written in anticipation of a renaissance in the American theater.[13] That he was too optimistic, at the moment, does not make the poem less excellent.

> When in from Delos came the gold
> That held the dream of Pericles,
> When first Athenian ears were told
> The tumult of Euripides,
> When men met Aristophanes,
> Who fledged them with immortal quills—
> Here, where the time knew none of these,
> There were some islands and some hills.
>
> When Rome went ravening to see
> The sons of mothers end their days,
> When Flaccus bade Leuconoë
> To banish her Chaldean ways,
> When first the pearled, alembic phrase
> Of Maro into music ran—
> Here there was neither blame nor praise
> For Rome, or for the Mantuan.
>
> When Avon, like a faery floor,
> Lay freighted, for the eyes of One,
> With galleons laden long before
> By moonlit wharves in Avalon—

> Here, where the white lights have begun
> To seethe a way for something fair,
> No prophet knew, from what was done,
> That there was triumph in the air.

Resisting the temptation to laud the style, and considering only the structure, we note first the implied comparison, in successive stanzas, between the epoch of achievement that the poet fancies is beginning in New York, and three previous high points in the culture of the Western world: Periclean Athens, Augustan Rome, and Elizabethan London. We note next the perfect grammatical and logical parallelism in the first two stanzas: the three "when . . ." clauses, the first stating a general characteristic of the period, the other two referring to two great authors (the Romans are more familiar as Horace and Virgil); and the concluding main clause, marking with characteristic understatement the contrast between "the glory that was Greece and the grandeur that was Rome," respectively, and the wilderness that was New York. In the last stanza, as is proper in approaching the climax, the plan is altered; there is only one subordinate clause, giving only one feature—the genius of Shakespeare—of the Elizabethan age; and four lines are devoted to the contrast not only between Shakespeare's London and what then existed on the site of New York, but between what then existed and what exists there now.

Similarly oracular, but almost opposite in mood and less precisely proportioned and articulated, is *Cassandra*. The prevailing temper is closer to that of the great Jewish prophets in their denunciations of Israel's iniquity than to the wild and mournful forebodings of the ill fated maiden of Greek myth; but in either case a rigid plan would be inappropriate. Nevertheless, the poem is by no means formless. The first four stanzas list America's shortcomings: her dollar-worship, her blind pride, her confident unreason. The next three repeat in varied forms the question, "What makes Americans so sure that they dwell on the ultimate peak of civilization?" The last five reiterate the general indictment of the first four: the acquisitiveness, the egotism, the willful blindness to past and present realities, that from a certain point of view appear to dominate the character of Americans as a people. And then comes the climactic question, "Are you to pay for what you have/With all you are?" That few hear the question and none heed it may seem an anticlimax, but is not; for it supplies the needed ironic objective confirmation of the truth of the indictment.

Another direct comment on life as the poet sees it, perhaps even more finely phrased than the preceding, and no less firm in the structure of its thought, is *Hillcrest*. The first stanza gives the setting —peaceful, lovely, remote from urban uproar. The second introduces the main theme—that such surroundings may induce a truer perception of ultimate facts and values than a person has possessed before. The next three stanzas list some of the illusions that may spring from too close and constant contact with one's fellows— regret for the past, fear of the future, cynicism based on a private disappointment, an exaggerated estimate of one's own wisdom. The next four stress the lesson in humility that in the environment of "Hillcrest" one may learn. And the last four proceed from this thought to a warning against too easy an optimism—a warning the force of which derives, as in *Cassandra*, from an unspoken affirmation, but a warning delivered in a different temper, in that the righteous anger there expressed has been tempered by the poet's surroundings into serenity that is only a little sad.

Robinson's longest reflective poem, *Dionysus in Doubt*, will be found by many readers to be among the least rewarding of the group; and one reason is the apparent failure in structure. The poet seems to be using the discursive method of the dramatic monologues, and it is hard to find any logical or rhetorical arrangement, any clear progression in the argument, any climax to the emotional appeal. In other words, he has forgotten that propaganda must be disguised, and has written a tract instead of a poem—and perhaps not even a very good tract, though his main points are well taken.

None of these faults appear in *The Man Against the Sky*, Robinson's fullest and most serious exposition of his views on ultimate problems, of what might be called his religious faith. The poem opens abruptly, with the picture of a lone symbolic figure, seen briefly and lost sight of as he moves across a hilltop looming dark against a flaming sunset. There follows a brilliantly visualized and deeply felt description, in a series of verse paragraphs ranging in length from twenty-four to forty-two lines, of the various ways a man may take through life; and these are then summed up, according to the ruling motive, the inward force that "drove or lured or guided him," in five lines,

> A vision answering a faith unshaken,
> An easy trust assumed of easy trials,
> A sick negation born of weak denials,
> A crazed abhorrence of an old condition,
> A blind attendance on a brief ambition,—

the last of these being the way of the confident materialist. Whatever his destiny, we are then told, "His way was even as ours"; for at the end we, like him,

> Must each await alone at his own height
> Another darkness or another light.

Thus is provided a transition to the question that Robinson regards as unanswerable. If there is nothing for man to live *toward*, why live at all? But the premise is not to be accepted; the poet declares his faith in "an orient Word that will not be erased," and then returns to his attack on the answers to his question that materialists have tried to give: Marx's "soft evangel of equality," strangely derived from economic determinism; and the equally absurd notion (as he regards it) of other social philosophers about living for some meaningless abstraction called "the Race." From this second attack on materialism the poet turns, almost as in the choral responses in a Greek drama, to a second confession of faith in a spiritual reality—"The Word itself, the living word"; an affirmation that grows in sweep and intensity through a resounding series of rhetorical questions, and comes back at last, thus ending the antiphony, to the one asked first, and declared now, as then, to be unanswerable:

> If there be nothing after Now,
> And we be nothing anyhow,
> And we know that,—why live?
> 'Twere sure but weaklings' vain distress

> To suffer dungeons where so many doors
> Will open on the cold eternal shores
> That look sheer down
> To the dark tideless floods of Nothingness
> Where all who know may drown.

Thus the vistas opened to the mind by the initial experience have been explored to the end; the awe and mystery remain, but the fears and doubts and denials and phantom faiths have one by one been confronted and finally dispelled. And the reader is left—unless alienated by a belief that is at odds with his own—with a sense of harmony and completion, "and calm of mind, all passion spent."

7

The line of division between Robinson's reflective and his dramatic poems is, of course, not always definite. Often a poem is held together not only by the singleness of the action, or the consistency (or consistent development) of the central character, but by some general comment, explicit or implicit, of which the poem's content offers an illustration. And the reader (unless, again, he is inhibited by disagreement with the statement) derives a double satisfaction from the completed portrait or story in itself and from its being placed in relation to experience in general and the world as a whole. The characters exist for their own sake, but they are at the same time inhabitants, with the author and the reader, of a "real" world that is at least partially coherent and intelligible. And, on the other hand, general statements about how the universe appears to function have little meaning for most people until brought into a specific relation to themselves or human beings not unlike them.

Some persons, therefore, will find their pleasure limited in reading *Haunted House, The Tavern, The Return of Morgan and Fingal* (which the poet called "merely an episode with overtones"),[14] and other poems almost purely dramatic, because the overtones seem to have only a remote and indistinct connection with the pattern of human existence as these readers have observed it. Others, in contrast, will be only partially satisfied with such pieces as *Credo, Cassandra, Modernities, The Spirit Speaking,* perhaps even *The Man Against the Sky,* because the author's direct exposition of what he regards as general truths so greatly outweighs the dramatic element.

The importance of each factor is of course relative. *The Man Against the Sky* is not without incidental drama; and one can read ethical implications into *The Return of Morgan and Fingal.* What matters most is that the two should be complementary and not competitive; and this condition, as a rule, Robinson is careful to preserve. Even in *Amaranth* and *King Jasper,* where the omnipresent allegory tends to make the characters bloodless and inhuman—to parasitize them, so to speak—anyone who is persistent enough to try a second reading may be surprised at how some of the people come to life.

Among the poems in which some sort of balance is kept between life itself and "a criticism of life," are those in which a dramatic account of a unique incident carries with it an implicit general application. *Cliff Klingenhagen,* for instance, would seem relatively pointless, its hero merely queer, without the perception of what it is that his action illustrates—that happiness may be found in schooling oneself to accept as a matter of course life's inevitable bitterness.[15] *Alma Mater,* again, has a central episode almost too bizarre to be worth telling for its own sake; but taken as a symbol of men's inescapable interdependence, their universal kinship as "children of the night," it awakens us to a chastening awareness of the conditions of our existence.

In *The Flying Dutchman,* on the other hand, it is the thought that is clearly dominant, and that needs to borrow interest from the dramatic element instead of lending it. The theme is the hopelessness of the search by "Science" for ultimate truth—unpromising material, one would say, for poetry. But by embodying the quest in a person endowed convincingly with human qualities, who is "Unyielding in the pride of his defiance" and "Fearless of in what coil he may be caught"; and who summons for the reader subconscious memories not only of the Flying Dutchman, but of the Ancient Mariner, of Odysseus, of Captain Ahab, and of the great historic figures of the Age of Discovery that once stirred our youthful adventurousness, the poet makes us in imagination partners in the endeavor, and thereby makes substantial and memorable his abstract proposition.

Sometimes, again, there is a nearly equal balance between the general and the specific, the philosophic and the dramatic. Such a skillfully proportioned double appeal is present in Robinson's early masterpiece *Captain Craig*. Conceivably it could be regarded as simply an exposition of the author's own philosophy, with the Captain serving merely as a mouthpiece; or as a purely dramatic work in which the Captain's opinions are introduced only to reveal his character. But to insist on either approach to the exclusion of the other would be to rob the poem of much of its vigor and richness. The Captain's situation, as well as his words, is a commentary on society's single-minded pursuit of material wealth and its complacent nonrecognition of any but its own standard of values. Likewise, his uncringing acceptance of his destiny, his unembittered estimate of human nature in general, his unfaltering effort to maintain a balance between extremes—between "flesh-contempt" and "flesh-reverence," between the optimism that is "blinded by the lights" and the pessimism that is blinded by the shadows—all these take on an added clarity and persuasiveness when present in a man whose ebbing life is companioned by obscurity, poverty, and pain. Without the philosophy, the Captain's story would be merely depressing; without the Captain, the philosophy would be cold. Taken together, they make a poem that is not always easy reading, but that quickens our awareness, deepens our understanding, widens our sympathies, and leaves us with a feeling of renewed well-being.

In *Merlin*, again, we need to call upon the underlying philosophy to help us understand the story and to rescue it from the charge of disunity that critics have almost unanimously brought against it. At first glance, Merlin's role as Arthur's counselor seems to have no connection with his role as Vivian's lover, except that he plays them both, and that King and mistress contend for his allegiance, each detesting the other. That both are disappointed in the end only seems to make the whole narrative more confused and pointless.

But if we look below the surface, we find that the disunity and aimlessness are only apparent, since Robinson's purpose is not to tell either story for its own sake (glamorous as is the idyl of the lovers amid the enchantments of Broceliande), but to make manifest in both of them his reading of the riddle of human destiny—as Merlin himself established Arthur and his kingdom "to be a mirror wherein men/ May see themselves, and pause." The crash of kingdoms and the anguished voices of dying men and of a dying social order (less a matter of course to his generation than to ours) were in the ears of the poet as he wrote; and the sickening sense of waste and folly that Merlin's foreknowledge cannot prevent him from feeling as he sees the lights going out in Arthur's kingdom is what Robinson himself was feeling as he watched World War I pursue its ruinous course. And therefore Merlin is presented as "such a lover of the world as to use Arthur and his empire as an object lesson to prove to coming generations that nothing can stand on a rotten foundation." [16]

The rotten foundation of Arthur's kingdom was his illicit love affair with his unrecognized sister, whence was born the treacherous Modred, and his marriage to Guinevere despite his knowledge that she did not love him. The rotten foundation of Western civilization would have been its economic and political imperialism, the ruthless sacrifice of moral ideals in the fierce pursuit of personal and national wealth and power: what Carlyle called the "Gospel of Mammonism," which accompanied the industrial revolution, which the great Victorian writers denounced to no avail, and which furnished to Karl Marx (in its profound and naïve materialism, on the one hand, and its creation and acceptance of a dehumanized proletariat, on the other) both positive and negative inspiration. "The world has paid enough/ For Camelot," says the dying Gawaine in *Lancelot*, in what Robinson called "the most significant line in the two poems." [17] But we in this generation see that payment still goes on.

As to Vivian (not to bruise her bewitching womanliness with

any crude and banal symbolism), we may perhaps, with Merlin, see her as the warm and breathing embodiment of all the beauty in the world that our senses can bring us; and without his love for her, Merlin's wisdom would have been incomplete, his life only half lived. But hers is also only half a life—or even less; and "her golden shell of exile" from the responsibilities of an existence shared with other human beings must eventually be broken for her as it is for her lover. No more than Merlin can she live forever within her enchanted walls. Having opened already for him to come and go, they must open again for her,

> "whose unquiet heart is hungry
> For what is not, and what shall never be
> Without her, in a world that men are making,
> Knowing not how, nor caring yet to know
> How slowly and how grievously they do it,—
> Though Vivian, in her golden shell of exile,
> Knows now and cares, not knowing that she cares,
> Or caring that she knows. In time to be,
> The like of her shall have another name
> Than Vivian, and her laugh shall be a fire,
> Not shining only to consume itself
> With what it burns."

But the "torch of woman," shining clearly in Vivian to no purpost but Merlin's passing pleasure and lasting wisdom, shines luridly in Guinevere to kindle "the time-infuriating flame/ Of a wrecked empire." What in each case corrupts the flame, making one too cold and the other too consuming, is what also corrupts the light that Arthur would have had shine before men: unwillingness to discipline the earth-bound desires of the small and transient personal self for the sake of a more inclusive and enduring good. And so another light is needed for the guidance of groping humanity: the "light that Galahad found"—which, as Robinson explained to an inquirer, "is simply the light of the Grail, interpreted universally as a spiritual realization of Things and their significance." [18]

Thus *Merlin*, which lacks unity as a pure narrative, is unified on a different level by the philosophy that the poet intends it to illustrate. How strong this philosophical motive is, appears in Robinson's statement that *Merlin* "was written in anticipation of" *Lancelot,* "and the two should be read together." [19] Under such circumstances the unity of action would be still more tenuous. In fact, there is simply no connection between Vivian and Guinevere except through what they represent as figures in a philosophic drama. It is only through an understanding of this deeper drama that *Merlin* is seen to have unity and direction.

The preceding analysis makes no claim to be more than tentative, or to do more than indicate certain avenues of approach to the problem of organic form, which other readers, according to their tastes, may wish to explore more thoroughly. By its very nature, this kind of undertaking can never be complete, since form in art is indeed organic. The "form" of a poem is something in which language and meter, rhetorical devices and over-all arrangement, subject matter and central theme, prevailing mood and controlling purpose, are all inextricably fused to make a whole that is not to be identified with the sum of its parts; and its contribution to the reader's pleasure, although great, is ultimately indeterminate.

chapter v: CHARACTERS:

A SPIRITUAL GENEALOGY

The previous chapter has shown that the content as well as the style of Robinson's poetry is rich and varied—that with equal fidelity and power he can embody in words a mood or emotion, a situation or character, a moral or metaphysical conception. But it is the second of these classes of subject matter with which he is most often concerned and in which the uniqueness of his achievement mainly lies. Moreover, with a few exceptions—including perhaps *Stafford's Cabin, The Tavern, Haunted House,* and *En Passant*—it is character and not situation that really counts; the story is not told for its own sake but for the sake of the people in it.

It is this centering of interest on individual human beings that, even more than his style, sets Robinson apart from other poets of the twentieth century; with the exception (as so often) of Frost and of the single success (*Spoon River*) of Edgar Lee Masters. Brilliant or moving portraits by other poets—Masefield's *Dauber* and Eliot's *Prufrock,* for instance, to draw upon the work of two poets almost antithetical in temper and talent—pay allegiance first of all to abstract ideas, to the critical intellect. One is an impassioned plea for realism as a principle in art and life, the other (not wholly different in theme, after all) a detached and all but pitiless unveiling of a man shrunk almost to a skeleton by the unsustaining fare of "high" society life. But Robinson's characters, in the main, unlike these two, have no other motive than mere existence.

This contrast calls for a few more words of analysis. Most twentieth century poets are concerned primarily with either themselves or the universe; with their private experiences, which they often seem to wish to offer as unique, or with traits, tendencies, "problems," which somehow seem more important than the fate of the individual persons in whose lives they are exemplified; in short, with either the singular or the symbolic. The creation of characters who have a sort of objective existence and an identity of their own, and whose main appeal is simply that they are people, has been left largely to the writer of prose.

This is not said in disparagement. The private and the universal have long been recognized as the particular province of the poet, whose special gift for turning them to artistic account has not been challenged. On the other hand, there seems no reason why the poet should surrender his interest in human character as such. There are even critics who have held that the supreme achievement of the poet, as of other literary artists, is the creation, for their own sake, of men and women who will live in the mind of the reader. It is to such an achievement by Robinson that the following chapter is devoted.

2

Though Robinson's characters are all individuals, they fall roughly into several classes, and among the members of each class one may discover a sort of family resemblance. The group of which the discerning reader perhaps becomes first aware, and which includes some of the poet's most vivid and stirring creations, is composed of persons who are failures in the eyes of the world but not (if the phrase may be used without committing Robinson to a theological dogma) in the eyes of God. For them, whatever wealth or fame or other treasures they may have once laid up on earth have vanished—snatched or worn or thrown away by Fate or Time or themselves. Yet in place of these tangible glories, after moth and rust and unreined passion have done their work, has come a faith that in some sense or other they are "saved," that in the sum of things their lives have counted, and that for them the future, on earth or elsewhere, can hold no terrors.

This is the central theme of *Captain Craig*, the thought as well as the style of which may have baffled readers whose eyes were still adjusted to the Gilded Age of America's "empire builders"; to whom world wars and decade-long depressions had not yet brought doubts that *doing* things is all that matters. It may not be without significance that the real-life model for the Captain, a friend of Robinson's early, struggling years in New York, was not a native American, but by birth a European and by choice a cosmopolite.[1] Endowed with great and varied talents, he had invested them not in commercial enterprises, nor even in a professional career, but simply in experience; and no financial dividends were forthcoming to compensate for the failing energy of old age. Yet, at least as he is presented in *Captain Craig*, beneath the shabby and soiled exterior there lives a personality that is warmed and lighted by a faith, inextinguishable and undefiled, in life's ultimate worth. His word to the young friends who gather about him is always one of hope and of good humor. Unembittered by the past, unafraid of the future, he shows by a last grand gesture his contempt for the funereal trappings of death with which so many Christians mock their faith, and requests that on its journey to the grave his body be accompanied by a brass band, with special emphasis on trombones.

Another and still more powerful illustration of the same general theme is to be found in the hero of a poem written a quarter of a century later—Fernando Nash in *The Man Who Died Twice*. For he, though certain of his gift, confident of his power to compose a symphony like none before, is unwilling to wait, not for fame but even for the music to come to him; and instead plunges, though not without a sense of guilt, into an all but fatal round of dissipation. The music comes at last, in a vision, to draw him back from death; the music that "he had always heard—/ And had not heard before"; music that would have been deathless had his own power to record it not been dead. But the stroke that follows the vision leaves Fernando Nash with no memory of the music itself but only with the

memory of having heard it; leaves him bereft of inspiration, empty
of ambition, content through the brief remainder of his life to beat
a drum for some evangelical group. Yet the Olympian if not the
Mephistophelian irony of such a fate is tempered to its victim by
what can only be called Divine Grace. His sin has been expiated,
and he carries with him the assurance, sealed and stamped by the
fact of his having been permitted to "hear" his symphony, that in
some incomprehensible way his life has not been wasted, and that
in his future farings all will be well.

This assurance, we may infer, is the peace that comes to Cavender
when, after twelve years of penance, he finds the courage to face the
evil in himself. It is the peace that Guinevere finds in her convent.
It is the "Light" that Lancelot sees at last, alone in the darkness,
where he has before seen only the fading face of a woman that in the
flesh he is never to see again. Once he would rebel:

> But the Voice within him said: "You are not free.
> You have come to the world's end, and it is best
> You are not free. Where the Light falls, death falls;
> And in the darkness comes the Light." He turned
> Again; and he rode on, under the stars,
> Out of the world, into he knew not what,
> Until a vision chilled him and he saw,
> Now as in Camelot, long ago in the garden,
> The face of Galahad who had seen and died,
> And was alive, now in a mist of gold.
> He rode on into the dark, under the stars,
> And there were no more faces. There was nothing.
> But always in the darkness he rode on,
> Alone; and in the darkness came the Light.

The triumph (as Robinson at least regards it) that is recorded at
the end of each of these poems is not only over the loss of things conventionally valued but over the still more corrosive sense of having
betrayed one's better self. It is a question whether the trial endured by these persons is harder or easier, their triumph greater or
less, than that of another group of people that we meet in Robinson's poems: those who, like Job in the great biblical drama, are
afflicted though guiltless; who in fact seem singled out to be the

pawns in a cosmic contest between Good and Evil. Certainly it is no easy victory that is won by the painter in *Rembrandt to Rembrandt*. And an even higher price (perhaps) is paid by other historical characters, in whose fidelity to a vision Robinson found a theme for poetry. Such are John Brown, Toussaint L'Ouverture, and Lincoln (*The Master*). Their world is far from Rembrandt's; the evil that they defy is more aggressive; the climax of their strife is more dramatic; but in essence their trial and triumph are the same. The three crusaders against Negro slavery die—in a hangman's noose, in a tyrant's prison, by an assassin's bullet; but in the long and painful struggle preceding the fatal climax they have been sustained by the vision—which history is slowly justifying—of ultimate victory for their ideals. What Robinson says in *Sainte-Nitouche* with reference to another sort of struggle will apply here:

> The fight goes on when fields are still,
>   The triumph clings when arms are down;
> The jewels of all coronets
>   Are pebbles of the unseen crown.

Such a triumph of the spiritual over the physical finds another stirring expression in *The Three Taverns*, in which the Apostle Paul, with neither regret nor pride, but with simple acceptance of his mission, looks back across the stormy years since the vision on the Damascus Road, and forward to the clouded future that awaits him in Rome.

It is not only with these figures from the heroic past, however, that Robinson is concerned. He has a vision of his own, which reveals in the strivings of his undistinguished contemporaries the same quality and the same value as in the actions by which history has been shaped. Thus he chronicles at length, in *Amaranth*, an experience that is in some ways the converse of Rembrandt's, telling of how Fargo, the would-be artist without talent, wandering in the "wrong world," is saved from the destruction that comes to Pink the poet and Atlas the painter by being able to look into the eyes of Amaranth (otherwise Truth) and accept the fact that he was born for more practical pursuits. The heroism of such an acceptance is less romantic than Rembrandt's, but perhaps no less admirable. After all, Fargo has no support in dreams of posthumous glory, which, however illogically, have often been a saving shield against the world's indifference; he must find satisfaction simply in the knowledge that he is doing useful work and doing it well.

Another kind of test that human beings often have to face, and often fail to pass, is that endured by Old King Cole, which for some reason Robinson chose to treat in the spirit of high comedy. Of all the sons since Cain whose actions have embittered their parents' lives, there have been none, the poet assures us, more graceless than these two fathered by the benign King. The townsfolk talk, scold, pity, and wonder how the old man can bear with such apparent calm the shame that to their notion has been cast upon him by the conduct of his sons. But he has other comfort than that provided by his pipe and bowl; "like One whom you may forget," he says to his visitor, with Robinson's accustomed mockery of merely nominal Christianity, "I may have meat you know not of." He, like the others, has found peace of mind in the shadow of what outsiders can only see as irretrievable disaster.

3

A second more or less clearly defined category of characters, again dependent on the basic Robinsonian principle of disparity between appearance and reality, includes those persons whose lives are outwardly illustrious but inwardly empty.[2]

The transition—logical, of course, and not chronological—between this and the previous group may be found in the protagonists of two late long poems: Nightingale in *The Glory of the Nightingales* and Matthias in *Matthias at the Door*. They save their souls in the end, one by dying and one by living. But their previous lives are of a different pattern from those so far considered. Born to greatness or to the easy achievement of it—great possessions and the power that these confer, a name written large for all to know, the honor and admiration of the multitude (not made less pleasant by some admixture of envy and fear)—they have found this outward splendor all but fatal to inward peace, and have been tempted by it to what is for Robinson the cardinal sin: callousness or cruelty toward other human beings. And they are only saved because events deprive them of their satisfaction with what they have had. As long as life flows smoothly for them, its waters are poisoned, for them and for others, by their egotism and insensitivity; only when—while retaining the material possessions and the power that have always been for them, as for most of their fellows, the mark of success— they lose the human ties that they have taken for granted, do they painfully win a peace that cannot be lost, and find a line of action to redeem their errors.

In a way, therefore, Nightingale and Matthias are still among the "elect." But there are others among Robinson's characters for whom, from the limbo of mere material wealth and social station, no redemption is destined. The most obvious and perhaps the least interesting (though, like most other characters in the long poems, he improves with repeated acquaintance) is King Jasper, the captain of industry in Robinson's self-styled "treatise on economics," whose kingdom was founded on the betrayal of his friend Hebron, and who finds no way to atone for this betrayal before retribution in the form of his friend's fanatical son strikes him down. His Victorian queen, Honoria, uncomprehending and unyielding in her loyalty to traditional ways, forestalls by suicide the bloody end of young Hebron's revenge.

A spiritual cousin of King Jasper is (oddly, it may seem) King Arthur, whose kingdom is built upon a quicksand of dishonor that is fated finally to engulf him. The glamour of his reign hides from all but a few the unconfessed sins of his early manhood; but it cannot avert the ruin to which they eventually give rise. Lesser men, to be sure, have often been guilty of such actions without incurring such catastrophic punishment. But a king who sets out deliberately to sway his people to a Christian life, and who presents himself as a pattern of moral perfection, is permitted no such frailty. And his kingdom falls.

Arthur and Jasper perhaps deserve what comes to them. At least they seem clearly to have caused it. If destiny was unkind, it was only through having endowed them with power, or the desire for it, without the strength to resist its corrupting influence. But for others the threads of life are tied in a different, and more confusing, though not less fatal knot. For they have wealth and a respected place in the world, without the temptation to evil that kings must face—and without, in fact, being guilty of evil, as far as we can see. And yet they also are destroyed.

One of them is Richard Cory. There is no hint here of hidden guilt: egotism impervious to others' needs, betrayal of friendship, or failure in duty to one's fellow men. We seem to be confronted here with the dark opposite of the Divine Grace that brings salvation to Captain Craig and Fernando Nash and Lancelot and the rest. Somehow Richard Cory is cursed with the inability to believe that life is worth living. No Light shines in the darkness, no Word breaks the silence in which he moves and has his being. No "celestial messengers" bring him a vision and a promise; no Amaranth guides him through and out of a wrong world; no voice firmly forbids him to pass through the door of death. The thing that in most men gives worth to life, even in the midst of suffering, has simply been left out of his makeup. And with only this thing lacking, and nothing to suffer except the lack of it, life becomes intolerable. But why this spiritual vacancy exists remains a mystery.

From another point of view, this lack may sometimes seem to be a gift, although an apparently malign one—the gift of seeing the hollowness, the worthlessness, of what men commonly and conventionally live for, or are at least satisfied with. For most practical purposes, one may infer, no faith is needed; an illusion will do as well. But what of the man, asks Robinson, to whom illusion is forbidden and faith not granted?

He asks it most explicitly in *Tasker Norcross*, a poem that probably only he would ever have thought of writing. "Tasker Norcross" is the pseudonym under which Ferguson conceals his own story, one of Robinson's "slow tragedies of haunted men." Norcross differs from Richard Cory in that he has few gifts (except wealth) and no graces. But he has the same fatal incapacity for illusion, and it destroys him:

"Could Norcross only not have known, I wonder
How many would have blessed and envied him!"

But he has no friends—and knows it. He has no religion—and is
aware of the vacancy in his life. For him, pictures, symphonies, and
architectural triumphs are merely groups of sensations that have
nothing to say—yet he perceives the pleasure that they bring to
others. Where most persons are able to find meaning and purpose
in the world, he finds a vacuum.[3] He is no worse than other men—
there are even suggestions of secret generosity, as in the line, "And
what he gave said nothing of who gave it," and in the surmise that
after his death, "The few there were to mourn were not for love,/
And were not lovely"—who live in relative contentment, because
they are unaware of any lack. But Norcross "Was given to know
more than he should have known,/ And only God knows why."[4]

Many readers will be surprised to find Shakespeare in this company of the doomed and haunted. Yet that is where Robinson has
Ben Jonson put him. In many ways he is the antithesis of Norcross
—possessed of transcendent gifts, and knowing that he has them;
honored, admired, envied, loved, and conscious of being so; un-
lucky only in a past romance, and anxious only for respectability
embodied in a grand house in Stratford—and able even in this ambition to see the absurdity of thinking it important. But just as
Norcross knows too much, Shakespeare sees too far—to where it
becomes absurd that *anything* should be thought important. He
steps with assurance along the heights, while Norcross wanders de-
spondently in the depths; but to one no more than to the other
does the movement have meaning. Shakespeare's

> lark may sing
> At heaven's gate how he will, and for as long
> As joy may listen, but *he* sees no gate,
> Save one whereat the spent clay waits a little
> Before the churchyard has it, and the worm. . . .
> "No, Ben . . . it's Nothing. It's all Nothing."

Norcross lacks

> The faith, or friend, or genius, or the madness
> That he contended was imperative.

Shakespeare has them all—the friend, the genius, and the madness —except the one that counts most. So at least his friend thinks:

> To me it looks as if the power that made him,
> For fear of giving all things to one creature,
> Left out the first,—faith, innocence, illusion,
> Whatever 'tis that keeps us out o' Bedlam.

It is true that Ben Jonson foresees for Shakespeare "a last great calm/ Triumphant over shipwreck and all storms," born perhaps of a late-found vision of something more secure than "a phantom world he sounded and found wanting." But whatever may be the ultimate fate of this Shakespeare (and whatever may be the unattainable truth about the historical Shakespeare), the salient feature of Robinson's portrait is an inner failure accompanying outward success. And the significant point, here, is that in dealing with a character of which almost any interpretation is possible, Robinson should have chosen the one described.[5]

4

From such persons as Tasker Norcross it is only a step to the place reserved for a greater number of Robinson's characters than are to be met with in either of the regions so far explored; a place to whose inhabitants the Fates permit neither outward nor inward success, neither the form nor the substance of security; neither material mansions to protect them as far as may be from the ills that flesh is heir to, nor houses not built with hands where mind and soul may be at peace.

Among these dwellers in the valley of the shadow are those who are paradoxically distinctive and interesting—to the reader— mainly because, as in the case of Norcross, their lives and characters are almost destitute of distinction and interest. The aphorism of F. H. Bradley is apposite here: "It is by a wise economy of nature that those who suffer without change, and whom no one can help, become uninteresting. Yet so it may happen that those who need sympathy the most often attract it the least." It is characteristic that Robinson should have undertaken to call the world's attention to these forgotten men and women.

One of them is Levi in *The Field of Glory*, who has neither the material wealth that might have given him, unlike Norcross, some satisfaction, nor the fatal power (which gives Norcross his appeal to *readers*) to see the cause of the vacancy and negation of his life; he can only suffer, in inarticulate bewilderment, the vacuity and inanity of life as he is condemned to lead it. No talent of any sort is given to him to put to use or bury; his portion is a "painful acre," the dependence on him of a selfish, bitter, and unloving mother, and the curses of those who fail to appreciate their relative good fortune in being able to experience the positive sufferings of war.[6]

Obviously an author must not paint such portraits too often. In the nature of things one cannot write too much about dullness without becoming dull. And even Robinson, with his penetrating eye for the spark of kindred humanity alight within the dingiest bodily dwelling, behind the drabbest curtains of spiritual commonplaceness, has relatively few characters of this sort; and most of them are presented posthumously, when "eloquent, just, and mighty Death" has conferred upon them some measure of distinction.

One of these persons is the man presented in the sonnet *Charles Carville's Eyes*; these were

> insufficient eyes, forever sad:
> In them there was no life-glimpse, good or bad,
> Nor joy nor passion in them ever gleamed;

only after his death did his acquaintances, in some way not quite clear, apprehend his human worth. Only death, again (in the First World War, although perhaps this fact is unessential), elevates to the level of acknowledged humanity the "always useless and not always clean" specimen whom his townsmen had spoken and thought of as "the Rat." Similarly, in *Inferential*, the observer of the coffined body's "unfamiliar grace" revises his estimate of "one whom I had honored among men/ The least." And the portrait of another seeming failure and human nondescript, Clavering, is also elegiac:

> I think of him as I should think
> Of one who for scant wages played,
> And faintly, a flawed instrument
> That fell while it was being made.[7]

It might be questioned whether these last four characters are correctly classified, since, with Robinson as attorney for the defense, they lose their original smudged and indistinct existence and take on the clear uniqueness that makes them men. But such a posthumous revaluation could hardly (were they real-life persons) be foreseen, to serve as a mitigation of the meager earthly condition of these seemingly disinherited sons of God.

More commonly, Robinson prefers to deal with lives distinguished by some ironic incongruity. And among poems of this sort, few are more appealing than the stories of persons whose dreams outrun accomplishment and become in the end a substitute for it; men and women who are indeed "pensioners of dreams" and "debtors of illusions," but who differ from their kindred in *The Valley of the Shadow* in that their dreams are not the result of opium but are the opiate itself.

It is true that Miniver Cheevy's illusions are somewhat strengthened by drink; but this, again, is not a cause but an effect of his refusal to face reality—a refusal that has seldom been so ingeniously and disarmingly justified as in the imaginings of Miniver. It is the quality of these imaginings that sets him above the kindred Vickery, whose gold mine at the distant mountain's foot is not so much a fact as a symbol—a symbol, as the poet himself says, of "human inertia." [8] With Bewick Finzer, however, we are back in the world of reality; for Finzer's "fond imponderable dreams" are the children of his desire to regain what once was his—not so much the half million dollars as the self-respect that vanished with it. On a more heroic scale, but still a portrait of one who seeks by dreaming of past glories to save some fragment of self-respect, is the characterization of Napoleon in *An Island*; in which the dethroned dictator asks, with the irreconcilable bitterness of "one the stars have disinherited," why he now finds himself alone on

A peak, where fiery dreams and far desires
Are rained on, like old fires;

drifting, helpless but defiant, toward insanity and death. Akin to the dreamers in their reluctance to face reality are those who waste their lives in trivial activities: like Atherton in *Atherton's Gambit* (if I have correctly interpreted a poem that even to chess players must be somewhat cryptic); or the player in *Doctor of Billiards*, whose "false, unhallowed laugh" as the "three spheres of insidious ivory" click is supposed to suggest that he is "throwing away a life . . . no longer worth living." [9] Here, too, we may perhaps note "the fiery-frantic indolence/ That made a ghost of Leffingwell," and that served to hide "the sorrow or the pain/ Within him" inspired by the sight of a world incurably corrupt. Another poignant portrait is *Bon Voyage*, in which a life dedicated to gaiety and glamour is left, when youth departs, without a motive.

Under another heading in Robinson's catalogue of failures come the stories of promise unfulfilled or talent misapplied: lives like those of Captain Craig or Fernando Nash, but without the saving grace that they are permitted to know; lives like that of the poet's brother Dean (memorialized in *The Pilot*),[10] who was too sensitive to endure the physical and emotional wear and tear of the physician's life that he somehow found himself leading, and from which he sought a fatal refuge in drugs; or like that of his other brother Herman (whose epitaph he wrote in *Exit*),[11] for whom, like Bewick Finzer and many another, financial misfortune meant a loss of self-mastery that in turn made the ruin irretrievable; or like those of many of the inhabitants of the weird "wrong world" of *Amaranth* (which was formally dedicated to the memory of his brother Dean).

Amaranth is the story of one success and many failures. Here are the two aggressive modernists in art, to whom the eyes of Truth bring sudden destruction: Atlas the painter, to whom "color . . . Was a long drunkenness," and to whose sobered glance, under the spell of Amaranth, his works are only chaos—and who thereupon kills himself; and Pink the poet, whose "enameled words/ Were dead while he was making puzzles of them," so that a reader "never read them twice in the same way"; and who, after looking in the eyes of Amaranth, says quietly, "Excuse me, while I go and hang myself." Here, also (to balance Pink), is Elaine Amelia Watchman, "Who writes, and writes, and writes"—presumably popular novels, although we are not told—but whom some hidden doubt compels to meet the gaze of Amaranth, whereupon she collapses into a small heap of dust. Here, besides, are the four engaging misfits who have learned to live with Truth but who are never to redeem their "mishandled heritage": Evensong the composer, Figg the lawyer, Styx the physician, and Flax the clergyman.

5

At this point it may begin to seem that almost all existence, to Robinson's mind, is a "wrong world" of some sort or other. Yet perhaps still sadder than any of the sufferers so far met are those condemned for no apparent cause to a solitary confinement of the soul.

Of course, loneliness—or perhaps one should say "aloneness"—is not always tragic or pathetic. For Robinson, in fact, it is almost a prerequisite to wisdom and peace. The Man Against the Sky moves alone "to failure or to glory":

> For whether lighted over ways that save,
> Or lured from all repose,
> If he go on too far to find a grave,
> Mostly alone he goes.

Lancelot rides alone to find the Light. Merlin leaves Vivian behind as well as Arthur, taking with him only the pitiful jester Dagonet, as he turns his back on the crumbling fabric built by human hands. Roman Bartholow and Matthias must pass through a long night of loneliness before they emerge into the sunlight of a new life. Alone, Rembrandt hears and heeds his "wiser spirit."

But this is for the few, the rare souls mysteriously elected for a special destiny. Their reward is unsought and unwanted by ordinary men and women, for whom the companionship and affection of others like themselves is what matters most. And since ordinary men and women make up a large proportion of Robinson's characters, his pictures of lonely people strike the note of pathos more often than that of triumph.

To be sure, the note is never shrill or strident. Robinson's shuddering abhorrence of anything that might be labeled "sentimentalism" [12] makes him keep the emotion firmly in check—by comic or ironic touches, by stress on seemingly trivial everyday details, by calculated indirection and understatement. Such is the tone, for instance, of *The Long Race* and *Reunion*, two sonnets that dramatize the slow but inevitable and irreparable destruction of human ties by time and separation. One pair of old friends "dredged an hour for words, and then were done"; for the other pair, "when there was at last a way to leave,/ Farewell was a foreseen extravagance." For all of them there remains the taste of ashes, and the sense of an implacable destiny.

These are mere episodes. In *Aunt Imogen* it is a person's whole life that is involved. Yet the near tragedy is not thrust upon the reader, who may very well carry away from a casual perusal only an impression of the festal mood of the children—"Aunt Imogen made everybody laugh"—rather than the woman's endurance of the lightning-like assault of terror and despair that comes with the recognition that her passionate longing for motherhood must always be unrealized: "For she was born to be Aunt Imogen." [13] The poem ends with her acceptance, as second best, since "there was no might have been," of the role of a beloved aunt.

The same sort of quiet reconciliation with the inevitable, told in the same quiet tones, appears in *The Tree in Pamela's Garden*, in which Pamela makes

> all Tilbury Town believe
> She sighed a little more for the North Star
> Than over men, and only in so far
> As she was in a garden was like Eve.

And having deceived her neighbors, she indulges in a gentle smile at their overheard wish that she might find a substitute for romance. She too has found a kind of contentment in the second best.

But for many of Robinson's other characters condemned to be alone, there seems to be no second best. The pathos of *The Poor Relation*—the picture of a woman whose gay and innocent and triumphant youth has been prematurely banished by poverty, illness, and obscurity—is all but intolerable.[14] Too gentle to feel resentment against life's pitiless injustice, too unsophisticated to try to philosophize it away, she can only ask in hurt bewilderment the old unanswered question, "Why?"

> Beneath her beauty, blanched with pain,
> And wistful yet for being cheated,
> A child would seem to ask again
> A question many times repeated.

At long intervals come former friends, "The few left who know where to find her," to pay brief and uneasy homage to a remembrance of "what she was":

> Her lip shakes when they go away,
> And yet she would not have them stay;
> She knows as well as anyone
> That Pity, having played, soon tires.

When they are gone, she suffers and waits,

> With no illusion to assuage
> The lonely changelessness of dying . . .

A portrait in some ways similar is that of Mr. Flood. But here the pathos is simultaneously relieved and intensified by humor, as the poet shows us the harsh lines of the lonely present being blurred, the faint lines of a happy past being brightened, by the genie from Eben's jug. But at the end the humor and the glamour go, and the world of unadorned fact is left.

It is not strange, since one of Robinson's main concerns as a poet is the relations between men and women, that he should often treat the theme of loneliness that is born of love betrayed or unreturned. Rarely, the betrayal is by death or some other external circumstance, as it is in *Reuben Bright* and *Annandale Again*; or (with a difference) in *The Mill*, where the husband's quiet desperation, issuing suddenly in self-destruction, leaves his wife in a world too empty to be endured. But more often the loneliness springs from some discord between the characters, as in the delicate and tender early sonnet called *The Story of the Ashes and the Flame*; the story might be "as old as human shame," but "he loved her all the same," and his only dream, however hopeless, is of her coming back. Still more poignant is the treatment of the theme in the later verses called *Tact*; with a "merry word" at parting, the woman masks from the man she loves her pain at learning that he does not love her:

> He saw no ruins anywhere,
> Nor fancied there were scars
> On anyone who lingered there,
> Alone below the stars.

Jane Wayland, on the other hand, in *John Gorham*, unlocks and partly opens her heart; but its riches appear as only glass and tinsel to the egotistical eyes of her embittered suitor. In *Mortmain*, also, it is the man who puts an end to an unsatisfying relation; but here it is the woman who is to blame for the waste of affection. For her heart has been buried for more than a decade in her brother's grave, while she has kept her lover waiting and hoping for an answer that were she honest she would acknowledge she can never give. A similar theme is treated in *Late Summer*, although this time the dead man is not a brother, and the woman is more defiant in her devotion to a ghost.

One may imagine of these two men, as of Jane Wayland, that they have spirit enough to survive and live down the loss. But no such hope is in near prospect for the disillusioned wife of *Eros Turannos*, whose utter surrender to love has left her no choice except to "Take what the god has given," however harsh and desolating it may be. In *London Bridge* and *The Clinging Vine* we have other pictures of the desperation—not quiet now—to which a wife may be driven by her husband's infidelity. *An Evangelist's Wife*, likewise, shows a woman near the breaking point as she listens to her husband's sanctimonious denials of adultery. Similar violent passions, which in this instance burst out in violent actions, occur in one of the grimmest of all of Robinson's tragedies, *The Whip*; in which, besides, we see again that it is not always the man who betrays nor the woman who suffers. When the narrator sees upon the drowned man's face the mark "Blue, curious, like a welt"—as from a whip in the hand of a woman filled with desperate hate of the husband whom she has wronged—he is disposed no longer to condemn the suicide.[15]

In this and some of the other poems mentioned, the stress is not on the actual loneliness but on the events that cause it or result from it. But still, in the end, the pain and seeming waste lie in the never-to-be-satisfied need of one heart for another. Whether the stroke is violent and fatal, or whether the suffering is slow and long, matters little.

In the second of these categories is *The Unforgiven*, where the husband hopelessly

> feeds with pride his indecision,
> And shrinks from what will not occur,
> Bequeathing with infirm derision
> His ashes to the days that were,
> Before she made him prisoner.

Here also belong the two sonnets called *The Woman and the Wife*, which the poet at one time considered "the best I have ever done or am likely to do." [16] In contrast to *The Unforgiven*—and with characteristic impartiality in his treatment of the sexes—Robinson presents the woman as the one who, having been persuaded against her better judgment to marry the man, and having learned that her forebodings were justified, rebels against a painful and false relation which her partner's pride insists on maintaining. Still a third picture of a marriage that has failed is given in the two sonnets entitled *Not Always*. This time, one infers, it is the wife's shortcomings which have brought about a situation that both partners have the wish but not the strength to put an end to.

So many poems on the theme of everyday unhappiness in marriage might well, if read consecutively, become monotonous. But occasionally Robinson introduces the macabre element that in his genius is so oddly allied with his characteristic emphasis upon the commonplace. One instance is the disturbing poem called *Nimmo*. Into Nimmo's pictured eyes the painter—from motives not wholly clear—put a look that made his wife afraid, so that she "fled from paradise"; and there remains only

> The calm of men forbidden to forget
> The calm of women who have loved and changed;

only, for Nimmo, what has now become "his bewildered and un-fruitful task/ Of being what he was born to be—a man."

In the longer poems, also, the theme constantly occurs. Another tale of loneliness, of bitter and bewildered estrangement from the person beloved, which becomes in the end too crushing to bear, is that of Gabrielle in *Roman Bartholow*, whose tragedy has been al-ready noted. Natalie, also, in *Matthias at the Door*, ends with her own hand a life of unendurable isolation, the penalty of marrying a man she did not love. The fault was not wholly hers; Timberlake, the man she *did* love, had more or less let her fall into the arms of Matthias, to whom he owed his life. But her false position becomes intolerable when her husband discovers the wrong she has done him, and to her remorse is added the horror of seeing his respect for himself and his love for her distorted into drunkenness and lust. He too, of course, is trying to escape from loneliness; and through some destined grace denied to her, the more dreadful loneliness that fol-lows her death and the death of the friend whom she and he had loved brings him purgation and not damnation.

6

There are in Robinson's poems, nevertheless, men and women to whom destiny is kind: who, if they have the physical well-being and the high station in society that are generally thought to consti-tute success, do not have to pay for these with moral ruin or a bank-rupt faith; or who, if such blessings are denied, do not miss them. Nor for them do peace and inner security, though sometimes pain-fully bought, come only at the end and at the cost of a lifetime of illness, poverty, loneliness, frustration, disgrace, or sense of guilt. Their ambitions and endowments correspond; for them the possible and the desirable more or less coincide; what they want, on the whole, is what they get, and what they get is all they need.

This harmony and proportion are found most often, in Robinson's view, in lives that are otherwise undistinguished. The admonition in *The Clerks* reveals a permanent attitude, although in later life he would probably not have stated it so directly:

> And you that ache so much to be sublime,
> And you that feed yourselves with your descent,
> What comes of all your visions and your fears?
> Poets and kings are but the clerks of Time.[17]

Isaac and Archibald, for instance, are "two old men"—that is all, and that is enough. Their happiness is simply in "all the warmth and wonder of the land" around them; in their thankfulness to God "for all things/ That He had put on earth for men to drink" and otherwise enjoy; and in their serene and undramatic faith that

> "there's a light behind the stars
> And we old fellows who have dared to live,
> We see it—"

Their most pressing problem is whether Archibald's field of oats was ready to cut. The chief worry of each—unfounded save in this trivial item itself—is that the other is falling into senility, beginning to lose his grip on life and on himself. From their serenity the shimmering landscape takes on, for the boy's eyes, an almost supernatural though subdued radiance; and while he looks away to the horizon, his fancy catches

> A flying glimpse of a good life beyond—
> Something of ships and sunlight, streets and singing,
> Troy falling, and the ages coming back,
> And ages coming forward . . .

Here there is nothing of Wordsworth's sententiousness about "rustic and humble life"; nor is there any intimation that rusticity and humbleness are the cause of virtue and contentment. But there is an assurance no less strong than in the work of the great prophet of English Romanticism that wealth and station are irrelevant to the "good life."

Sometimes, even, this life is achieved in circumstances that to unperceptive eyes might seem to warrant pity or derision: like Uncle Ananias and his luxuriant world of "lies," justified by the fact that "every child who knew him, far or near,/ Did love him faithfully"; or like the mother in *The Gift of God*, whose utter illusion about her mediocre son serves as well as if it were the truth in bringing to her life a fulfillment that few achieve.

Yet one would rather have a love, after all, that need not borrow from illusion, like that in *Vain Gratuities*. The wife here, like the mother in *The Gift of God*, is to her acquaintances an object of pity:

> Never was there a man much uglier
> In eyes of other women, or more grim:
> "The Lord has filled her chalice to the brim,
> So let us pray she's a philosopher,"
> They said.

But here it is she who sees truly, and they who deceive themselves:

> But she, demure as ever, and as fair,
> Almost, as they remembered her before
> She found him, would have laughed had she been there;
> And all they said would have been heard no more
> Than foam that washes on an island shore
> Where there are none to listen or to care.

To the characters in this group that we have so far met, happiness has apparently been free, a gift not needing to be earned—though of course it may have been paid for in ways not stated. But to other persons, though it comes before life's morning has passed, and promises a sunlit, tranquil day, it does not come of itself but as a result of conscious effort and struggle, of the renunciation of more immediate, tangible, and seductive goals; or of the wisdom, bought by trial and error, to distinguish between mirage and substance.

Such would seem to be the state of Cliff Klingenhagen, who gives his guest the wine and keeps the wormwood for himself:

> And when I asked him what the deuce he meant
> By doing that, he only looked at me
> And smiled, and said it was a way of his.
> And though I know the fellow, I have spent
> Long time a-wondering when I shall be
> As happy as Cliff Klingenhagen is.

What the wormwood symbolizes, among other things, we may infer from another sonnet, relating the fortunes of Shadrach O'Leary, who "was a poet—for a while," but who was eventually able to place in perspective "the small, ink-fed Eros of his dream," and thus become "a man to know—/ A failure spared, a Shadrach of the Gleam." He has drunk the wormwood of acknowledged defeat, and found happiness. Or, to change the symbol, he has looked, like Fargo in *Amaranth*, into the eyes of Truth, and by his humility has been saved and not destroyed. What he sees is also what "The Contented Metaphysician" sees in *The Burning Book* while

> He considers the tinder that flies
> And the quick flame pursuing.

The book on which he has worked so long, and which was to be "a way to make others to gaze/ On God's face without falling," is being turned into the ashes that, as he now knows, are all it ever was. Henceforth, he will be

> attended
> By the large and unclamoring peace
> Of a dream that is ended.

In love, also, the clouds may clear and troubled waters become calm; not every voyage ends in shipwreck. Among the fortunate is Alcestis in *As a World Would Have It*, Robinson's retelling of the old Greek myth. But in this version the trial that she must undergo is not the sacrifice itself—the dying to save her husband's life—but the necessity after her redemption of breaking down the wall of reserve built in Admetus's mind by mere incredulity at any woman's making such a sacrifice, and perhaps also by shame and injured pride at owing so much to one whom he had so undervalued. When she succeeds, no barriers remain to living happily ever after.

A tale with the same ending, told of modern people and in a lighter vein, is *Talifer*. Because destiny has prepared for Talifer, in the person of Althea, a blessing that was "more than he deserved," he must undergo a "probation" in the form of a foolish marriage to a woman who, along with a prodigious bent for scholarship, has all the beauty and all the warmth of a white marble statue carved by one of the classic Greeks whom she so much admires.[18]

Talifer, following a not-unheard-of path through bewilderment and disillusion to good sense, finds Althea ready to take him back without reproaches, and with only affectionate mirth for his folly and discomfiture.

A somewhat similar comedy, with the parts reversed, is presented in *Rahel to Varnhagen*, in which the young man listens with amused, if not a little bored, tolerance to his older companion's dramatic recital of her romantic past; a tolerance that she forgives, not without some touches of exasperation, as a sign of his unshakable confidence in the enduring quality of their mutual love.[19]

Such cheerful stories, however, can hardly be considered typical of Robinson's work. More often, the cost of happiness, when it comes, is so high that one wonders whether it has been, or ever can be, fully paid. At the end of *Roman Bartholow*, for instance, Bartholow has the world all before him, and does not doubt that the new life will be fair. Yet the question lingers whether the future can be wholly unshadowed by the horror of what has passed—his own long despair, his betrayal by the man who had been his savior, the suicide of the woman whom he had once loved. Is the happiness that he and the others in this group find at last, with or without a painful apprenticeship, *altogether* without alloy? Does Cliff Klingenhagen's wormwood lose at last its bitter taste for him? Or, rather, is Robinson's final view about the quality that human happiness most often has—when it *does* come—expressed most clearly in *Firelight?*

> Ten years together without yet a cloud,
> They seek each other's eyes at intervals
> Of gratefulness to firelight and four walls
> For love's obliteration of the crowd.
> Serenely and perennially endowed
> And bowered as few may be, their joy recalls
> No snake, no sword; and over them there falls
> The blessing of what neither says aloud.
>
> Wiser for silence, they were not so glad
> Were she to read the graven tale of lines
> On the wan face of one somewhere alone;
> Nor were they more content could he have had
> Her thoughts a moment since of one who shines
> Apart, and would be hers if he had known.

7

It will have been evident in the foregoing analysis that the lines of classification are not always sharp, straight, and unyielding; that sometimes the boundary between success and failure is hard to draw, and that often the balance in which happiness and misery are weighed is hard to read.

Sometimes uncertainty arises because the story is not told to the end. Conceivably what seems like perfect happiness may be shaken into chaos—even by blind physical forces, whose influence on human life Robinson seems usually inclined to depreciate. Such is the unexpected sequel to the story in *The Book of Annandale*, a story whose main characters, at the end of this particular poem, would seem to be firmly established in the small company of fortune's favorites. And their contentment seems all the more secure for having been earned: on Annandale's side by the struggle through a period of blank uncertainty following the death of his first wife, the partner in a genuine if youthful love; and on Damaris's, by her long fight to free herself from a promise given to her dying husband that she would never love or marry another man. Yet their overflowing cup of happiness has hardly been tasted when an automobile accident leaves Annandale such a shattered fragment of himself that his friend the doctor concurs in what he believes to be the victim's unspoken wish not to go on living, and helps him to its fulfillment. For the "Why?" of such a catastrophe the doctor has no answer:

> It may be they offended fate
> With harmonies too much in tune
>
> For a discordant earth to share
> Unslain, or it may just have been,
> Like stars and leaves and marmosets,
> Fruition of a force unseen.

And we need hardly be told that Damaris, who her husband admiringly declared "knows everything," long afterward "May still be asking what it meant."

Such a reversal might occur to anyone whose happiness depends

on the existence of another person: to Talifer or Althea, to Rahel
or Varnhagen, to Admetus or Alcestis (since death would hardly
relinquish its hold a second time); perhaps even to the couple in
Firelight or to the wife in *Vain Gratuities*. Or again, perhaps even
those who, like O'Leary and Fargo, have escaped from the "wrong
world" as far as calling or occupation is concerned may still be vul-
nerable at some other point. Only those are secure, like Captain
Craig, Rembrandt, Matthias, and Bartholow, who have painfully
won independence of external things. And even in considering
their lives, perhaps we ought not to forget the uncomforting words
of the Mother Superior in the convent where Guinevere has found
final refuge, to a nun who thinks she knows the answer to her question but wants to be assured:

> "We who love God
> Alone are happiest. Is it not so, Mother?"—
> "We who love God alone, my child, are safest,"
> The Mother replied; "and we are not all safe
> Until we are all dead. We watch, and pray."

On the other hand, some of the failures are not irretrievable. The
particular "dark house" in which many a character is left at a
poem's end may not be a prison forever. The lovers, for instance,
whose happiness depends upon another person and is therefore
always in danger of being lost, always have the chance of recovering
it by finding a new object of affection. The cheated partner in *Eros
Turannos, The Unforgiven, The Clinging Vine, London Bridge,
John Gorham*, and the other dramas of loss or disillusionment may
conceivably form a new attachment to a more worthy person. However black the future may look to those involved, "to the serene out-
sider," often, "There still would seem to be a way" of escape. Time
may be kind as well as cruel. The separation of the lovers in *The
March of the Cameron Men*, with a barrier between them that was
revealed though not erected by the permitted death of a husband
deservedly abhorred, may seem the end of everything for them, as
the last stanza of the unsought song suggests:

> When he left you again there were stars in the way
> Of his eyes, and he wandered alone
> In a dream that would mock him for many a day

With a music unheard and unknown;
Till at last he awoke, and remembered, and found
All there was that remained of it then.
There was only the sound of the world going round,
And the March of the Cameron Men.

Yet as they part the woman declares that "there will be a time for you to bless me/ That all has ended well."

Even those like Luke Havergal, Lorraine, Natalie, Gabrielle, the miller and his wife, and others who choose to take the unretraceable step, pass beyond judgment: "we do not know/ How much is ended or how much begun." So, likewise, such God-forgotten men as are shown in *Tasker Norcross* and *The Field of Glory* may sometime fall heir to another life and a kinder destiny:

When even Levi, tired of faith,
Beloved of none, forgot by many,
Dismissed as an inferior wraith,
Reborn may be as great as any.

Only the rare vicious persons who live contentedly with evil—Aaron Stark, Bokardo, the cruel or callous member of each pair of sometime lovers—seem to be without hope of redemption.

And even when the story is all told, or a situation is described where no change seems possible short of death, we are often at a loss to say just how the accounts of the characters stand—whether the sum of all the entries gives a balance of happiness or misery, of failure or success. What of the equivocal hero, for instance, of *Llewellyn and the Tree*: the worm that turned at last, and fled from a wife who was "shriller than the sound of saws"; taking with him the "roses" that fate had tossed in his path in the form of what seemed to detached observers a somewhat tarnished enchantress? The shabby sidewalk salesman of "fictive merchandise" insists to the old acquaintance who has stumbled upon him:

"I've tried the world, and found it good,
For more than twenty years this fall."

And to the acquaintance it seems, indeed, that "those worn satiric eyes/ Had something of immortal youth."

Again, what of the clergyman Vanderberg in *Sainte-Nitouche*, who after the death of his mistress finds a dubious reconciliation with life in a return to orthodoxy—yet with thankfulness and not repentance for the adventure that the orthodoxy of others called a sin? [20]

> We grant him idle names enough
> To-day, but even while we frown
> The fight goes on, the triumph clings,
> And there is yet the unseen crown.
>
> But was it his? Did Vanderberg
> Find half truth to be passion's thrall,
> Or as we met him day by day,
> Was love triumphant, after all?

And what of the still more elusive seeker for "the sunken crown" in the sonnet so named? What also, of the mysterious Flammonde, whose past career and present essential character are shielded so impenetrably from his fellow townsmen that they can only admire from a distance his masterful acts of magnanimity that straighten so many warped perspectives in their cramped lives? Why is he here, instead of acting on a wider stage? How balance against the postulated grandeur that was missed the limited and unspectacular success that was achieved? And how appraise the spiritual estate of the philosophical panhandler in *Peace on Earth*? And how measure what life has meant to the dying adventurers in *The Klondike*, resolved to "hold our thoughts north while we starve here together,/ Looking each his own way to find the golden river?" And what of Leonora, saved by death (one somewhat hesitantly infers) [21] from descent along the primrose path? What of "Job the Rejected," to whom his rival's tragedy brings no triumph? What of the poet in *Caput Mortuum*, still "Unfailing and exuberant all the time" despite his "old defeat . . . In Art's long hazard"? And in *Old Trails*, after the long struggle to success, what ominous note, if any, "when old echoes ring too long," makes the narrator "wish the bells in *Boris* would be quiet"? [22]

And what of some of the subsidiary characters in the long poems: Vivian in *Merlin*, "whose unquiet heart is hungry/ For what is not," to whom the lover that she found beneath the magician's robes will return no more; Penn-Raven in *Roman Bartholow*, who can cure his friend's spiritual affliction yet yield to passion for his friend's wife; Umfraville in the same work, who seeks with only partial success in fishing, the classics, and philosophy some compensation for the sort of perpetual quarantine imposed on him by his incredible ugliness; Timberlake in *Matthias at the Door*, whose commendable gratitude to Matthias for saving him from a fiery death brings tragedy into both their lives; Doctor Quick in *Talifer*, who, somewhat like Aunt Imogen, is destined to only vicarious enjoyment of the domestic bliss which he has so much desired; and many others whose lot is likewise mixed?

To these questions no certain answer is possible, any more than a certain answer is possible to similar questions concerning people in real life. For even were our perceptions less limited, even were external appearances more important, human beings are ultimately unclassifiable. It is true that individual lives tend to fall into one or another of several general patterns, for the world is not chaotic. On the whole, men and women desire the same things, fear the same things, and take the same means to possess what they desire and avoid what they fear. But at the same time, every person is unique, and every story is indeterminate, as far as human vision can reach. It is therefore the part of reason as well as charity not to be too officious in cataloguing and labeling our fellow human beings, nor too quick to praise or pass sentence, to envy or even pity; but rather, on the one hand, to respect their unique integrity, and, on the other, to acknowledge our common humanity.

Perhaps no more fitting final remark can be made, characteristic in tone as well as content, than the imagined ironic consolation offered by the dead man in *Inferential* to the acquaintance who is now inclined to modify the severity of his former judgment:

> I might as well have heard him: "Never mind;
> If some of us were not so far behind,
> The rest of us were not so far ahead."

chapter vi: CHARACTERS:

THE CREATOR AND HIS CREATURES

Such are the members of the human family, as Robinson sees it, and such are their relations with each other. Our next concern is with the relation between them and their creator. What is the essential aspect or quality of their existence, for him? By what means does he give them body and breath, bring them living before his readers? And finally, how does he himself feel toward the creatures of his imagined world?

To the first of these questions the general answer is easy, in the light of what has already been said about Robinson's sharp distinction between outward and inward failure or success. What Robinson mainly cares about in his characters is the inward world of the individual—the thing that before the birth of psychology men could without embarrassment call the soul. He is not greatly concerned with human behavior as such, but rather with its hidden springs; and not with what happens *to* people but with what happens *in* them. Why does Reuben Bright tear down his slaughterhouse after the death of his wife? Why does Cliff Klingenhagen drink his wormwood so cheerfully? Why does the rich man in *Karma* make an unaccustomed gift of a dime to the Salvation Army? [1]

There is, of course, a poetry of description and a poetry of action. The hero of the *Odyssey*, though he is not the hero of Tennyson's *Ulysses,* is familiar with "cities of men,/ And manners, climates, councils, governments"; he contends with the monstrous Cyclops and slays Penelope's presumptuous suitors. The partly heroic pro-

tagonist of *Paradise Lost* rallies his fallen followers among the
darkly visible flames of Hell, fights his way through Chaos, and amid
the odorous and glowing bowers of Paradise ravishes (in effect)
their lovely mistress.

But the conflicting powers in Robinson's poems characteristically
have for their battleground (like Milton's *Samson Agonistes*) the
minds of the characters. "A man's foes"—and his friends—"shall be
they of his own household." Rembrandt in his dark hour listens
alternately to the counsel of his evil and of his good spirit, and
finally heeds the latter. Fernando Nash, faced with essentially the
same decision, listens to the evil counselor within his mind; and of
the body-destroying debauchery that follows we are told little,
whereas we are given in minute and magnificent detail an account
of the soul-saving symphony that the composer is allowed to hear—
in his mind. That no one will ever hear it played by actual human
beings on substantial instruments apparently does not matter.

This almost exclusive concern with inward experience rather
than with outward actions, with psychic rather than with physical
conflict, has been mentioned already as one barrier to an understanding of Robinson's poetry. It is also one obvious cause, if not
the main one, for his failure in his cherished ambition to be a successful playwright.[2] And in addition it leaves many of his poems
without intrinsic interest for many potential readers. The part of
life that to the poet is most real and significant is to the majority
of persons most of the time imponderable and unimportant. It is
no "unseen crown" that they are eager to wear or read about. A
society that builds its homes physically and socially around television sets (as perhaps any society would do if it had the chance)
is unlikely to find the time or the inclination to follow the tortuous
spiritual Odyssey of a Captain Craig, a Roman Bartholow, a Matthias, a Fargo.

Such generalizations are dangerous, however, for something of the
sort *did* happen (before the days of television, to be sure) when
Tristram became a best seller. This, like Robinson's other long
poems without exception, and despite its source, is a drama of souls
and not of swords; its substance is not action but emotion, and emo-

tion so intellectualized, even in the lovers, that its kinship to the raw passion that fills the divorce courts is scarcely recognizable.[3] And yet it was as a story of raw passion, gaining not only respect but admiration by its sheer force, by its irresistible superiority to traditional ties of family or of court, to conventional moral codes devised for the government of common men's desires, that the legend of Tristram and Isolt was first conceived. The magic potion drunk by the lovers was a symbol, an explanation and a justification, of a love whose absolute sway could be neither explained nor justified by reason and common sense. It enabled the poet to lead the lovers, forever blameless, changeless, and naïve, through a fairy-tale world where their adventures and not their feelings, much less their thoughts, are the source of interest.

This externality, and the device that made it possible, Robinson violently rejected. "The fool potion . . . ," he declared heatedly, "has always been an incurable source of annoyance to me." This "impossible and wholly superfluous concoction," which took away the lovers' "wits and wills," leaving them "denatured and turned into rabbits," into a "pair of impossible and irresponsible morons," became finally, in fact, an irresistible challenge to tell the story in what he considered to be purely human terms.[4]

In the resulting poem, some readers will feel, the lovers are "denatured" in a different way. Their folk-tale simplicity is metamorphosed into ultrasophisticated intellectualism. Like the lovers in a French classical tragedy by Corneille or Racine, they discourse lengthily in impeccable meters about the conflicting claims of love and honor, anatomize in detail their own motives and emotions, and discuss the correct values to be assigned, in the equation of life, to fate and free will. Passion is vaporized into speech, and although this is periodically interrupted by breathless embraces, we begin to question whether a love that is so much talked about but so rarely evident in real action is as overpowering as it is declared to be. Robinson's own feeling while working on the poem—"I am still in doubt as to some of the mushy parts" [5]—may be shared by some readers of the completed work.[6]

This general situation helps to explain, perhaps, why Isolt of

Brittany comes to occupy so large a place in the poem; why she is made, as many readers feel, the most memorable character; and why even Mark, toward the end, wins some of our sympathy away from the lovers. The latter, deprived of their original function as the exemplars of an irrational and overwhelming love, which finds a natural outlet in violent action, remain ill adapted to the analytical and introspective roles in which Robinson casts them. Mark and the other Isolt, however, whose parts in the tragedy have always been more or less passive, leaving them time and occasion (which the early narrators ignore) for reflection on their own and the general human lot, and who are forced to find within themselves, if anywhere, some sort of compensation for the irretrievable loss of what they most desire, are characters to whose portrayal Robinson's genius is exactly suited.

Why *Tristram* caught the public fancy is not wholly clear.[7] At any rate, Robinson's other Arthurian poems caused no such sensation, although they involve the same sort of transformation of the original materials. In the medieval treatment of the many legends drawn into the Arthurian cycle, including Malory's great compilation, *Le Morte d'Arthur*, character counts for little. Action comes first, with numberless combats in which blood flows and heads roll freely, as giants, enchanters, and wicked knights receive their due. This crudity is accompanied unexpectedly by emphasis on a highly sophisticated code of etiquette, governing every detail of knightly conduct, covering every contingency in the relations of knights with each other, with their liege lords, and with the other sex, in general and in particular. Over all this plays the light of a poetry born of the writers' sense of being surrounded by a fresh and joyous world, yet one often strange and sometimes fearful.

In Robinson's poems, on the other hand, action for its own sake never occurs, and the social or the natural setting exists only to illumine the motives and reflect the moods of the human figures. And in presenting these the poet is always probing toward the subtle, central core of character. Arthur is neither a peerless warrior nor a moral paragon, but a fallible and bewildered human being, grappling with forces within as well as outside himself which he can neither control nor even fully comprehend. Merlin is not a wizard but a man of the world; emerging from a past that is not mysterious but only vague, testing the claims of romantic love with a self-possession which, though inquiring and generous, belies his supposed isolation from feminine society; and retiring at last, regretful but unembittered, from a world that is not yet ready to be ruled by wisdom. Vivian is not a witch (much less, as Tennyson makes her, a mere wanton) but an intelligent woman, calculating, though not coldly, how to win the one man whose love she thinks might match her own.

By a similar process Guinevere becomes, not the admired heroine of a courtly (and perhaps largely literary) convention that made "true love" possible only outside the bonds of marriage, nor an adulterous wife callously disregarding a queenly duty to be a pattern of fidelity, but a person confused and caught, like her husband, in a web of conflicting desires and loyalties. Less single-purposed than Isolt of Ireland, less self-reliant than Vivian, she resents the false position in which she has been placed by Arthur's assumption of the right to marry her without consulting her inclination, and thus is able to rationalize her liaison with Lancelot. Lancelot himself is simply an ordinary decent man, of moderate intellectual and moral capacity, pulled this way and that by his loyalty to Arthur, his love for Guinevere, and his remembered vision of the Grail.

Those who have wondered why Robinson, so resolute in facing the modern world with its skepticism, its restlessness, its complexity, should have turned back to the apparently primitive world of romance at which he gibes, though genially, in *Miniver Cheevy*, may find an answer in what has just been said; for underneath the surface simplicity, the glitter and glamour of a childhood world, within the relations between men and women so haphazardly established by chance accretions to the central story, there are latent all the mental conflicts and spiritual crises by which man since the birth of civilization has been beset. No modern tensions can rack the soul more fearfully, no modern mazes of the mind can be more tortuous, than those surrounding the dwellers in Arthur's kingdom.[8]

In his historical portraits, also, it is the inward and spiritual grace or gracelessness by which the career of his subject has been shaped that is the poet's first concern. Toussaint L'Ouverture, Napoleon, John Brown—all men of action, of elemental power—are shown upon a stage where the action is over, and upon which death is about to drop the curtain. Toussaint in one of Napoleon's prisons, Napoleon himself on Saint Helena, John Brown hours only away from the scaffold, unlock their hearts and lay bare what they consider to have been the driving powers and guiding principles of actions whose significance to many beholders would only be spectacular.

The same emphasis is evident in the poems that are mainly of Robinson's own invention. In *Captain Craig* the central character neither acts nor tells a story; he simply reveals, both directly and inferentially, in talking to his tolerant young friends, the hard-won faith that illuminates the seemingly sordid close, and justifies the seemingly fruitless adventures and endurances, of his life. *Roman Bartholow* and *Matthias at the Door*, among others, are accounts of life's mysterious ministry to a mind diseased, in which the causes and symptoms of the illness and the stages of the cure are minutely although sometimes obscurely chronicled. And the shadows are deepened and the mazes through which the reader moves are made more intricate by the fact that the other characters in the story, whose destinies are involved in that of the protagonist, are also torn by inward conflict—to such an extent, indeed, that the salvaging of one life is often achieved only at the cost of wrecking another, or others. Thus Gabrielle and Natalie kill themselves because the former cannot live without, nor the latter live with, the husband who in each case has become a stranger. In each story, also, the friend in love with the wife finds his position more than usually complicated by the fact that in *Roman Bartholow* Penn-Raven is the spiritual creditor, and in *Matthias at the Door* Timberlake is the spiritual debtor, of the husband.

The shorter dramatic poems are often marked by the same intense introversion. Three of Robinson's obscurest stories—*Her Eyes, Old Trails*, and *Sainte-Nitouche*—are clear at least in one respect: each records a struggle in the soul that has only an ironic relation to the person's outward life and the world's estimate of him. In the many brief dramas of domestic discord— *The Clinging Vine, London Bridge, The Woman and the Wife, The Unforgiven, An Evangelist's Wife,* and others—the tension characteristically springs from the fact that one partner is coming at last to find intolerable what the other—more stubborn, selfish, callous, or cruel— wishes to maintain before the world: the lie that they any longer have a life in common. Or sometimes the end has come through one partner's irreparable breaking of faith, and the drama lies in the other's inner reaction to an unforeseen and overwhelming loss. Such are *The Story of the Ashes and the Flame, Eros Turannos,* and *The Whip.*

Whatever the outcome, it is always determined by forces arising from within the characters involved, not by those acting from without. Nothing has changed Nimmo; only Francesca's image of him has been changed, by a hint of evil in his pictured eyes, put there by the painter, or by the devil, or by herself. Matthias returning to Natalie after an absence inspired by the revelation of her love for Timberlake, finds her

> As he had left her. The one change he found
> Was in his world, which he had taken with him
> And brought home with him.

And the same principle holds in other situations than those involving love. Whether "The Dark House" is a craving for alcohol or is something else, it is a creation of the mind of the man who is imprisoned there. Robinson himself is certainly speaking when Captain Craig declares:

> "for 'tis the mind
> That makes you craven or invincible,
> Diseased or puissant";

as he had spoken in *The World* in his earliest volume:

> And so 'tis what we are that makes for us
> The measure and the meaning of the world.

The same thought appears in *Peace on Earth:*

> "Your world is in yourself, my friend,
> For your endurance to the end."

And in view of these passages we may safely assume that we hear the voice of the poet himself when Lancelot muses:

> "Sometimes I wonder if this be the world
> We live in, or the world that lives in us."

2

In fact, Robinson deliberately refuses to draw the line between the "real" and the "imaginary" that we apply in our normal rule-of-thumb test for sanity. In *Avon's Harvest*, for instance, the power of mind-created entities is so great as to destroy the life of their creator—not indirectly by bending his will to suicide, but against his will, directly and violently. It is true, apparently, that the person with whom these deadly psychic forces are associated is actually near when Avon's two seizures occur. But no physical contact took place.[9] Whatever killed him was "unreal," for on the second and fatal occasion his door was locked from the inside, and when it was broken down there were "no signs of any visitors." Nevertheless, his wife "heard him when it came," and he died, horribly. Yet, aside from this one obsession, the poem contains no hint that he was not perfectly sane.

Avon's visitation is unique in its mystery and malignity. But others of Robinson's characters also entertain unearthly guests. Of these the most genial and informative is the "He" of *Why He Was There*: "there he was in his old chair, serene/ As ever . . ." Aware of his host's unspoken question, "And how far will this go on?"

> [He] smiled: "I was not here until you came;
> And I shall not be here when you are gone."

This seems relatively clear; and yet the lines have a queer twist. "He" may exist only in the mind of the man who sees him and hears him, and yet his answer is his own.

Of the same family, although her nature is less immediately clear and yet finally more consistent, is Laramie in *Cavender's House*. Her first appearance to Cavender, following his midnight entry of an empty house, does not surprise him; and her face and voice are no different to his senses than they were twelve years before. This changelessness itself, of course, is strange; but only slowly, as past events come inferentially to light, and as we note Laramie's refusal to tell her husband anything that he does not already know, does the conviction come that she has been called into existence solely by Cavender's will—by his intense desire to know whether the jealousy that led him to kill her was or was not based on fact.[10] She cannot tell him, of course; but by recalling her he seems to find (within himself, obviously) the answer that he seeks, and though it confirms his guilt (which lay not so much in the final act of violence as in his long refusal to understand the woman he had married), it brings him peace.

The reader who wants the line drawn sharply between what is real and what is not may say that the poem is to be interpreted simply as a dream. But when Robinson does introduce unquestioned dreams, like those of Matthias and King Jasper, they have all the disproportion and incoherence that we expect of dreams; whereas what happens in *Cavender's House* is, for the most part, as connected and purposeful as normal waking experience.[11] This statement will not quite apply to the vision—or whatever one wishes to call it—in which Fernando Nash hears a ghostly performance of his great unwritten symphony. Unfamiliar forces are at work, and there is a nightmarish touch in the orchestra of dress-suited rats who appear on an occasion previous but similar to that which brings the climax. Yet the symphony itself, although one movement tells of madness, proceeds with the assurance of inspiration guided by conscious art; and the composer listens, serene and satisfied, to what he knows is *his*, hearing in the music "All he had known and had not waited for" through wasted years. This is not the stuff that dreams are made of—not, at least, our every-night, sleep-fogged dreams that morning makes dim.

A similar strange world, where the dreamer's experience is illumined and ordered, although not with the light and logic of everyday existence, is that which Fargo explores in *Amaranth*. The poet tells us without equivocation that it *is* a dream: "So Fargo slept again and had a dream."[12] Yet it is a dream whose connection with his waking life we may guess at with some assurance. Once he had aspired to be a painter; but coming to realize that the world of art was the "wrong world" for him, he had abandoned it and found peace and satisfaction in the more prosaic pursuit of manufacturing pumps. Now, after ten years, his dream comes to take him back; and although his anguished "Why?" at first receives no answer, the reader may take it as reflecting a never quite extinguished desire to venture again in "Art's long hazard."

But also, it is evident, there are around him (that is, within him) powers that are working to save him from a wasted life. These, embodied in Amaranth, guide him safely through this new circle of the Inferno, created by the twentieth century mind, and enable him to look with the eyes of Truth upon its inhabitants: to see them as illustrations of what happens to those who try to live in the wrong world or to take the wrong way out. Thus he views without illusions Pink and Atlas, who respond with suicide to the truth that "modernism" in art is, at least for them, a false Messiah; Elaine Amelia Watchman, who "liked writing more than she liked truth,/ Or life," and who follows the example of her many well bound volumes and collapses into a handful of gray dust; Figg, Flax, Styx, and Evensong, whose acceptance of the inevitably failing roles in which they have been cast is marked by an "inextinguishable grace" that hints at high achievement could they have found their proper sphere; Ipswich the inventor, whose last device is an infernally seductive drink that makes his followers hear siren songs of another world where failure is forgotten and salvation can be had for the asking, and whose "abrupt and festive exodus" with his scarecrow crew has a quick and fatal end; and, in the background, the importunate, obscene, Yahoo-like "grave-diggers," who it would seem from Fargo's experience do not always wait until a person is dead to perform their office.[13]

From this analysis *Amaranth* emerges, like the other poems that have been mentioned, as a reflection of two basic convictions, two unwavering intuitions, in the poet himself. One is that it is only the inner life of the individual that really matters: the life of the reason, the will, the passions, the affections, the image-making power. The outward world of physical appearance, of manners and fashions, of bodily contact and conflict, of the seemingly accidental impact upon human purposes of unintelligent brute force—all this, which is also the stuff of life, with which the literary artist traditionally deals, scarcely exists in Robinson's poetry.

The other guiding principle, which prevents the poet's world from dissolving, as far as many readers are concerned, into an "unreal" dream or abstraction, is his intense perception of the distinct identity, the unique position and attributes, the existence as an end in itself, of the individual person. This, though itself intangible, provides a stable nucleus around which elements of experience can be organized, and upon which their significance depends.

3

This constant concern of the poet with the inward life of his characters naturally affects his method of presenting them. For one thing, as just noted, the details of a person's physical appearance receive, as a rule, relatively little emphasis. We may or may not have a mental picture of the person Robinson is writing about, depending on how our imagination works. But if we do, it is usually one that we have put together ourselves, after we have somehow been given a conception of the essential nature of the man or woman.

Captain Craig, for instance, is unforgettable. But we never learn whether he is tall or short, stout or thin, nor what his features are like, nor what is the color of his eyes or hair. Miniver Cheevy and Mr. Flood are memorable, but not because we are given a scrap of information as to what they look like. Even in presenting his feminine characters, although Robinson's chivalrous regard for those who deserve it is at all times manifest, it does not extend, in the early poems, to taking note of their physical charms. Whether Lorraine's complexion was as dark as her destiny must have appeared to conventional minds we are never told. Of the more fortunate Damaris, the heroine of the poet's first extended treatment of love between the sexes, *The Book of Annandale*, not one physical attribute is mentioned. The same is true of Aunt Imogen, despite the quivering pathos with which she is drawn.

Two almost startling exceptions, in the early poems, to this habitual neglect of people's appearance occur in *Richard Cory*, already quoted, and *Aaron Stark:*

> Withal a meagre man was Aaron Stark,
> Cursed and unkempt, shrewd, shrivelled, and morose.
> A miser was he, with a miser's nose,
> And eyes like little dollars in the dark.
> His thin, pinched mouth was nothing but a mark.

It is true that every word expressive of a physical trait has spiritual overtones, and that these words are interspersed with others directly expressive of character. Yet the passage as a whole, like the description of Richard Cory, evokes so forcibly a visible person, reveals in the poet so sharp an eye for visual detail, that one wonders why these two descriptions stand alone among the poems published during the twenty years following the appearance of Robinson's first volume.[14]

In the blank-verse novels, beginning with *Merlin*, which occupied Robinson increasingly during his last twenty years, some attention is paid to how the characters look. Yet the charming Althea in *Talifer* captivates by her personality and not her appearance, of which the only detail mentioned, casually, is her "orange-colored hair." Her rival, Karen, after being called an "ivory fish," is formally introduced by a mere five lines of description. And Zoë in *King Jasper*, although she seems to embody the saving grace of humanity as a whole, is pictured only as "a slight young woman,/ Impredicably firm, fair to behold."

The nearest approach to a set portrait is that of Natalie in *Matthias at the Door*, which is not too long to be quoted entire:

> a . . . vision
> Of a slim woman's easy stateliness,
> Which never failed or faltered, or was false
> To its design. An edible cleanliness
> Of countenance that hungry time forgot,
> A straight nose, and large eyes that you called hazel,

> And a firm mouth, made a face fair enough
> To serve, or to be served. Over it all
> Was a close crown of hair—a tawny bronze
> Of shades and changes. Natalie called it red.

One can visualize the person if one wishes: slim build, tawny-bronze hair, hazel eyes, straight nose, firm mouth—an agreeable but unexciting ensemble. The real effect comes not from what is said, but from what is suggested about qualities too subtle to be seen directly. The face is "fair enough to serve"—that is, to be not conspicuous for any defect; but the unexpected alternative "or to be served" imparts a sudden queenly dignity. Yet it is not so sudden, after all; it has been prepared for by the emphasis on some intangible quality of her stateliness which makes it seem to the reader natural, inevitable, right. The "cleanliness of countenance," again, is surely not mere freedom from dirt; it bespeaks a cleanliness of mind that has left her face as yet unsoiled by any surrender to sordid aims and that sets her apart still farther from the common run of human beings. And then at the end, lest she seem too cold and remote, comes the human touch: "Natalie called it red"—and we can imagine the smile with which she did so, gaily arming herself against envy's accusation of pride.

Yet, with all its reliance upon nonvisual suggestion, this is perhaps the most literal and detailed description of a character's appearance that can be found in Robinson's poetry. Even the face of Umfraville, which has apparently determined his lonely destiny, is not pictured but only suggested, as being

> a face made more for comedy
> Than for the pain that comedy concealed,
> Socratic, unforgettable, grotesque,
> Inscrutable, and alone.

Even the Arthurian poems do not compel us to revise our judgment, despite the vividness of our recollections—the blue-black hair and violet eyes of Isolt of Ireland; the white hands, white face, and gray eyes of Isolt of Brittany; the gold hair, fair complexion, and blue eyes of Guinevere. For closer scrutiny reveals that these details are remembered simply because they are introduced so often, almost as leitmotifs, to the exclusion of other details. Furthermore, these features are traditional; a retelling of the story that changed them or left them out would scarcely be possible. Yet in Robinson's version they hardly matter; there would be no essential loss if the characters' appearance were left wholly to the reader's imagination. Their physical traits do not have the independent vigor, the originative force, that such traits have in the character drawing of such writers as (to take an obvious example) Dickens. They borrow rather than lend vitality, and become effective in proportion as they cease to be substantial and sharply defined, as they tend toward the figurative and the symbolic. Thus in the portrait of Isolt of Brittany, the one of the three heroines mentioned in whose re-creation Robinson is most original, the recurrent stress on her white hands, white face, and gray eyes suggests with cumulative force her fragility, her purity, her isolation from the dust and heat, the haste and heartiness, of the general life.

In other words, Robinson's use of physical appearance as a method of characterization is most successful when it is least direct, when he follows (to borrow a phrase used in the portrayal of Laramie in *Cavender's House*) his "proper native way of indirection." What power this way can have appears in the picture of Vivian as Merlin sees her waiting, crimson-gowned, in the "flame-shaken gloom," beside the gleaming table whose food and wine are an almost sacramental prelude to the consummation of a long-treasured dream that has now become a tyrannous desire:

> It seemed
> A flower of wonder with a crimson stem
> Came leaning slowly and regretfully
> To meet his will—a flower of change and peril
> That had a clinging blossom of warm olive
> Half stifled with a tyranny of black,
> And held the wayward fragrance of a rose
> Made woman by delirious alchemy.

Before leaving the whole subject of appearance, one ought to mention the short poems in which, without a set description yet with reference to some physical feature, we get lightning flashes of insight into the vital core—the focus of feeling and thought—of a human being. We remember Flammonde, with a "glint of iron in his eyes"; Bewick Finzer, with

> The broken voice, the withered neck,
> The coat worn out with care;

the Poor Relation, whose childlike bewilderment at life's harshness is visible "Beneath her beauty, blanched with pain"; the errant Llewellyn's "worn satiric eyes," which still have "something of immortal youth"; Old Archibald, who "twinkled in his chair" when he told of cutting down the trees that were "thieves of light"; Nimmo, with a "velvet light" in his eyes—until the "painter put the devil in those eyes," and made his wife, Francesca, afraid; the self-possessed mendicant of *Peace on Earth*, whose

> unshaved, educated face,
> His inextinguishable grace,
> And his hard smile

remain with us as with the poet; and the mysterious stranger in *En Passant*, whose "famished eyes were lit/ With a wrong light." A rare instance of a similar technique in the long poems is the "malignant oily swarthiness" of Avon's unnamed incubus in *Avon's Harvest*.

Two things strike one in looking over this list. One is its brevity —the fact that when Robinson could do this sort of thing so well, he did it so seldom. The other is that these snatches of revelation so often center in the eyes—the most changeful, elusive, and inward-leading part of a person's physical make-up.[15]

4

So much—too much in proportion to its importance in Robinson's work—for the revelation of character through appearance. More frequent, and on the whole more telling, is the use of action. Yet action is not Robinson's proper element, either, even when it is introduced for the portrayal of character rather than for its own sake. The fault that most readers find with the longer poems, besides the difficulty of the style, is the fact that so little happens.

Tristram has been mentioned already in this connection. What does the hero, "the loud-accredited strong warrior," *do* in the 4,000-odd lines? He passionately embraces Isolt of Ireland; hurls Andred against a wall; wanders half mad through the forest until he is rescued and lets himself be sullenly seduced by Morgan; goes to Brittany and kills the monster Griffon; subsequently lets himself be married to Isolt of Brittany; goes back to England and enjoys a sort of belated, extralegal honeymoon with the first Isolt at Joyous Gard; swoons away when he hears that Mark has kidnaped her; and returns to Cornwall to embrace her once more and die at the hands of Andred.

From these events, it is true, a substantial dramatic narrative might be made, in which the characters would come to life in their actions. But in Robinson's poem the events are related almost as briefly and baldly as they are in the preceding paragraph. Ten lines are enough for Tristram's rough treatment of the spying Andred; ten more are given to his seduction by Morgan; Griffon is taken care of in five; the marriage to Isolt of Brittany is never told of at all, but is presently found to have occurred; the voyages are taken for granted; ten lines or so again suffice for the catastrophe; and the dramatic possibilities of swoons and kisses are soon exhausted. So the poem is made up mostly of observation, analysis, and talk.

The other Arthurian poems are also characterized by what seems like a deliberate avoidance of action; and so are the long narratives of modern life. *Roman Bartholow* is almost as long as *Tristram*, but an adequate summary of the action is given by the poet himself in ten words: "One man knocks another down . . . and a woman drowns herself." [16] And this lack of incident is typical of the poems in this group. In them all there is perhaps only one really memorable bit of action: the scene in which Matthias, after the complacent pride that had kept him decent has been destroyed by the discovery that Natalie had never loved him, is moved by drunken lust and anger to try to possess her by force, and is repulsed by a blow.

The short poems, perhaps surprisingly, make far more effective use of action. Although Aaron Stark is probably presented to the eye more vividly than any other character in the poems, long or short, what really clinches the scrap-iron structure of his character is an act—the laugh that reveals, in its unmeasured contempt for those who would offer him pity, the absolute corrosion of whatever humanity he may have once possessed. Flammonde, likewise, though with less obvious finality, is set apart by his appearance; but his true distinction is established by his perception of spiritual needs that Tilbury Town has hitherto ignored, and by his simple and effortless way of seeing that they are met. In *Richard Cory*, on the other hand, appearance is belied by action, and much of the effect is in the contrast.

There is also the wife in *Ben Trovato* who removes her rings and puts on unaccustomed furs in order to bring a last hour of happiness to her blind and dying husband. A similar restrained intensity of revelation is found in the doctor's telling of *How Annandale Went Out*. Reuben Bright and Cliff Klingenhagen likewise live for us, perhaps more simply, mainly in what we see them do. *Llewellyn and the Tree* and *The Burning Book*, although more complex, both turn on a crucial act in which an unexpected strength of character asserts itself—in the former against convention and a nagging wife, in the latter (a common theme in Robinson's work) against the self-created tyranny of a mistaken ambition.

Of course, the most obvious way of presenting a character is for the author simply to tell what that person is like—not in appearance only, but in reality, at heart. Thus Aaron Stark is "shrewd," "morose," and "a miser." Llewellyn at his last appearance shows, among other traits, an "unholy guile." Reuben Bright is not "any more a brute than you or I." Lincoln in *The Master* is "The saddest among kings of earth." Oakes and Oliver in *Two Gardens in Linndale* are "Two gentle men as ever were." King Mark is said to have

> A nature not so base as it was common,
> And not so cruel as it was ruinous
> To itself and all who thwarted it.

Honoria, King Jasper's queen,

> Would have been royal anywhere, and apart
> With her distinction in a multitude
> Or on a throne.

But this directness, as the reader at this point will not be surprised to learn, is comparatively rare in Robinson's work. His usual
relation with his characters is simply that of a human observer,
whose knowledge of them is only inferential. And therefore, rather
than telling us what they are, he more often chooses to tell us how
they act—which is not the same thing as *letting* them act, as in the
instances above, in crucial situations, but involves the casual or
habitual actions of everyday existence. Richard Cory "fluttered
pulses when he said,/ 'Good-morning' "; Miniver Cheevy "kept on
drinking"; "year after year" Aaron Stark "shambled through the
town"; Flammonde "borrowed graciously" what he needed to live;
Lincoln "Met rancor with a cryptic mirth"; the mother in *The Gift
of God* "wears a proud humility"; "howsoever mild" Llewellyn was,

> Priscilla was implacable;
> And whatsoever timid hopes
> He built—she found them, and they fell;

Vanderberg, playing the part that he has set himself after the death
of Sainte-Nitouche, "scoured the shrine that once was home/ And
kept himself a clergyman"; the beauty celebrated in *For a Dead
Lady*

> No longer trembles at applause,
> Or over children that are sleeping—

as she once trembled at applause because of the fullness of her heart
at having made people happy, because of her gratitude for what she
felt to be the return of the love for them, the love for life as a whole,
that she could not help pouring out; and as she once trembled over
sleeping children because her own innocence and purity responded
to theirs, and because they wakened her perhaps as yet not wholly
conscious need for the fulfillment in motherhood of a life whose
opening had been so fair.[17]

But the poet does not always place upon his reader, as he does
here, the obligation of drawing the proper inference from what the
eye can see. He assumes at times—what at other times he refuses to
assume—the awareness of thoughts and feelings that find no immediate and obvious outward expression. Aunt Imogen, while she
"made everybody laugh," was

> covering, like a scar, and while she smiled,
> That hungering incompleteness and regret—
> That passionate ache for something of her own.

Concerning his heroine in *Tact*, the poet is free to observe, as the man she loves without return does not,

> The ruins of a day that fell
> Around her in the dark

as she smiled a last goodbye. Levi is "sick with nameless rage" at the "harsh, inhering claims of home" that keep him from "The Field of Glory" that war offers to his imagination. In the same way the poet reads for us the hearts of the devoted husband and wife who share the warm "Firelight" of home (though each reserves a memory less happy) and enjoy "The blessing of what neither says aloud."

This method, used in many of the shorter poems with an economy that begets vigor, becomes standard practice in the long narratives. Nothing is easier for a poet of Robinson's introspective turn than mentally to place himself in a certain situation and record the thoughts, the feelings, the unsought images, that flow through his mind. There can be no question of the effectiveness of this technique in the delineation of character; but there is equally little doubt that its success with the reader who is not a devotee depends on the exclusion of all except salient items.

The following passage (the length of which is essential to the illustration) will do as well as any. It tells of Tristram's feelings on his return to England after his long sojourn in Brittany:

> Incredulous after Lancelot's departure
> From Joyous Gard, Tristram, alone there now,
> With a magnificence and a mystery
> More to be felt than seen among the shadows
> Around him and behind him, saw the ocean
> Before him from the window where he stood,
> And seeing it heard the sound of Cornish foam
> So far away that he must hear it always
> On the world's end that was for him in Cornwall.
> A forest-hidden sunset filled long clouds
> Eastward over the sea with a last fire,
> Dim fire far off, wherein Tristram beheld
> Tintagel slowly smouldering in the west

To a last darkness, while on Cornish rocks
The moan of Cornish water foamed and ceased
And foamed again. Pale in a fiery light,
With her dark hair and her dark frightened eyes,
And their last look at him, Isolt of Ireland
Above him on the stairs, with only a wall
Waist-high between her and her last escape,
Stood watching there for him who was not there.
He could feel all those endless evening leagues
Of England foiling him and mocking him
From where it was too late for him to go,
And where, if he were there, coming so late,
There would be only darkness over death
To meet his coming while she stood alone
By the dark wall, with dark fire hiding her,
Waiting—for him. She would not be there long;
She must die there in that dark fire, or fall,
Throwing herself away on those cold rocks
Where there was peace, or she must come to him
Over those western leagues, mysteriously
Defeating time and place. She might do so
If she were dead, he thought, and were a ghost,
As even by now she might be, and her body,
Where love would leave so little of earth to burn,
Might even by now be burning. So, as a ghost
It was that she would have to come to him,
On little feet that he should feel were coming.
She would be dead, but there might be no pain
In that for him when the first death of knowing
That she was dead was ended, and he should know
She had found rest. She would come back to him
Sometimes, and touch him in the night so lightly
That he might see her between sleep and waking,
And see that last look in her eyes no more—
For it would not be there.

The poet's immediate purpose in recording this reverie is to prepare for the entrance, in the next line, of Isolt in the flesh. And he
may also wish to assure the reader, after the interlude in Brittany,
of the unabated strength of the old love. But both purposes might
have been served more briefly; and it may seem that the poet, having identified himself with his hero, simply surrendered to the pleas-

ure of clothing in words the sunset-begotten dream of a love long cherished and hopeless of fulfillment.

Yet there can be no doubt that the poet, as always, is fully aware of what he is doing, although the execution may be open to criticism. For one of "the qualities in which he was unlike his contemporaries"—"perhaps, two hundred years in advance of his time"—was, so he averred to a friend during one of his early summers at Peterborough, "his absorption in the unconscious and semi-conscious feelings and impulses of his characters." [18] It is evident, however, that the age caught up with him sooner than he expected; for what he does is hardly distinguishable from what has been done by the more moderate practitioners of what has come to be known as the "stream-of-consciousness" technique in fiction.

5

Passages akin to the one just quoted are scattered through all of Robinson's long poems. Lengthy as they are likely to be, however, they do not make up the major portion of those works. It is a safe estimate that at least half the lines are dialogue. Increasingly as he grew older, Robinson inclined toward letting his characters be revealed through their own words and the words of others.

The poems in which this method is used may be divided, on the basis of form, into four groups. In one, the speech of the characters is only an added means, along with those already mentioned—their physical appearance, their choice of actions in decisive moments, the author's direct exposition, and the author's observation of their customary behavior and of the working of their minds—of bringing them clearly and fully into the reader's view. Here, as perhaps one might expect, belong all the long poems except *Avon's Harvest* and *The Man Who Died Twice*, but (since such a composite approach demands a certain scope) only a few of the shorter pieces: four in rhyme—*Old King Cole, Hector Kane, Mr. Flood's Party,* and *Two Gardens in Linndale*—besides one sonnet, *Lingard and the Stars;*[19] four blank-verse narratives of medium length—*Mortmain, Lazarus,*

Nicodemus, and *Sisera;* and an experiment in alcaics, *Late Summer.*

A second form is the dramatic monologue—a poem entirely in the words of one person, the revelation of whose character is the main purpose of the piece, although other characters may be incidentally delineated. Here are to be included *The Clinging Vine, How Annandale Went Out, An Evangelist's Wife, The Woman and the Wife, Lisette and Eileen, As a World Would Have It, Horace to Leuconoë, Partnership, Rahel to Varnhagen, An Island, The Three Taverns, John Brown, Rembrandt to Rembrandt, Toussaint L'Ouverture,* and *The Prodigal Son.* These pieces also are in a variety of metrical forms, from the sonnet to blank verse. Although Robinson's use of the dramatic monologue has been often noticed, readers as a group would probably place only *Rembrandt* among his most successful works.[20] It is curious, although not clearly significant, that the last nine of these pieces deal with historical or biblical characters, and that *As a World Would Have It* retells the Greek myth of Alcestis. Only five are original in subject.

But whatever may be one's general opinion of Robinson's work in the dramatic monologue, strictly defined, he undeniably achieved in a modification of this form some of his greatest triumphs. These poems are told in the first person, but the interest centers on a second character, of whom the narrator is the friend and confidant. The list includes the justly popular *Ben Jonson Entertains a Man from Stratford; Captain Craig,* the most complete revelation of Robinson's character and genius in his early manhood; *The Man Who Died Twice,* which one might find reasons for calling Robinson's greatest work; *Llewellyn and the Tree,* with its high and delightful comedy; *Tasker Norcross,* in which sympathy and restraint subdue a subject matter that might have been judged absolutely unpoetic; *Sainte-Nitouche* and *The Growth of "Lorraine,"* in which dubious battle is followed by victory that in the poet's view can seem dubious only to the unseeing; the eerie, obscure *Nimmo* and *Old Trails; Inferential* and *Peace on Earth,* two whimsical Robinsonian warnings against smug or hasty judgments on our fellows; *Avon's Harvest,* already analyzed as a frightening study of the obsessive power of evil; and, over against this last picture of total spiritual (and thence physical) eclipse, the sun-flooded *Isaac and Archibald*.

The reasons for this success are not immediately obvious. Perhaps one factor is that in maintaining the familiar tone assumed by the narrator, as in a quiet and friendly conversation, Robinson avoids the supersubtle suggestions and the exasperating involutions of style that mar so many of his verse novels. Again, the narrator is a character in his own right, winning the other's confidence through his willingness to listen and his refusal to sit in judgment, yet commanding respect for a point of view of his own, and hence the perfect recipient of a confession—in which, again, the style is relatively direct.[21] There is also a chance for the narrator, more naturally than in stories told in the third person, to clarify by restatement, interpretation, or question, when there is need to do so, the words of the primary character.

The fourth group is made up of dramatic dialogues: formally dramatic in *On the Way*, *Genevieve and Alexandra*, and *Demos and Dionysus*, where, as in a printed play, each speech is preceded by the name of the speaker; and informally in *John Evereldown*, *John Gorham*, and *London Bridge*. The first three are (to venture a personal opinion) rather flat; the blank verse never seems to come alive. In the others, especially *John Gorham*, where Robinson shows his gift for combining the lyric and the dramatic, the results are happier.

In the study of Robinson's creation of character by means of dialogue, an obvious starting point is what the characters say about themselves. Many, like their creator, are given to introspection, not in any morbid fashion, but because they wish to understand themselves and their relation to the world. Lorraine's restlessness, her willfulness, her honesty, and her ultimate loyalty to her better self could hardly be revealed more movingly than in her own confession, especially when it is framed by her lover's quiet acceptance of it. Old King Cole's cheerful transcendence of the affliction of having two worse than worthless sons—

> "They'll have a bad end, I'll agree,
> But I was never born to groan"—

shines for the reader through his words, even if they make little impression on his sleepy auditor. The self-evaluation of Vanderberg in *Sainte-Nitouche*—

> "But there's a guidance for the man
> Who stumbles upward for the light"—

and of Llewellyn—

> "I've tried the world, and found it good,
> For more than twenty years this fall"—

though in each case it is questioned by the friend who repeats it, is a crucial factor in the reader's final conception. John Evereldown, seen by Tilbury Town's casual observers as a "skirt-crazed reprobate," takes on tragic intensity as he cries,

> "God knows if I pray to be done with it all,
> But God is no friend to John Evereldown."

The doubt that we feel in the first part of *John Gorham* as to which person deserves our sympathy disappears as we read the last appeal of Jane Wayland, where the wall of raillery that she has built to shield her love from common eyes is shattered by the sudden fear that it has also deceived her lover, whose egocentric blindness she is not yet willing to acknowledge.[22]

In the longer poems, as so often happens, the process is different. Occasionally, it is true, we get the same swift and brilliant revelation that occurs in the passages just quoted. Isolt of Brittany, for example, makes an unforgettable answer to her father's gentle urging that she end her dreams of a past that is dead:

> "I am not one
> Who must have everything, yet I must have
> My dreams if I must live, for they are mine."

But as a rule the self-portraiture is done gradually—sometimes, it would seem, almost painfully—with many small brush strokes that in some cases achieve in the end a decisive effect but in others leave the picture dim or blurred. Norcross, Rembrandt, and Fernando Nash pass on to the reader with energy and clarity the self-knowledge by which they are damned or saved. But Napoleon's mental wanderings (in *An Island*) are never quite drawn together and placed in focus, as even madness must be when it is the subject of art. Even *Toussaint L'Ouverture*, despite the poem's lofty theme, the skillful use of leitmotifs, the power of many of the lines, and the pathos of the situation, never quite seems to bring its hero to life. And in most of the verse novels, where self-analysis is only one means of characterization, many readers will wish that it had been used more sparingly.

One question that always arises for the reader in connection with self-portraiture is, "How far can it be trusted?" May the speaker not be trying sometimes to deceive his hearer, as, in one of the instances given, the mention of Llewellyn's "unholy guile" might suggest? Or, since so many of Robinson's characters are eager for illusions, may not the speaker himself be at least partly deceived, as Vanderberg is thought by his friend to be: "I knew him—better than he thought"?

Such queries are sometimes, though rarely, answered by a direct statement of the poet, as noted in the preceding section. But more often the answer comes from what other characters say. This natural approach Robinson uses indirectly in some of his best short poems. Not having space for the actual words, he summarizes in terse and luminous phrases what people say about a certain person, though sometimes their talk clarifies the picture less by plain statement than by inference. Tilbury Town has its say about Old King Cole, Richard Cory, Pamela, the wife in *Vain Gratuities*, "A Man in Our Town," the son who to his mother is "The Gift of God," the ill treated wife in *Eros Turannos*:

> We tell you, tapping on our brows,
> The story as it should be.

Yet the Town's opinion is not merely the shadow that makes the truth shine brighter; we know how the popular mind works, and therefore its judgment of a person gives us, when we have made the proper allowances, a measure of positive insight into that person's character.

In those poems, also (as we have seen), where the narrator is a friend of the central character, we profit from the friend's comments because his position is known. His office is that of Horatio at the end of *Hamlet:* to tell an imperceptive and skeptical world the true story of a person doomed to fare far from the beaten track. Similarly, in the long poems told in the third person there is sometimes a character set apart from the others by a temperament at once detached and sympathetic, whose often lengthy comments about his companions, made either to them or to others, may generally be taken at face value. Umfraville in *Roman Bartholow*, Timberlake in *Matthias at the Door*, Doctor Quick in *Talifer*, and Evensong in *Amaranth* (not to mention Amaranth himself and Zoë in *King Jasper*), all occupy such a position and perform such a function (and sometimes appear to be present for no other purpose).

In addition, naturally, we often come to know a character through what is said of him in the give-and-take of ordinary conversation, as when Matthias, Natalie, and Timberlake discuss Garth's life and death, or when Isaac and Archibald each talk about the other with the boy. "Ordinary conversation," however, is not common among Robinson's characters, whose speech, however lengthy, is always intended to clarify a particular point.

But what usually guides us in the longer poems, though often by imperceptible stages, to the poet's intended conception is a general tone pervading everything that a person says and reflecting his unique vision of the world around him and within him: the distinctive scale of values that he applies to experience; his will to harmonize the actual with the ideal or his willingness to accept their divorce; the quality of his response to contacts with his fellow human beings.

The words of Captain Craig, dying in destitution and obscurity after a lifetime of unsuccess, are radiant with youth and hope, with the innocence and eagerness of "the Child within the man" that he bids each hearer find, qualified by a serene wisdom sprung from a sober second sight of a world not designed to be a child's plaything. In the speech of Fernando Nash it is a more lurid light that we become aware of—a kind of Purgatorial fire, burning away his betrayal of such a compact with the divine Power as few men are permitted to make. Lingering pride at having been chosen above other men, passionate self-reproach for having failed, humble gratitude for undeserved forgiveness guaranteed by the dream-performance of his great Third Symphony, all find a voice as he tells his story, and as he pauses from time to time to assure himself and his hearer, "I had it—once."

At another outpost of human experience, what Ferguson says about himself under the pseudonym of Tasker Norcross paints for us, gradually, the picture of a man imprisoned for life in a changeless limbo whose deathly light reveals only the blankness of floors and walls on which no shade or brightness ever comes, and whose blank silence is never broken by any music—divine, human, or infernal. Or, turning to a situation that is easier for most of us to imagine, the thing that makes Natalie the most gallant and heartwarming heroine in all the longer poems is the unfailing honesty with which she speaks—not from indifference to others' feelings, nor from an affectation of frankness, still less from any impulse to give pain; but from respect for herself and for those whom she addresses, hatred of subterfuge and insincerity, trust that the Power that rules the universe is on the side of truth.

So in the Arthurian poems it is the speech of each character taken as a whole that plays the largest part in achieving the poet's purpose of humanizing the misty figures of medieval legend. It is in Merlin's speech that we read most clearly his human passion and affection for Vivian, his human inability to alter the events that he has been able to foresee, his human pity for Arthur, and his human surrender at last to the assaults of Time. In what the character himself says, likewise, are visible Gawaine's resolution—before the death of his brothers—to take nothing seriously; the struggle in Lancelot between his dying passion for Guinevere and his living memory of the Grail; the moral weakness of the mighty Tristram and the moral strength of the frail Isolt of Brittany when each is for the first time brought to recognize that destiny is stronger than the will of a human being.

Not all the characters, of course, are drawn with equal power. The most ardent admirer of Robinson must admit that some are at least relatively unsuccessful. Such failures are due, perhaps, not to lack of clarity in the poet's conception, nor to lack of skill in applying the techniques that have just been analyzed, but to his inability to *feel* his way into the character and identify himself with it. To use his own terminology, "cerebration" overbalances "feeling." If the chararacters called into being in the shorter poems of Robinson's early and middle periods by means so economical and apparently simple are often more alive than those that are delineated at length and in detail in the later and longer works, it is only because the intellectual conception is embraced so much more closely and strongly by the indefinable creative power that men have agreed to call "imagination," for which technique can never be a substitute.

6

But although Robinson's methods of characterization may have become more elaborate as he grew older, and although the failure of imaginative power (from which the greatest artist at the peak of his career is never entirely secure) may have become more frequent, his attitude toward his characters does not change. From the beginning to the end, he thinks of them and treats them, as he thought of and treated people in real life, with a scrupulous and almost fastidious regard for their integrity, with an unreasoned and unqualified acceptance of the Kantian principle (which may also, if one chooses, be called Christian) that human beings are always to be treated as ends and never as means.

It has been said already that the men and women in Robinson's poems exist for their own sake, to play their unique parts in the spectacle (and whatever else it may be) called "life." There are, of course, obvious exceptions in Robinson's last two poems, *Amaranth* and *King Jasper*. That they *are* exceptions, one may add, is an equally obvious factor in limiting their appeal; and perhaps it also indicates a weakening of the poet's imaginative grasp of the concrete, individual character.

But if Amaranth is only a pair of eyes and a voice, Captain Craig is a man, and his words are his own, even though they may also at times be Robinson's. The same is true of King Cole, of Merlin, and of other characters—even some in the late poems, such as Timberlake and Doctor Quick—who are called on to be oracular. If Zoë impresses the reader as being mostly a musical voice emanating from a sort of disembodied glow, she has no sisters among the other heroines. And if King Jasper himself loses some of his humanness because he symbolizes the merits and defects of American capitalism historically considered, Matthias and Nightingale carry no such handicap.

Likewise, *Vickery's Mountain* is not a sermon against idleness, nor *Aaron Stark* a denunciation of avarice, nor *Reuben Bright* an argument for vegetarianism, nor *Doctor of Billiards* "a plea for the suppression of vice." [23] Miniver Cheevy and Mr. Flood personify neither an indictment nor a defense of the use of alcoholic beverages, although Robinson doubtless felt a degree of kinship with them, especially the latter, who was conceived during the era of Prohibition. *How Annandale Went Out* has only an oblique connection with the moral issues involved in euthanasia. *John Evereldown* does not advocate celibacy; *The Growth of "Lorraine"* contains no moral or sociological comments on fallen women; *Talifer* is not a tract against education for women nor in favor of divorce. What we are given in every instance is the response of a particular person or persons to a particular situation.

This fact fits with another already noted—that Robinson rarely takes sides for or against his characters. Tennyson's grudge against Guinevere as the architect of the ruin of Arthur's world, which vitiates the dramatic appeal of the *Idylls*, has no counterpart in Robinson's Arthurian poems. Browning's love affair with Pompilia (who becomes a sort of reincarnation of his dead wife), which adds intensity to the drama while it distorts the history of *The Ring and the Book*, has no parallel in Robinson's many stories of marital discord or frustrated romance.

So it is with the world as a whole that lives in his poetry. The rain falls alike upon the just and the unjust. Misers and murderers carry no visible mark upon their foreheads. Martyrs and Good Samaritans move beneath no halos. Flammonde is as far from any overt admiration on the part of his creator as he is from the understanding of Tilbury Townspeople. King Mark incurs no malediction for his initial vengefulness, gains no praise for his tardy forgiveness, is repaid with no verbal pity for his final frustration. No tears are asked for the fate of either Isolt. For the most part Robinson gives the impression of sharing the unexpected detachment of Lorraine's lover as he reads her last letter—of never being "surprised or grieved" at anything that people do or that they have to endure.

This dispassionate presentation is due mainly to the poet's profound humility, which is really a sense of inescapable oneness with his fellows. "But for the Grace of God" is the title of only one of his poems, but it is a theme implicit in almost all.[24] "Why," he seems to be always asking himself, "did such misfortune come to another and not to me? What did he do that he should suffer thus? What have I done that I should not?" Or if some act seems inexcusable, the question may be, "How do I know that in the same situation, subject to the same pressures, I might not have done the same?"

And this constant comparison not only determines his refusal to condemn those for whose deeds he can only have abhorrence, but forbids him to insult with pity those who are the apparently casual victims of the mysterious economy of the cosmos. What he *does* feel is perhaps best expressed by the term "compassion"—the indentification of oneself with the sufferer, the impulse to share his burden and so lighten it.

> If we divide suffering and dross, we may
> Diminish till it is consumed away.

So wrote Shelley, another man doomed to an implacable awareness of the world's pain; and although Robinson has less inclination to leap from a concrete experience to the formulation of a metaphysical principle, he has the same intense desire to lessen the suffering of his fellow beings and has the same intuitive perception that in this way it may be done.

In the background of this attitude, no doubt, is the elementary and unregarded principle of Christianity pronounced by Jesus in the words, "Inasmuch as ye have done it unto one of the least of these my brethren, ye have done it unto me." But this would have meant little to Robinson, who was not accustomed to mouthing other people's sentiments because he liked the sound, had it not expressed a personal intuition of "human solidarity"; a conviction that in a world which in so many ways seems alien and hostile, men and women are bound together by their common humanity, which validates certain claims upon, and certain obligations to, each other.

This does not mean that Robinson's attitude is dictated by duty or theory. The fact is that he *likes* people. Shy, austere, fastidious, distressed by the taste of the general public ("as for the democratization of art, there ain't no such animal" [25]), and distrustful of its intelligence (as he makes plain in *Dionysus in Doubt*), with no capacity or desire to be a "popular" poet, he nevertheless distinguishes the person from the mob; and piercing the armor of apparent nonentity, he finds a human being like himself and lends an attentive ear to his unique variant, comic or tragic, of the story common to mankind. It was not because of the human associations that his work on the New York subway project galled his spirit, for between him and the illiterate laborers there seems to have been an unaffected friendliness. Nowhere in his writings or his life is there a hint of the *heartlessness* that one is sometimes tempted to think rules increasingly in the modern world: in totalitarian states, in industrial organization, in modern art and literature. Somber as his portrayals of human character often are, they are never even remotely suggestive of the purpose that a celebrated contemporary novelist ascribes to one of his characters, and that the reader may fairly ascribe to the novelist himself: "forcing humans to be fully, *verbally* conscious of their own and other people's disgustingness . . . of the fact that you can't do without your fellow humans, and that, when you're with them, they make you sick." [26] Such a sentiment Robinson would have regarded as the expression of a warped and envenomed personality, who might have served, like Aaron Stark, as the subject of a sonnet, but who even then would have been transformed so that, like Robinson's other unpleasant characters, he would not have been himself an object of disgust.

On the other hand, clearly, Robinson is no sentimentalist. His works are crowded with people who suffer through no visible fault of their own; yet neither the poet nor (as a rule) his characters declaim against the injustice of God or fate, or the inhumanity of man. What the poems say is simply, "This is the way things are." Pain is a fact, and men and women must bear it as they can: silently if possible, the poet seems to feel; yet, if driven to cry out, like Job (perhaps even like Job's wife), having the right to do so without incurring the censure of those more fortunate; or having even the right, if the suffering be judged unbearable, to seek a refuge in death. If we want a word for the poetic effects that result from such an attitude, it is not "sentimentalism" but "pathos."

Nothing will more clearly illustrate the poet's refusal to exploit his characters' unhappiness than his treatment of suicide. If the Freudian critics ever get around to Robinson (perhaps when they have finished with Herman Melville), they will have much to say about the unconscious will to death that they are sure to find evidenced in the twelve or, if one counts Pink and Atlas in *Amaranth*, fourteen instances of self-destruction in Robinson's poetry.[27] Yet such a theory seems scarcely necessary. Like Samuel Johnson (among others whom the world honors), he found in life "much to be endured" and relatively "little to be enjoyed"; and especially was this true when he considered not his own life but the lives of others. Unlike Johnson, however, he looked upon Christian dogmas, including the proscription of suicide (for which the churches have assumed an authority that is not found in the Gospels), as man-made and not God-inspired. And he took to heart, as few do, a command that *is* found in the Gospels, "Judge not that ye be not judged."

He is therefore not "surprised or grieved" or angry or contemptuous when a person decides that he has lived long enough. Nor—and this is the main point at present—does he try to arouse such emotions in his readers by exploiting any rebellion against, or acceptance of, religious dogmas; or any feeling, in regard to the person involved, of kinship or superiority. He remarks in a letter concerning an acquaintance rumored to have committed suicide: "A suicide signifies discouragement or despair—either of which is, or should be, too far beyond the scope of our poor little piddling human censure to require of our ignorance anything less kind than silence." [28] And this attitude toward actual persons is maintained toward the imagined characters in his poems. They have identities of their own; they are to be treated as ends in themselves and not as instruments to be used; their words and thoughts and actions are to be recorded and not judged.

It should be added that this attitude of judgment withheld, of interest generous but detached, is not due to any premise of determinism, any assumption that the characters are the products or puppets of environmental forces. The full discussion of Robinson's stand on the issue of freedom versus determinism is reserved for the following chapter; but here it may be said that the naturalistic —and nihilistic—viewpoint just described, which is present in so much twentieth century fiction, such as Dreiser's *An American Tragedy* and the early novels of Ernest Hemingway, is almost exactly opposed to Robinson's. For his characters are, within limits, self-determined. They do not, of course, always create the alternatives among which they are compelled to choose; but the choice is their own, and by a series of such choices they become what they finally are.

This principle of self-determination is, I take it, mainly what we mean when we speak of "human dignity." It is what makes Shakespeare's tragic heroes tragic and heroic. It is what makes Milton's Satan the dominant figure in at least the early books of *Paradise Lost*, and makes Samson so much more heroic than Adam, against whom the cards are stacked. It is what redeems from mere insanity the madness of Captain Ahab in *Moby Dick*. It is what redeems from mere inconsequentiality the different madness of Don Quixote. It is one thing that saves Robinson's world from being the "prison house" that so many critics have accused him of making it.

7

And as this principle of self-determination separates pathos from sentimentalism and tragedy from melodrama, so it is a main source of the distinctive quality of a feature of Robinson's characterization that has until now only been glanced at; namely, his humor. His regard for the integrity of his characters does not permit us to pity or scorn them, but it allows us to laugh at them. Having acknowledged their spiritual independence, we can let ourselves be amused by the incongruities in which that independence sometimes issues. "But," as the boy in *Isaac and Archibald* observes, "there's a laughing that has honor in it." And if our laughter at Robinson's characters does not always confer honor, it is always friendly: "And I may laugh at them because I knew them."

It is, incidentally, almost exclusively in his characterization that Robinson's humor is to be found. Of purely verbal humor there is almost nothing in his work: only a few puns on the word "water," to which he was apparently prompted by Prohibition, as when Fernando Nash, discussing with himself the possible means of suicide, remarks: "There's always water; but you don't like that." Perhaps one ought to mention, also, the whimsical portrayal in *Theophilus* of an irredeemable scoundrel whose name means "lover of God."

Equally rare is the comedy[29] of action and situation, except where it reinforces the comedy of character, as in *Fleming Helphenstine;* for in this sonnet it is not the situation itself that is amusing, but rather this particular victim's inability to rescue himself except by precipitate flight.

Nor is Robinson's forte the comedy of ideas, the sort of thing that is so inevitably and agreeably associated with Bernard Shaw. The only poem in which he makes a notable attempt to entertain his readers by placing familiar ideas in an unexpected and absurd light is *Dionysus in Doubt,* also a product of Prohibition; as when, with a happy stroke of wit, he compares democracy in its leveling aspect with Procrustes' bed, into which any guest, by "stretching" or "cleaving," could be made to fit:

> "One man no longer than another
> And every man thereby a brother."

The main source of comedy, as Robinson interprets the human scene, is the same thing that is often the source of tragedy: a disparity of vision that gives the same fact, or the same experience, a different look and meaning for one person than for another, or for people in general. This is apparently what Robinson has in mind when, referring to *Captain Craig*, he speaks of his "notion of 'semi-intellectual' humor, which is to me the only real kind—that is, the only kind that has to do with the realities." [30] It is characteristic that one of his first essays of this sort—one of the few gleams of humor in *The Torrent and The Night Before*—involves himself: pointing out to his "Dear Friends," with a wry but not bitter smile, the gulf between their view of his chosen career and his own:

> So, friends (dear friends), remember, if you will,
> The shame I win for singing is all mine,
> The gold I miss for dreaming is all yours.

In the dramatic poems comedy results if the disparity is never perceived by the character mainly involved, as in *Miniver Cheevy*; tragedy, if it is perceived and cannot be accepted, as when Matthias learns the truth about Natalie's feeling toward him. [31] If it is acknowledged and surmounted, the result may again be pure comedy, as in *Talifer*. Or if it is seen and accepted, but without the power to escape, we have, as in Mr. Flood or in Styx, Figg, Flax, and Evensong, what may be called tragicomedy.

There is, of course, no derogation of the last group in the fact that they choose a seemingly unheroic compromise. Robinson is always friendly as he raises the curtain that separates the way human beings see themselves from the way they are seen by others—who may or may not see truly. The smile is tender with which he looks upon the mother in *The Gift of God*:

> Blessed with a joy that only she
> Of all alive shall ever know,
> She wears a proud humility
> For what it was that willed it so,—
> That her degree should be so great
> Among the favored of the Lord
> That she may scarcely bear the weight
> Of her bewildering reward.

The reward, of course, is in having a son who in her eyes is perfect —although to others he is the subject "Of many smiles and many doubts"; it is not she but her friends who have to suffer (although not seriously) when her desire to share her happiness causes them to be "caught and tortured for the truth." And why should anyone be-grudge her the happiness that she finds in her illusion?

> And should the gift of God be less
> In him than in her motherhood,

what does it matter?[32]

The same quality is present in the portrait of Vickery, who dreams of the hidden gold, to which he alone has the key, at the foot of the far-off mountain "Blue in the west"; who has "a tear for worthy men" possessed of no such golden secret, while he dreams—and dreams. A still more charming dreamer is Miniver Cheevy, who was "born too late": as a medieval knight he would have worn his armor gracefully; as an Italian Renaissance nobleman, "He would have sinned incessantly"; but as an ordinary twentieth century man in the street, he finds—after he has "thought, and thought, and thought,/ And thought about it"—that there is nothing better to do than keep on drinking. To the same family belong the "Veteran Sirens," so tenacious in their embrace of the illusion of youth and passion, when in reality they stand "So far from Ninon and so near the grave." [33]

Robinson's greatest triumph in the creation of this sort of charac-ter is Mr. Flood. The contrast between dream and reality is soft-ened, the pathos that in the poems just mentioned lies below the sur-face is here brought into view, by the fact that what is now illusion was once truth. It is some remnant of self-respect that makes him pause "warily" to make sure that no one sees him lift the jug. The relic of a once acute intelligence is present in the grace and irony with which he can jest (borrowing a line from Omar Khayyám) about his defeated and derelict life: "The bird is on the wing, the poet says"—as if Eben Flood needed a poet to tell him. The lines that picture how,

> as a mother lays her sleeping child
> Down tenderly, fearing it may awake,
> He set the jug down slowly at his feet
> With trembling care, knowing that most things break,

cause one to wonder whether his tenderness for what is now his only treasure may not be mingled with the memory of children of his own, with whom all ties have long been broken, and whether this loss may not have helped him to his melancholy knowledge "that most things break." The courtliness with which he addresses his other self gives us a glimpse of the social position that he once graced. In his singing of *Auld Lang Syne* are echoes of a heart-warming fellowship that once was his. But, lest the pathos swell into a flood of sentimentalism, the poet from time to time throws a less romantic, though still not unfriendly, light upon the scene; in which we note the frequency of Eben's resort to the jug, his mere pretense of restraint, the two moons shining on his whisky-misted world.

In *Uncle Ananias* the picture is different. Our smile is only a little for the old man and the prodigality of his trespasses against truth, for he and his world are defended against disaster by the un-shakable adoration of his young audience. What does amuse us is the thought of the discomfiture, in his presence, of the town's solid citizens, whose inherited Puritan assumption that happiness is a re-ward reserved for industry and truthfulness is here so blithely chal-lenged. And the question occurs to the reader, although not clearly to them, "Who is most deluded, after all?" Thus "thoughtful laugh-ter" (the admirable phrase of George Meredith) is often hovering on the edge of Robinson's humor.

Such laughter also plays over the rare portrayals of the comedy of love, as in *Rahel to Varnhagen* and *Talifer*. But in a third such comedy, *Llewellyn and the Tree*, the laughter becomes almost hilarious, and is only thoughtful at the end. The first comic incon-gruity is between Llewellyn's blissful dream of marital paradise and the small Inferno that Priscilla, shrill and implacable, makes of the reality. The second is between Priscilla's mental picture of her husband—"Not knowing quite the man he was"—as a worm who will only writhe while remaining prostrate, and the real man who is capable of being goaded into explosive rebellion. The third is between what Llewellyn sees as "roses" tossed in his path by Time (or Providence) and what Tilbury Town sees as mostly made up of "civet, coral, rouge, and years." The crowning incon-gruity is that between the penitential confession of error and resultant ruin that most of the Town would have thought proper to the occasion of Llewellyn's meeting with an old acquaintance, and his actual, cherished, sustaining pride in "his one victory." And finally, as we look back over the poem to relish more fully its special quality, we begin to perceive the implications of the fact that the tree is the Tree of Knowledge, and to remark the parallels—which, entertaining as they are, have a final half-serious note—with the biblical story.

The same delightful disparity between what society expects of a person and what he may assert his right as an individual to feel and do is the theme of *Old King Cole*. Tilbury Town resents the father's persistent cheerfulness in the face of his sons' notorious misdoings, and even tries, with the boldness of assured righteousness, to impress upon him the impropriety of his behavior:

> And Old King Cole, with many a puff
> That haloed his urbanity,
> Would smoke till he had smoked enough,
> And listen most attentively.
> He beamed as with an inward light
> That had the Lord's assurance in it;
> And once a man was there all night,
> Expecting something every minute.

But his expectation is foiled by his own dullness; he goes to sleep while King Cole is talking, and retains for the benefit of the other townspeople only a dim recollection of what sort of defense the old man offered.

King Cole suggests the "droll derelict" of *Peace on Earth*, who sees how he must appear to the eyes of respectability, and who balances against this perception, without bitterness, a perception of the insecure foundation upon which respectability is often based. And this attitude, in turn, calls to mind Captain Craig. A pauper has no right—so runs Tilbury Town's logic—to act as if he were a preacher ordained and paid to tell people what they ought to believe and how they ought to live. The humor lies partly in the Captain's resounding defiance of this dogma, his exultation, even, in the incongruity that from such depths of destitution he should avow a confident and joyous creed; partly in the fact that, after all, it is not the people of Tilbury Town but a few patient friends who have to listen to him; and partly in his half-admitted perception of this fact, which leads him to order, by way of compensation, a posthumous attack on the bastions of propriety by providing for a brass band—with trombones—in his funeral procession. Thus he enjoys in anticipation, as his young friends later do in fact, the Town's incomprehension of the whole affair:

> for men stopped
> And eyed us on that road from time to time,
> And on that road the children followed us;
> And all along that road the Tilbury Band
> Blared indiscreetly the Dead March in Saul.

From these lines "the large humor of the thing" emerges unconquerably.

There is just a touch of this large humor in the otherwise unsmiling portrait of Fernando Nash, who, knowing that he "had it —once," having listened to "the drums of God" and to His "golden trumpets," can after that experience believe that he is doing penance and serving God by beating a drum for a group of lunatic-fringe revivalists. One may also feel a certain largeness in the humor of Merlin's emergence from his beard and wizard's robes to play with Vivian the roles of a man and woman in love, so vastly at variance with the pictures of them that exist in the imagination of the world outside Broceliande. And perhaps beside Merlin may be placed Ben Jonson's Shakespeare, a magician also of sorts, who can create worlds of his own, but whose concern for the one that is to most men real and is to him "a phantom world he sounded and found wanting," is an imposing house in Stratford—which, urgently as he desires to possess it, he knows to be a phantom like the rest.

From this world of ambiguities, where one person's vision of himself and his world may be not only absurdly different from that of another person or of people in general, but also whimsically at odds with another view of his own, we move in *Isaac and Archibald* into the clearer and simpler universe of boyhood. The boy accepts without more than a passing wonder the incongruity between his world and that of his aging friends: his world where the miles are long and dusty, where the hours stretch out into a day that is almost infinite, with another always beyond, where the taste of "worm-ripe" early apples is a sufficient justification for living, and where the whims of two old men about the proper time to cut a field of oats and about each other's supposedly failing faculties are mysterious but natural; their world where miles and days are short, with the end in sight, but where the sense of brevity adds a tang rather than a taint to "all things" (like cider) that God has "put on earth for men to drink" and be thankful for, and where their sight begins to be dim only for things near at hand.

It may be emphasized, as a final word, that Robinson's humor is always *good* humor. Here, as elsewhere in his work, the reader is aware of the breadth of his sympathy and the depth of his charity, of the warmth of his affection for his fellows. But here also we meet face to face a quality that in much of his work remains far in the background, though never absent; namely, the faith, or rather the perception, that life is self-justified. "I've tried the world, and found it good," Llewellyn says; and so, these poems make one feel, has his creator. If the incongruities of human existence are sometimes painful, they bring at other times a brightness, a grace, a savor, to a world of which, with all its shortcomings, the poet is glad to be a part.

chapter vii: VERITIES

Glimpses of Robinson's philosophy have been caught many times already—in his views about poetry, in the attitude toward life that is implicit in certain qualities of his style, in the ideas that help to give his poems organic form, in his choice of people to write about and and in his attitude toward them. The work of any author inevitably reflects his beliefs, and particularly must this be true when they are held with such consistency and conviction as are Robinson's.

The general unity of his thought, however, may not always be apparent, for it is a matter of temperament rather than logic. He would no doubt have agreed with Emerson (to whom he renders high homage in early letters[1]) that "a foolish consistency is the hobgoblin of little minds." He is correct in denying that he is a systematic thinker, and it was honesty as well as modesty that led him during his life to discourage attempts to extract from his writings a complete and coherent philosophy. In a friendly letter to a graduate student who had chosen to do a thesis on this aspect of his work, he remarked: "I still wish that you were writing about my poetry—of which my so-called philosophy is only a small part, and probably the least important." [2] And on another occasion he went even further: "It annoys me to hear talk about my philosophy of life. I am not a philosopher. I don't intend to be one." [3]

This attitude is characteristic. We need not doubt that he is in sympathy with the "Contented Metaphysician" in *The Burning Book*, who, after years of labor on a projected masterpiece, sees that it is not for him to save the world, and burns the manuscript; thereby escaping, like Fargo, from the "wrong world," where

> "There are philosophers who delve and starve
> To say again what others have said better;
> There are wan moralists and economists
> Who write with screaming blood to save a world
> That will not read them and will not be saved." [4]

On the other hand, Robinson has strong personal convictions, which he sees no more reason to conceal than to flaunt. There is something in him, after all, of the unreasoning self-confidence of genius, the unconsidered acceptance of Emerson's ringing challenge: "Trust thyself: every heart vibrates to that iron string." And there is always present in his work, as he confided to Smith with reference to "many of my verses" in *The Torrent and The Night Before*, "a conscious hope that they might make some despairing devil a little stronger and a little better satisfied with things—not as they are, but as they are to be." [5]

Even when (as is most often the case) he is not stating his convictions directly, they underlie his stories and his portraits, are implicit in the things that happen to his characters and in what they do and say and think. If we are to understand how the poet wishes us to take these events and these people, we need some knowledge of the philosophical climate of the world that they inhabit.

2

Among Robinson's beliefs about the nature of the world, there is one that is more deeply rooted than all the others, and that serves as the initial premise in all his reasoning about ethical and social problems. This conviction is best expressed by the term "antimaterialism." "My 'philosophy,'" he declared in the letter to a student mentioned above, "is mostly a statement of my inability to accept a mechanistic interpretation of the universe and of life." [6] And to another inquirer he gave a similar answer: "There is no 'philosophy' in my poetry beyond an implication of an ordered universe and a sort of deterministic negation of the general futility that appears to be the basis of 'rational' thought." [7]

Both these statements belong to the poet's later years; but the belief in an ordered universe and in some meaning and purpose present in the world was a basic principle of his thought from the time when he began to think about such matters at all. The negative emphasis, however, the feeling that materialism must be attacked,[8] apparently belongs to the latter half of his life. From the beginning, to be sure, he had resented the usual American assumption that success is to be measured in dollars: first, because, as held by his father and the majority of his fellow citizens in Gardiner, it caused him intense mental discomfort in his early manhood (and may even, in a small way, have warped his entire life); and second, leaving all personal grievances aside, because he was convinced, on the basis of both intuition and observation, that such a standard was restrictive and degrading in its effect on human life. But many years seem to have passed before he advanced from the perception of this particular evil to the realization that it was only one result of a general disbelief, overt in the minority, tacit in the majority, in anything more than a physical reality. His apparent slowness in reaching this conclusion is odd, for in the spring of 1891 he read with enthusiasm Carlyle's *Sartor Resartus* ("I . . . am completely soaked with its fiery philosophy" [9]), the first big gun in the Victorian counteroffensive against Utilitarianism, Positivism, and other manifestations of the widening desire of men in the Western world to take their destiny entirely into their òwn hands, and to dismiss God as an unnecessary hypothesis. Possibly it was World War I that made Robinson feel the need to announce to the world his conviction that Western civilization stood on a "rotten foundation." [10]

At any rate, *The Man Against the Sky* is his first as well as his most powerful attack on materialism as a philosophy. It was not his last, however; for although he had stated his position once for all, and only once again felt called on to devote a whole poem to the issue (elaborating one aspect of it in *The Flying Dutchman*), there are enough references to it in the later poems—*Rembrandt to Rembrandt, Cavender's House, Matthias at the Door, Ponce de*

Leon, The March of the Cameron Men, and *King Jasper*—to show, as do his letters, that it was never far from his thoughts.

Robinson's rejection of philosophical materialism rests upon three arguments. There is, first, the traditional idealist criticism of the naïve realist—that the latter's position depends on an assumption at least as irrational as any made by his opponents. As F. H. Bradley shows at the beginning of *Appearance and Reality,* no philosopher can ignore metaphysics. The only choice is between adopting an unsound metaphysics—that reality is what the senses tell us it is, and nothing more—and facing the fact that this is not only an assumption but a demonstrably false assumption, and that a more satisfactory starting point is needed. From this point of view, the materialist is not too much but too little of a skeptic, of a "rationalist"; not too critical but too credulous. While heaping ridicule upon revealed religions and their acceptance of a supernatural order, he accepts as a private revelation the testimony of the senses, whose pretensions to supply an adequate account of ultimate reality will simply not stand examination.

This point of view is stated, with unwonted acerbity, in a letter which Robinson wrote to Will Durant in 1931. Durant had asked him for a brief statement of belief, to be published, along with those of other more or less noted persons, in a volume entitled *On the Meaning of Life;* and in making his request he had apparently said something from which Robinson inferred an acceptance of the materialist viewpoint.

I told a philosopher once that all the other philosophers would have to go out of business if one of them should happen to discover the truth; and now you say, or imply, in your letter that the truth has been discovered, and that we are only the worse off, if possible, for the discovery. This is naturally a cause of some chagrin and humiliation for me, for I had heard nothing about it. It is true that we have acquired a great deal of material knowledge in recent years, but so far as knowledge of the truth itself is concerned, I cannot see that we are any nearer to it now than our less imaginative ancestors were when they cracked each others' skulls with stone hatchets, or that we know any more than they knew of what happened to the soul that escaped in the process. It is easy, and just now rather fashionable, to say that there is no soul, but we do not know whether there is a soul or not. . . . The cocksureness of the modern "mechanist" means nothing to me; and I doubt if it means any more to him when he pauses really to think. His position is not entirely unlike that of an intrepid explorer standing on a promontory in a fog, looking through the newest thing in the way of glasses for an ocean that he cannot see, and shouting to his mechanistic friends behind him that he has found the end of the world.[11]

A second objection to a materialistic metaphysics seemed to Robinson to lie in the apparent incongruity of using the mind to deny its own existence; of imagining that somehow atoms (not to get into the mazes of current nuclear physics, which do not affect the principle) arrange themselves in a sort of mechanism which then is able to discover, describe, and manipulate the atoms themselves of which it is nothing more than an aggregation. And a similar intrinsic absurdity is equally present when any other operations (such as those related to art or ethics) of what may no longer be called "the mind" are reduced to their assumed atomic origins. This might be called a commonsense reply when materialism presents itself as a "commonsense philosophy." It is at any rate a retort that Robinson makes at some length in *The Man Against the Sky*. The materialist "may have built"

> A living reason out of molecules
> Why molecules occurred,
> And one for smiling when he might have sighed
> Had he seen far enough,
> And in the same inevitable stuff
> Discovered an odd reason too for pride
> In being what he must have been by laws
> Infrangible and for no kind of cause.

But a much stronger motive to opposition was Robinson's conviction that human life, if taken on the terms of the materialist, is a mere insane welter in which happiness is overwhelmingly outweighed by pain. Over and over, both in his poetry and in his letters, he comes back to the nightmarish thought of what life would be like if it were nothing more than w'.at our senses—and reason working merely with the data that the senses supply—declare it to be. Like so many poets before him—among them Shelley, Tennyson, Arnold[12] (the Arnold of *Dover Beach*, speaking for himself, not the Arnold of *Culture and Anarchy*, speaking as England's schoolmaster), and his near contemporaries Hardy and Housman —he found himself driven to accept as a fact, which he must find some way to live with, the predominance of evil in man's life on earth. And one could only live with it, he felt (like Shelley and Tennyson, at least), if one believed that there is more in life than meets the eye, that there is some hidden plan and purpose, some justification for existence that sense and reason do not discern, some continuing aim even for the individual life after the body has ceased to have an identity.

Writing to Hermann Hagedorn about *The Field of Glory* and its rather pathetic central figure, Robinson explained: "The world is peppered with his kind, and I simply drew his picture to let people see what they thought about it in the light of contemporary materialism. If materialism is true, than parenthood is assuredly the greatest of all crimes, and the sooner the much advertised 'race' is annihilated, the better." [13] A few years later he put the same thought into *The Man Against the Sky*, in passages already quoted [14] and others:

> Why pay we such a price, and one we give
> So clamoringly, for each racked empty day
> That leads one more last human hope away,
> As quiet fiends would lead past our crazed eyes
> Our children to an unseen sacrifice?

And he continues the argument in the letter to Will Durant.

If a man is a materialist, or a mechanist, or whatever he likes to call himself, I can see for him no escape from belief in a futility so prolonged and complicated and diabolical and preposterous as to be worse than absurd; and as I do not know that such a tragic absurdity is not a fact, I can only know my native inability to believe that it is one. . . . But if life is only what it appears to be, no amount of improvement or enlightenment will ever compensate or atone for what it has inflicted and endured in ages past, or for what it is inflicting and enduring today. Only the most self-centered and short-visioned of egoists, it seems to me, will attempt to deny the truth of a statement so obvious.[15]

The reader who is familiar with Robinson's poems and letters will appreciate how unusual is the extremity of the language that is

here employed, and therefore how intense must have been the
writer's feeling. The same intensity prevails in almost all his references to the theme. It bursts forth in *The Children of the Night*:

> And if there be no other life,
> And if there be no other chance
> To weigh their sorrow and their strife
> Than in the scales of circumstance—
>
> 'Twere better, ere the sun go down
> Upon the first day we embark,
> In life's embittered sea to drown,
> Than sail forever in the dark.

Half a lifetime later, the old physician in *Ponce de Leon* who tries
to bring peace of mind to the dying adventurer observes

> "that if the world is only this,
> We are remarkable animate accidents,
> And are all generated for a most
> Remorseless and extravagant sacrifice
> To an insatiate God of nothing at all."

And toward the end of *King Jasper* Robinson makes Zoë say,

> "No God,
> No Law, no Purpose, could have hatched for sport
> Out of warm water and slime, a war for life
> That was unnecessary, and far better
> Never had been—if man, as we behold him,
> Is all it means."

In these and similar utterances, two different arguments against
materialism appear to be implied. One is that human beings, logically and in fact, would not go on living if they did not believe in
something more than a material reality. Thus we have a pragmatic
justification for such a belief; and one might argue in addition, although Robinson nowhere clearly does so, that the evident univer-
sality of this belief (since people in general do go on living as long
as possible) bears some sort of testimony to its truth. The other line
of reasoning begins with the premise that a world so cruel and
chaotic as this appears to be could not imaginably have evolved by
mere chance (or—what is the same thing for the seeker of meaning

—by a mechanical process). "When I look at this life without the rosy spectacles and try to see it as a thing in itself, as the final word, it is too absurd to be thought of. You've got to add something, just to make sense." [16] The second premise is that the creation of the world by a malignant or irresponsible Deity (a Being possessed of intelligence and will) is still more difficult to conceive. In the early sonnet *Kosmos* he asks:

> Is God a jester?—Does he laugh and throw
> Poor branded wretches here to sweat and strive
> For some vague end that never shall arrive?

And many years later he said, "apropos of Hardy's pessimism, that Hardy's blunder, both philosophical and artistic, was his reiteration of the idea of God jesting with mankind." [17] The conclusion is that the remaining hypothesis of a transcendental Power, or Purpose, not evident in the operations of the physical world but somehow in accord with the basic ideals and aspirations of the human mind, is the one for rational people to accept. What degree of validity such reasonings may have is a question about which philosophers have disagreed.

3

Some of the passages quoted above bring us to the threshold of the long-labored subject of Robinson's "pessimism," which began with Harry Thurston Peck's widely quoted comment in the *Bookman*, with reference to *The Torrent and The Night Before*, that "the world is not beautiful to him, but a prison-house." [18] The discussion of this topic has been largely a threshing of chaff; but although only a careless reader can accuse the poet of anything that can legitimately be called "pessimism," the fault of such critics has lain not in exaggerating the darkness of the picture but in overlooking the light. The grimness is not only in such direct statements as those just quoted, but in the somber fate by which so many of his characters are overtaken. The reader is familiar with this picture already, and it needs no further emphasis, except as a confirmation of the poet's sincerity in his assertions about the lot of humanity "if materialism is true."

Among those who see only the shadows in Robinson's panorama of human existence, there are some who support their opinion (assuming that everybody's character except their own can be "explained" in what purport to be scientific terms) by the theory that Robinson's outlook is clouded by his personal experience; and their view will of course not be affected by his specific denial, at the end of the letter already quoted at such length: "These remarks, which to some readers might seem a little severe, are more the result of observation and reflection than of personal discomfort or dissatisfaction. As lives go, my own life would be called, and properly, a rather fortunate one." [19]

The accuracy of this statement is, however, attested by the evidence. It is true that in his life there were prolonged periods of agonizing unhappiness, when his abnormal sensitiveness to human suffering in general was intensified by the desperateness of his personal situation.[20] But at no time did he indulge in bitterness or self-pity, never did he lose his sense of humor, never was he deserted by his faith in "the Light." "Admirable, all through this time," says his friend Mason with reference to one of the most painful of the periods mentioned, "were his half serene, half humorous detachment from his surroundings, the long stride and quizzical smile with which he walked through all incongruities." "The great art of life," he told this friend, "is to suffer without worrying." [21]

This side of Robinson's character has been too often overlooked. The critics who have exhausted their vocabularies in applying to his personality, or to his style, or to the kind of people whom he pictures, or to his view of the world in general, such adjectives as "negative," "bleak," "bare," "starved," "cold," "wintry," "withered," "black," "shriveled," "blighted," "chilly," "shivering," "forlorn," "thwarted," "stunted," "meager," "undernourished," "frugal," "dark," "gloomy," "gaunt," "stark," and "somber," and such nouns as "desolation," "decay," "defeat," "narrowness," "stinginess," "sterility," "failure," "despair," "melancholy," "distrust," "defeatism," "waste," "worthlessness," "weariness," "repudiation," and "rebellion" —all these critics have to this extent missed the mark.[22]

To Mason's statement should be added the comments gathered by Mrs. Richards from the poet's early acquaintances. One of his elementary-school teachers wrote of him: "He was a highly sensitive child, looking at the world objectively, for the most part, and quick to observe the humor in everything." [23] A later friend recalled that he "always saw the humorous aspect of things." [24] A high-school mate stressed as "the quality most clearly apparent" in him "*patience!*—patience, and an unruffled good humor." [25] Mrs. Richards herself concludes that he "was from his childhood singularly surrounded by groups or clubs of congenial spirits." [26] His statement to his sister-in-law that "at the age of eight or ten he had realized that he was different from the boys who liked only athletics and playing ball, and sometimes wished he had not been born" [27] reflects an experience that is probably not uncommon in childhood and not of any particular significance.

Returning to his later life, Carl Van Doren says that "he was humorous about himself" and stresses his apparent liking for the company of younger persons.[28] At Peterborough, according to Rollo Brown, "Always at the beginning of the summer when I first saw him he startled me with his cheerfulness." [29] Robinson himself, from the time of the "prison-house" comment to the end of his life, always showed unaffected bewilderment and irritation at being called a pessimist. He commented to Karl Schriftgiesser in regard to *Talifer* that "some of the critics . . . resent my being cheerful. I don't see why. It is not unusual, even for me. For in all my dramatic poems there is an undercurrent of comedy and humor." [30]

Another fact that seems not to have occurred to many critics is that the ratio of "failure" to "success" in his poetry does not necessarily correspond to the ratio in what he saw as "real life." For literary history would seem to demonstrate that in the nature of things "failure" is more interesting than "success." Shakespeare's comedies, with all their "love and beauty and delight," are trivial beside his tragedies. If it is invidious to compare *Paradise Regained* with *Paradise Lost*, there are *Comus* (lovely in its way) and *Samson Agonistes*. Even Browning, in his best work, like *Andrea del Sarto* and *The Ring and the Book*, gives the lie to the pulpit optimism of *Rabbi Ben Ezra*. Robinson was simply formulating the attitude of all his great predecessors when he argued: "I have been criticized for writing so much about 'failures.' Well, isn't it the people who fail who are more interesting than the others? They are—at least for the purpose of dramatic poetry. There is nothing poetic, and usually nothing dramatic about anyone who is a 'success.' " [31] "Somehow model citizens don't make good poems," he observed on another occasion.[32] Also apposite is a remark in a letter to Mason: "I think there are more victims of good luck in the world than there [are] of the other kind, and I must confess that I find them uninteresting as a lot." [33]

It is surely evident at this point that such easy labels as "optimism" and "pessimism" do not help us to approach the elusive truth about a subtle and complex personality and body of poetry. In this personality and this poetry—which are essentially one— perhaps the most distinctive and compelling trait is an intense and involuntary awareness of the spiritual pain that human beings inevitably or willfully endure. But this awareness issues not in bitterness or hopelessness or dreams of escape to an earthly or unearthly paradise, nor in a servile pretense that whatever is, is right; but in a serene, clear-eyed, humorous, compassionate, steadfast reliance on life's essential if indefinable worth.

This conclusion is confirmed by an examination of Robinson's poetry. The critics who find it a spiritual Siberia have simply not read it as it deserves to be read. One thing that they have failed to note, especially, is that his statements about the preponderant painfulness of life always begin with "if": "if materialism is true . . ."; "if this world is only this . . ."; ". . . if man, as we behold him,/ Is all it means"; "if there be nothing after Now . . ." But materialism is *not* true; this world is *not* "only this"; life *does* mean more than "man, as we behold him"; there *is* something "after Now." "You know that I'm not a materialist," he wrote to Hagedorn. "As

a matter of fact, I suppose I'm the damnedest optimist that ever
lived." [34] Life's landscape may be grim, but hope is there:

> Where was he going, this man against the sky?
> You know not, nor do I.
> But this we know, if we know anything:
> That we may laugh and fight and sing
> And of our transience here make offering
> To an orient Word that will not be erased,
> Or, save in incommunicable gleams
> Too permanent for dreams,
> Be found or known.

There is in the universe a Power and a Purpose too limitless to be
comprehended by the mind, established by a syllogism, described
in words:

> Shall we, because Eternity records
> Too vast an answer for the time-born words
> We spell, whereof so many are dead that once
> In our capricious lexicons
> Were so alive and final, hear no more
> The Word itself, the living word . . . ?

Again, in *The Three Taverns* Paul declares:

> Many with eyes
> That are incredulous of the Mystery
> Shall yet be driven to feel, and then to read
> Where language has an end and is a veil,
> Not woven of our words.

In similar terms Garth's ghost answers Matthias's persistent ques-
tioning about the soul:

> With a few finite and unfinished words
> That are the chips of brief experience,
> You restless and precipitate world-infants
> Would build a skiff to circumnavigate
> Infinity . . .

The poet himself says in writing to a student: "I suppose you will
have to put me down as a mystic, if that means a man who cannot
prove all his convictions to be true." [35] And again: "nothing of an
infinite nature can be proven or disproven in finite terms—mean-

ing words—and the rest is probably a matter of one's individual
ways of seeing and feeling things." [36]
Robinson's own individual way of seeing and feeling things
seems always to have been the same as in the verses quoted above.
What he sees as a world where suffering is paramount is redeemed
by what he feels about its ultimate purposefulness. "You mustn't
forget the redemption," he wrote to a friend with reference to
Merlin and its ending, "even if you don't see it";[37] and this might
almost have been his motto from first to last. Nowhere (despite
the "prison-house" comment) is the note of redemption sounded
more strongly than in his first volume; as, for instance, in *The Altar*,
an earlier and more explicit statement of the theme of *The
Town Down the River*.

> Alone, remote, nor witting where I went,
> I found an altar builded in a dream—
> A fiery place, whereof there was a gleam
> So swift, so searching, and so eloquent
> Of upward promise, that love's murmur, blent
> With sorrow's warning, gave but a supreme
> Unending impulse to that human stream
> Whose flood was all for the flame's fury bent.
>
> Alas! I said,—the world is in the wrong.
> But the same quenchless fever of unrest
> That thrilled the foremost of that martyred throng
> Thrilled me, and I awoke . . . and was the same
> Bewildered insect plunging for the flame
> That burns, and must burn somehow for the best.

The same faith is reiterated in the last line of *Credo*—"I feel the
coming glory of the Light"—and in the words with which, in
L'Envoi, the poet bids farewell to the reader of *The Children of the
Night*.

> Now in a thought, now in a shadowed word,
> Now in a voice that thrills eternity,
> Ever there comes an onward phrase to me
> Of some transcendent music I have heard.

Such statements prepare us for what we learn from the letters to
Smith: that at about this time Robinson was being converted (if he

needed to be) to metaphysical idealism. He had been rereading *Sartor Resartus*, and concluded: "If the book is anything it is a denial of the existence of matter as anything but a manifestation of thought. Christianity is the same thing, and so is illuminated commonsense." [38] He had also been reading Mary Baker Eddy; and while not accepting Christian Science "as anything apart from the spiritual wisdom that is latent in us all," he added, "but I do believe in idealism as the one logical and satisfactory interpretation of life." [39] Despite its strong attraction, however, he was objective enough to ask himself whether such a philosophy might not be merely an escape. "Perhaps idealism is the philosophy of desperation, but I do not think so." [40]

Some readers may feel that there *is* sometimes a desperate note in the poems and letters of this period; and it would seem that later, as he gradually conquers his own temptation to despair, he becomes less insistent on so positive and specific a formulation of his faith. Less tortured by life's evil, although not less fully aware of it, he does not feel so strongly impelled to the simple denial of its existence that is latent in the absolute idealist position. A stronger intuition of the purposiveness of life permits him to acknowledge that the Gordian knot of evil cannot be so easily cut, and that, although evil must always be fought against, no immediate victory is in sight.

Even in the *Captain Craig* volume, the statements of faith are less frequent, less extended, and less direct than in the poems published earlier. Old Isaac, looking forward to the end of earthly life, tells his young companion:

> "The shadow calls us, and it frightens us—
> We think; but there's a light behind the stars."

The marchers in *Twilight Song* proclaim:

> And we trust now the gleam,
> For the gleam never dies.

Captain Craig himself for the most part steers clear of metaphysics, although between the lines of his plea for a heroic and harmonious life on earth, we can read his basic idealism.

When his next volume, *The Town Down the River*, made its appearance, Robinson was no longer young; and his native disinclination to public confessions of faith, increasing with age, prevented him then and thereafter, except for the great outburst in *The Man Against the Sky*, from more than relatively rare and oblique affirmations of belief. But in the words of his characters we hear at intervals echoes of the old unfaltering confidence in life's ultimate justification. The regenerate Roman Bartholow tells Umfraville:

> "Nature has ways, you say, not reasons. Well,
> They lead us, if we find and follow them,
> Strangely away from death."

Doctor Quick comforts Althea in *Talifer* by assuring her that although God's laws

> "are said
> To be obscure; yet my belief in them
> Uncovers them, and sees them occupied
> Not far from where we live."

And in *King Jasper* there is even an apparent restatement, put into the mouth of Zoë, of the absolute idealism of the poet's early years: "All a man sees is less than what he is/ Without it, if he knew." But then comes a question that in his youth Robinson would perhaps not have allowed himself to ask: "Is he ever to know?" The poet can ask it openly now because, at the end of his life, he is surer than ever that the answer is "Yes."

4

But it is not mainly in direct statements of this sort, even when we can be sure that Robinson is speaking in his own person, that we find the fullness of his affirmation of life's value. It is rather in the general tenor of his poetry, in his treatment of his characters, in the stories in which he involves them. And these justify the inference that he never went back on the creed that he expressed to Gledhill when still in his twenties: "The universe is a great thing, and the power of evil never put it together. Of that I am certain and I am just as certain that this life is but one little scene in the big show." [41] He is perfectly right in his later declaration, "If a reader doesn't get from my books an impression that life is very much worth while, even though it may not seem always to be profitable or desirable, I can only say that he doesn't see what I'm driving at." [42] A final clinching utterance is recorded by Mason, who dates it 1901, "the lowest, most hopeless, and most monotonous period of his long struggle with poverty and obscurity." In "discussing the free will problem," Robinson "opined that there was no use trying to find out [the truth about it], though thousands had wasted their lives in the attempt." To his friend's despairing cry, "But how is one to get strength to live without knowing?" he answered, "Isn't the mystery and vitality and energy of the whole thing enough to give interest and confidence?" [43]

It is true that only a few of his characters have stories with what is known as a happy ending—although these few should not be over-looked. *Isaac and Archibald* and *Talifer,* to take but two, one early and one late, cannot have been the work of a man who despaired of human happiness. *Old King Cole* testifies to the poet's respect for a degree of "optimism"—so long as it is honest—that Tilbury Town considers almost indecent. *Captain Craig* is more complex, but a main theme is certainly the weighing of the extremes of optimism and pessimism; and although the conclusion is that some kind of compromise, or reconciliation, is what human beings should strive for, still, if one had to choose between the extremes, he would do better to be "blinded by the lights" than "by the shadows," to take his chance with the "demon of the sunlight" that tempts to unearned cheerfulness. If he would not miss the best that life has to offer, he must "learn to laugh with God."

> "Because one half of humankind
> Lives here in hell, shall not the other half
> Do any more than just for conscience' sake
> Be miserable? Is this the way for us
> To lead these creatures up to find the light,—
> Or to be drawn down surely to the dark
> Again?"

And almost with his dying breath Captain Craig declares, "There is no servitude so fraudulent/ As of a sun-shut mind.[1] "

The Captain does not deny, on the other hand, "That sunshine has a devil of its own," who prevents his worshipers from ever seeing anything unpleasant—or from understanding how a poet who sees unpleasantness all about him can be other than an "emissary of gloom or of despair." [44] *The Man Against the Sky* was so widely misread that a note of pleased relief creeps into a letter from the poet to a friend who did not miss the point: "You are entirely right in assuming that the title poem is not a dirge. My purpose was to cheer people up." [45] And toward the end of his life, still dogged by this defect in his readers, he remarked: "Of course I am never really bitter, or anything but cheerful and full of metaphysical joy and hope, but people don't seem to understand that and so call me all sorts of names which also they don't understand. So far as I can make out, most people are so afraid of life that when they see it coming their first impulse is to get behind a tree and shut their eyes. And for some odd reason they call that impulse optimism—which has always seemed funny to me." [46]

This would seem to dispose of the charge of pessimism, but a few more comments may make still clearer the general picture of human life that the poems present. One is that, unlike many contemporaries and even many Victorians, Robinson refuses to emphasize—almost, in fact, refuses to acknowledge—the actual viciousness that exists in human nature. He may indulge in fierce generalizations against his countrymen, as in *Cassandra* and *Dionysus in Doubt;* he may deride, in *Captain Craig* and other poems, the smugness and spiritual blindness that prevail in Tilbury Towns everywhere; he may even be driven, as in *Fortunatus*, to express his sense of the pervasive horror of the human past by such nightmarish metaphors as "the breathing of the beast/ That has been history since there was man." But when he has to do with particular human beings, his harshness deserts him.

Hence, he only skirts the edges of the Inferno whose existence he is too honest to deny, the home of such as Aaron Stark and Bokardo, Priscilla in *Llewellyn and the Tree*, the wives in *The Unforgiven* and the really horrible *The Whip*, the men in *Karma* and *The New Tenants*, Modred and Morgan in the Arthurian poems, the evil genius in *Avon's Harvest*, Caiaphas in *Nicodemus*, the dreadful Jael in *Sisera*, the partly symbolic young Hebron in *King Jasper*. But except for Bokardo, who perhaps is after all more weak than vicious, Jael and Hebron, who are abhorrent partly for what they represent, and Avon's ghoulish antagonist in a poem that is in many ways unique in Robinson's work, the evil in these characters is simply taken for granted. Even Modred, when he appears in person in an Arthurian fragment published separately, is suave and persuasive, and his egotism and malice are only to be inferred. The fact is that Robinson was temperamentally incapable of hating another human being. And a man who cannot find it in his heart to hate or despise his fellows has in him at least one of the ingredients of optimism.[47]

It is also to be noted—and here again Robinson is far from many contemporaries—that although his characters suffer, they are not thereby corrupted or morally destroyed. Captain Craig defends a world that would seem to have used him shabbily; the Poor Relation is bewildered but not embittered; Aunt Imogen draws from her fated loneliness only an increased tenderness; Clavering and Leffingwell seem rather to gain than to lose humanity through the buffetings of fate; Tristram and Isolt are ennobled and not degraded by their long frustration. Even those who find life unendurable depart without self-pity, without protest, without loss of dignity. They do not whine or cringe or bluster, they simply do quietly what they consider to be best. External events may destroy but not subdue them, may impose defeat but not extort surrender. In Robinson's poems, as Lloyd Morris has finely said, "humiliation is a casualty to which the human spirit is never subject." [48]

Perhaps this makes the situation worse. That such fineness and strength should prove unavailing in the face of mere blind destiny may be considered the essence of pessimism. After all, if those authors were right who make human beings merely the creatures of environment (or heredity, or unconscious urges), without will, without reason, without a self except as a focus for sensations, then what happened to such beings would not greatly matter. If, on the contrary, the self is real, if man is morally superior to the accidental or mechanical forces which surround him, is it not shocking that he should be so much at their mercy?

Robinson would doubtless have said, "Yes, *if* . . . if materialism is true, if . . ." But it is *not* true. "The songs all count." "Something is here that was not here before." There are "lives wasted that will not be lost—/ Not even if thrown away." And such statements are not merely defensive. They are a part of the affirmation implicit in the spirit of all his writings. We have seen already that the note on which he regularly chooses to end his poems is one of reconciliation. Charles Carville's unspoken thoughts are heard at last, even though he is dead; Vanderberg "died right"; the person described in *But for the Grace of God* "brought a sorry sunbeam with him then,/ But it beams yet"; the Contented Metaphysician smiles as he burns the manuscript of the projected *magnum opus* which has claimed so many years of his life. And the long poems, grim as they may seem at first reading, are not really so. Arthur's and Jasper's kingdoms crash, but others will replace them. Fernando Nash hears his symphony before he dies. Cavender's doubts are dispelled. Bartholow, Malory, and Matthias are all healed of their soul-sickness (although the cost is high), and life begins for them once more. Fargo escapes at last from his dream-hell; and even concerning his companions who do not escape, the last word has not been said. Amaranth tells them (and Amaranth is Truth):

> "I hope you may all live
> Until you are all sure you are not sorry,
> Even here in the wrong world, that you were born." [49]

Only in *Avon's Harvest*, among the longer poems, does destiny seem senseless, the waste of a man's life unmitigated. Only a few of the shorter poems are like *The Whip* in telling a story that is wholly painful. And what such rare pieces show is only the mystery of life and not its malignity. Robinson was indeed true to his early resolve: "I am inclined to be a trifle solemn in my verses, but I intend that there shall always be at least a suggestion of something wiser than hatred and something better than despair." [50]

5

There would seem, therefore, to be small excuse for those who have failed to perceive that Robinson's attitude toward life is essentially affirmative. There is, however, an explanation, if not a defense, of such a failure.

The optimism that has been traditionally dominant in Western society since the beginning of the so-called Christian era, the bulwark erected against the forces in the world that experience shows to be inimical to man's dearest desires and fondest hopes, has rested upon one or another of three systems of thought: first, Christianity, with its revelation of a merciful God and otherworldly rewards; second, the "religion of nature" that arose in various forms in the eighteenth century, giving rise to Romanticism in literature and democracy in politics; and third (more vaguely defined but no less distinct), a utilitarian, humanitarian, "scientific" concept of an attainable "earthly paradise" that will make irrelevant the dreams of a supernatural or spiritual realm supposed to have been created as a refuge from life's unpleasantness.[51]

It is Robinson's rejection of these three traditions that has baffled so many of his readers and made his affirmation seem so tenuous. For few persons of any persuasion are yet ready to admit the possibility that he may be right: that the social chaos of the present century has demonstrated the inadequacy of each of these three traditions as an integrating principle in contemporary life.

Robinson's rejection of the humanitarian position is implicit in what has been said about his views on "materialism," and needs no further comment. Turning to his attitude toward nature, we find it to be akin to that of the ancient Greeks and the writers of the Renaissance. It involves an intense perception of nature's beauty, some sense of its restorative power, but hardly anything of the Romantic faith in its function as a revelation of the Divine, a mediator between man and God.

He can, indeed, when he chooses, describe nature as vividly as the Romantics. In *Merlin* nature provides for the hero's first arrival in Broceliande a background quivering with ecstatic light and sweetness, and for his last departure from Camelot, one ominous with storm and gloom. In *Tristram*, also, as well as in *Roman Bartholow*, *Matthias at the Door*, and *The March of the Cameron Men*, nature is described intimately and accurately, although less for its own sake than for its symbolic value. It *is* described for its own sake in *The Dark Hills* and the late sonnet *As It Looked Then*, which simply exist as re-creations of momentary moods wrought by nature's magic.

In a few passages Robinson approaches the Romantic attitude. In *Isaac and Archibald*, *Hillcrest*, *Monadnock Through the Trees*, and *The Sheaves*, nature is definitely something more than a source of pleasure to the senses. It is not in itself divine; but it restores the soul no less surely than the green pastures and still waters of the Psalmist:

> And when the time came for the long walk home
> With Isaac in the twilight, I could see
> The forest and the sunset and the sky-line,
> No matter where it was that I was looking:
> The flame beyond the boundary, the music,
> The foam and the white ships, and two old men
> Were things that would not leave me.

The glare and turmoil of the Town Down the River never robbed the poet of his serene appreciation of nature's beauty and healing power, born of a boyhood in Maine and nourished, after a decade of urban alienation, by a quarter-century of summers in a region ruled over by Mount Monadnock. Once toward the end of his life he remarked whimsically to Mrs. MacDowell, "I rather think the old fellow will miss me a bit when I'm gone." [52]

Over against this feeling, however, there are hints of a response more somber. *Pasa Thalassa Thalassa*, for all its loveliness, suggests a world alien to man's affections, indifferent to his sufferings, destructive of his desires, untouched in any way by his transient existence. In *The Wilderness*, again, and even to a greater extent, Nature is cold and hostile. She calls, indeed, but her voice is siren music that to heed would be death. And Shakespeare in his darker mood is made to anticipate Tennyson's nightmare of "nature red in tooth and claw":

"Your fly will serve as well as anybody,
And what's his hour? He flies, and flies, and flies,
And in his fly's mind has a brave appearance;
And then your spider gets him in her net,
And eats him out, and hangs him up to dry.
That's Nature, the kind mother of us all.
And then your slattern housemaid swings her broom,
And where's your spider? And that's Nature, also.
It's Nature, and it's Nothing. It's all Nothing."

This fits in with what Robinson told Mrs. Richards in a letter: "I'm afraid, on the whole, that there isn't much comfort in nature as a visible evidence of God's infinite love. It appears to be a shambles and a torture-chamber from the insects up—or should we say down?" [53] Of course Robinson's own views are not to be read into the lines he gives to Shakespeare; and his personal comment obviously expresses only one part of his feeling about the natural world. But his work as a whole gives relatively little comfort to the many persons in our day who have inherited a vulgarized and unreflective version of the Romantic religion of nature.

A much larger number of readers will be baffled or alienated by Robinson's even more decisive dismissal of various types of Christian "orthodoxy." This antagonism springs from several sources. As a young man he was angered (as many young men have been) by the frivolity—the apparently exclusive concern with outward forms and appearances—of what often passed (and passes) for Christianity. He wrote to Harry Smith from Gardiner in 1896: "it does make me positively sick to see the results of modern materialism as they are revealed in a town like this. . . . And when I add to this a vision of Trinity Church in Boston and a reflection of what it stands for, I begin to feel like breaking chairs, and wonder if a time is ever coming when the human race will acquire anything like a logical notion of human life—or, in other words, of Christianity." [54] And a little later, after rereading the Gospel of John, he declared: "The popular misinterpretation of Christianity makes me sick." [55]

A calmer expression of a similar view is found in a letter to Mrs. Richards some thirty-six years later, in which, besides, he disposes matter-of-factly of dogmatic Christian theology. In regard to the latter his position seems to be identical with that of Matthew Arnold—and many other eminent Victorians—some sixty years earlier: that it is simply no longer believable.

Leaving out the Romans and the Methodists, there doesn't seem to be much left of the churches but the buildings. Even the Romans will have to contrive some sort of symbolic compromise before long; and as for the Methodists, who come nearer to ruling us than we suspect, they are perhaps more an incorporated and shrewdly organized ignorance than they are a church, and the Church of England is more like a social club, with music and trimmings, than like anything in the Scriptures. The Christian theology has so thoroughly crumbled that I do not think of any non-Roman acquaintance to whom it means anything—and I doubt if you do. The Christian ethics might have done some good if they had ever been tried, or understood, but I'm afraid it's too late now. There's a non-theological religion on the way, probably to be revealed by science when science comes definitely to the jumping-off place.[56]

This unquestioning assumption that traditional Christian theology is obsolete goes along with a sort of religious relativism that a study of comparative religion makes hard to evade. From the variety, not to say the contrariety, of religious beliefs, and the passionate devotion that these conflicting faiths have inspired in millions of people through hundreds or thousands of years, it is not unreasonable to conclude that all claims to exclusive possession of "the truth" are equally baseless and presumptuous. In *Peace on Earth* the sharp-tongued truant from respectability inquires (undoubtedly with his creator's approval):

> " 'Do I believe in God?' Is that
> The price tonight of a new hat?
> Has he commanded that his name
> Be written everywhere the same?
> Have all who live in every place
> Identified his hidden face?
> Who knows but he may like as well
> My story as one you may tell?"

Returning to Christianity in particular, we find Seneca in *Mortmain* taking for granted that

> "a grim God that watches each of us
> In turn, like an old-fashioned schoolmaster,
>   . . . no longer satisfies,
> Or tortures our credulity with harps
> And fires."

This is, of course, one of Robinson's characters speaking, but the casualness of the assumption, in its context, suggests that the poet accepts it, just as he apparently accepts as normal the experience of Matthias, whose conventional success has been accompanied by conventional Christianity, which fails him in his hour of need:

> Matthias wondered now if ever his faith
> Was more than a traditional convenience
> Taken on trust, a plaything of a childhood
> That with his ignorance had survived too long.

A different source of dissatisfaction with the religion accepted by most Americans is stated by Captain Craig: that it still darkens men's lives by its fears and threats, and by denial of any good in earthly life:

> "You have made
> The cement of your churches out of tears
> And ashes, and the fabric will not stand.
>
> .   .   .   .
>
> And at the fairest and the frenziedest
> Alike of your God-fearing festivals,
> You so compound the truth to pamper fear
> That in the doubtful surfeit of your faith
> You clamor for the food that shadows eat.
> You call it rapture or deliverance."

Again, we cannot be quite sure that these are Robinson's opinions, but most of his references to the poem, as well as the general tone of the work itself, suggest that the Captain's philosophy is not far from his creator's.[57] We may note, also, the similarity of the last lines to what is said in *Amaranth* about the fatally delusive doctrine of Ipswich the Inventor, who appears to stand for extreme evangelical Christianity.[58] And the same point of view is present in the obviously personal *The Spirit Speaking,* dated "Christmas, 1929":

> As you are still pursuing it
> As blindly as you can,

You have deformed and tortured it
 Since ignorance began;
And even as you have mangled it,
 The Letter has killed man.

Because a camel cannot well
 Go through a needle's eye,
No jealous God has ever said
 The son of man must die;
Only the God that you have made
 Has mocked you from the sky.

Going back thirty-five years, to *The Children of the Night*, we find,
as so often, that Robinson's basic beliefs have not changed:

And if God be God, He is love;—
And though the dawn be still so dim,
It shows that we have played enough
With creeds that make a fiend of Him.

It is a little hard to reconcile this attitude with the view expressed
to Mrs. Richards that Christian theology is dying, if not quite dead.
But no doubt the poet in these pieces is hitting at the smugness of
many nominal Christians who are ready to judge others according
to forms and codes which they themselves adhere to only from habit
—or perhaps only pretend to adhere to. And he may be implying
that it is precisely such distortions of the original teaching as are
here condemned that are incredible to modern minds and therefore
discredit religion as a whole. Robinson's own view, of course, is that
of the essential Christian protestant of all ages: that the character
and teachings of Jesus express the loftiest ideal of human life with
which man has ever been presented—an ideal which the churches as
a whole have always tended to obscure, distort, or devitalize, although he naturally recognizes that in their own ways they have
often done good. He speaks in an early letter of "the utter fallacy
of all existing notions of religion—popular notions, I mean," [59]
and this is his permanent view.

Another issue on which Robinson is at odds with orthodoxy,
either Christian or "materialist," is immortality. "Personal" survival
after death—the continued life of the self as we know it, with all its
necessary limitations, and accompanied by the memory of earthly

life, without which the concept would seem to have little meaning—
seems to him both improbable and undesirable. We find him saying
in the first of *Two Sonnets* in *The Children of the Night:*

> No, I have not your backward faith to shrink
> Lone-faring from the doorway of God's home
> To find Him in the names of buried men;
> Nor your ingenious recreance to think
> We cherish, in the life that is to come,
> The scattered features of dead friends again.

And long after, he makes Cavender say:

> "If memories of so galled and sorry a life
> As this must follow us when we go from here,
> We are all damned indeed."

Of course, we do not really *know;* and there may be those who, like
Gabrielle, prefer ignorance.

> "You've said we never die,"
> She answered,—"and almost as if you knew it;
>
> .   .   .   .
>
> Yet I am no more sad than I am happy
> For cleaving to at least one ignorance
> Where even the smallest of us are as great
> As are the giants."

Robinson himself is more positive in his beliefs, but he acknowledges
that no one has a right to dogmatize, one way or the other. Writing
to thank Mrs. Richards for a memorial article about his brother Dean,
he assures her "that it would mean a great deal to him if he knew
about it. Maybe he does, though I doubt it, and don't really wish to
believe that whatever may be coming for us is to be shackled with
memories of so scrappy a link of existence as this." [60] To the same
correspondent, later, he expressed the same sentiment, speaking of the
death of a woman who "had, apparently, an absolute faith in meeting
her friends. I doubt if she meets them, but I don't know that she will
not. My notion of immortality, and I have some sort of notion,
doesn't include the memory of this rather trivial—and for most
people much worse than that—phase of existence." [61]

On the other hand, Robinson also rejects, and on the whole more
decisively, the idea that death involves complete extinction of the

self. "If . . . our being had no onward auguries," "If there be nothing after Now," then life is futile and had best be ended at once. But he does not accept the premise:

> "There is more of me,
> I hope, than a pathetic mechanism
> Grinding itself to nothing. Possibly not,
> But let me say there is."

This tentative assumption made by a character in *The March of the Cameron Men* is stated more positively by Garth's ghost in *Matthias at the Door:*

> "There's more of you for you to find, Matthias,
> Than science has found yet, or may find soon."

And both passages echo what the poet had said in his own person long before, in one of the *Octaves* in *The Children of the Night.*

> Where does a dead man go?—The dead man dies;
> But the free life that would no longer feed
> On fagots of outburned and shattered flesh
> Wakes to a thrilled invisible advance,
> Unchained (or fettered else) of memory.

That this is a personal confession of faith is confirmed by two passages in the poet's letters to his friend Smith: "Life itself is no joke to a great percentage of us, and all things seem to point to an improvement of our condition when they are explained. I am not preaching, but I believe in immortality. I can't help it." [62] In the second he refers to his mother's death, a blow which struck him with terrible force: "She has gone ahead and I am glad for her. You see I have come to look on death as a deliverance and an advancement (*vide* 'Kosmos,' 'Two Sonnets,' etc.) and I am very glad to be able to stand up and say that I am an idealist." [63]

Robinson never becomes more definite than in the *Octave* quoted above in trying to define, picture, or in any way put into words the future state of whatever it is that survives the physical death of the individual. All that he can affirm with assurance is that "we shall go on somehow or other." [64] He does, however, specifically reject the notion of deriving satisfaction (as some persons apparently do) from the thought that the chemical elements of the body will ultimately nourish other forms of life. For him, as for Shakespeare's gravedigger, such a notion is merely comic. "I get no comfort out of turning into grass, and cannot believe that the great Whatever-it-is would have gone to so much trouble as to make you and me (not to mention a few others) for the sake of a little ultimate hay." [65]

In this connection one more comment may be made on Robinson's "pessimism." No doubt many readers apply this epithet because so many of his characters die prematurely. But he would say, as does Garth's ghost, "What the world had for them is theirs." His belief is that of Penn-Raven:

> "And if life, as I view it, has a reason,
> Death is among the least of little things."

This view, which Christians accept in theory, he accepted in fact—simply and unostentatiously, as he accepted the days and seasons. "I didn't detect, or feel, anything like despair in my work," he wrote to his Catholic friend William Walsh with reference to the *Nicodemus* volume. "If it is there, it ought not to be, for it isn't in me." And he added, as a simple statement of fact, "my faith . . . in its way, is probably as strong as yours." [66] What baffles people in regard to this faith is its very simplicity.

For the rest, his final position appears to be that the whole problem is beyond the capacity of reason, and the words that reason must rely on, to deal with. *Cavender's House* and *Matthias at the Door* both discuss at length the problem of life after death, but in a manner too cryptic to do more than exasperate those who want simple and definite answers—such as the churches have always been willing to supply. Those who prefer other answers must wait. " 'The world was made in order, and the atoms march in time.' It is a damned queer time to us who are here now; but it is all right and we are all going to hear it as it is—when the mortal wax gets out of our ears." [67] The same whimsical note, mellowed by time and touched by imagination into poetry, is heard in the words of Amaranth as Fargo's dream begins to fade:

> "Never be sorry for the dead—
> Lament them as you may, or treasure them;
> And never build a stairway for a swallow."

6

The reader may still feel that Robinson's "philosophy" is mainly negative, since our present mode of being seems to him "so galled and sorry a life," "so scrappy a link of existence"; and since the future state that he believes in is not capable of being pictured or reasoned about. Even if we join the poet in rejecting, as presumptuous and impossible, all attempts to prove that "materialism is true," and agree (or are able) to share his intuitive belief in some guiding and justifying "Whatever-it-is," we may still wish for some inkling as to *how* so sorry a life can be justified.

This need seems to have been felt at times by the poet himself; and he found a partial answer in the familiar theory that spiritual growth, or advancement, comes only through effort, endurance, suffering. There is an echo of this thought—and undoubtedly of his thinking about the basis of whatever worth his own poetry might have—in the words of one of the characters in *The March of the Cameron Men:*

> "I wonder why
> So many of our songs and melodies
> That help us to forget, and make us happy,
> Are born of pain, and oftener of defeat
> Than victory."

This is, of course, an old story with the poets. But their experience is, for Robinson, only one illustration of a universal principle, which he accepted from the first. He declares in an early letter to Smith: "All I can see to life, as an occupation, is a kind of spiritual exercise (or at least a chance for that) by which we may, if we will, put ourselves beyond it." [68] Such was also his answer to the early criticism that he looked on life as a "prison-house." "The world is not a 'prison-house,' but a kind of spiritual kindergarten, where millions of bewildered infants are trying to spell God with the wrong blocks." [69]

It need scarcely be remarked that this is a traditional view in Christian thought; and it is appropriate that the first explicit statement of it in Robinson's poetry should be in his portrait of Paul in *The Three Taverns.*

> If the world
> Were not a world of aches and innovations,
> Attainment would have no more joy of it.

This thesis the Apostle then proceeds to elaborate.

> The power that holds the world,
> Away from God that holds himself away—
>
> .   .   .   .
>
> Was not, nor ever shall be, a small hazard
> Enlivening the ways of easy leisure
> Or the cold road of knowledge.

The sense here present of life's recalcitrance and of the high price in effort and sacrifice demanded for the good it has to offer is expressed again in *Roman Bartholow*, when Umfraville observes "How much of easy death in life there is/ Where life is easy." Even young Hebron, whose very presence seems an infection and a blight upon all beauty and virtue, plays his part in the cosmic economy, as Zoë notes even while proclaiming,

> "I hate him—
> His ignorance, I should say—and his inflamed
> Assurance of his power to serve the world
> When he is doing his ruinous worst in it;
> Which is his way, and the world's way, of growing."

In the last line of this quotation the concept of growth through struggle and suffering seems to be applied to the universal as well as to the individual life; an application which Robinson had already made in *Merlin*, nearly two decades before, in the sage's final summing-up of the significance of the world drama in which his own part is ended.

> "All this that was to be
> Might show to man how vain it were to wreck
> The world for self if it were all in vain.
> When I began with Arthur I could see
> In each bewildered man who dots the earth
> A moment with his days a groping thought
> Of an eternal will, strangely endowed
> With merciful illusions whereby self
> Becomes the will itself and each man swells
> In fond accordance with his agency.

Now Arthur, Modred, Lancelot, and Gawaine
Are swollen thoughts of this eternal will
Which have no other way to find the way
That leads them on to their inheritance
Than by the time-infuriating flame
Of a wrecked empire." [70]

The same general view is asserted with less solemnity but with no less intensity in Robinson's letters, both early and late. It is in three different letters to Smith written in 1896 and 1897. "My religion seems to be a kind of optimistic desperation and the deuce only knows what will come of it." "There's a good deal to live for, but a man has to go through hell really to find it out. The process is hard, but the result pays. If it didn't there would be no universe. This may sound obscure, but it isn't." "This world is a grind and the sooner we make up our minds to the fact the better it will be for us. That, to my mind, is the real optimism. The world is as good as it can be, but God knows that's bad enough." [71] Twenty-odd years and one World War later, he repeated himself almost *verbatim* to Mabel Dodge Sterne: "The world is a hell of a place; and if life and the universe mean anything, there is no reason to suppose that it will ever be anything else. This, as I understand it, is the true optimism." [72]

The doctrine set forth in these passages is one that has often been used in the attempt to reconcile the existence of evil with the existence of an all-good and all-powerful Deity. But it is present in Robinson with a difference. In him it is not the accompaniment of a congenital optimism like that of Browning (whom it is clear that Robinson as a young man admired, but whose ebullient cheerfulness he later found unendurable).[73] Nor is it the uneasy attempt of Christian theology by Procrustean measures to force experience and observation to fit a dogmatic conception of the Divine Nature: "It is said that God tempers the wind to the shorn lamb, but we aren't told who did the shearing." [74] Nor does it involve, as does the idealism of Hegel, the heartless sacrifice of human values to a brazen idol of logic.

What it does derive from is simply what Robinson regards as an indisputable fact of experience: that what is worth having is usually to be got only by persistent and often painful effort; and that even involuntary suffering and sacrifice do sometimes refine and ennoble those of whom they are demanded. Writing to Mrs. Richards of a person's changed appearance that he infers to have been "the result of trouble and pain," Robinson concludes: "I'm afraid this is true of many things that are agreeable and fair to see. Unfortunately it is too often true of a little intelligence and human understanding in many who would otherwise be almost unendurable in their abundant ignorance." [75]

From this general conception Robinson passes naturally to another salient point in his philosophy: that inability or unwillingness to change or grow under the impact of events in the world of time means death. Only those who can change as the world changes will endure to the end and be saved. The philosopher in *The Burning Book* gives up the dream that time has shown to be false, and finds freedom and happiness; Bewick Finzer clings to his dream and drags out a life as "futile as regret." Aunt Imogen's dismissal of her hope of marriage marks the beginning of a new life; the woman in *Late Summer* spurns marriage in order to embrace a ghost in the tomb of a dead love. Lorraine's "growth" ends in death; but Avenel Gray in *Mortmain* chooses never to live. Napoleon on Saint Helena looks back and dies; Rembrandt, at the bottom of an almost equal descent from glory, looks forward and lives.[76]

It does not follow that those who do not have the power or will to change are necessarily to be condemned. The reason for their lack we do not always understand. Their destiny after death we do not know. Concerning their lives on earth, and those of their more fortunate fellows, we can only say, "This is the way things are."

7

And yet we cannot be satisfied to say only this. By our very nature we are bound to ask, "Why do some succeed and others fail? Is it in themselves that their strength or weakness lies, and are they therefore responsible for what befalls them? Or are their destinies determined by forces over which they have no control?"

These questions were touched on in the analysis of Robinson's attitude toward his characters. On the one hand, he is loath to judge them, because of his feeling that they not only "might have been but would have been" very different people if they had been endowed with a different "make-up" and "environment." [77] On the other hand, he respects them, and asks the reader's respect for them, on the ground that they are autonomous and responsible: that what they *are*, if not what happens to them, has been theirs to determine. The faith confessed in an early letter is implicit in his work as a whole: "what I am after is the courage to see and to believe that my present life is the best thing for me, and that every man has it in his power to overcome whatever obstacles may be in his way—even that seeming obstacle we call by the name of Death." [78]

These two positions are logically irreconcilable. Yet some kind of reconciliation is necessary in any literary work that undertakes to deal seriously with human experience. It is equally intolerable to our moral feelings that a person should be held completely responsible for what he does and is, and that he should be freed from any responsibility whatever. Fortunately, however, an artist need not be logical. In Shakespeare's tragedies, for instance, we find one set of statements suggesting that the protagonist *is* responsible for the tragic denouement, and therefore deserving of our respect as a free being and not a mere puppet; and another set indicating that he is the victim of circumstances or of other men's evil schemes, and therefore free from our condemnation as being weak or vicious. If we regard Othello as a free agent, acting within the bounds of sanity and responsibility in his treatment of Desdemona, we can acknowledge a sort of strength in his character even though we must judge him to be, at the least, reckless and brutal. On the other hand, if we regard him as the victim of Iago's machinations (plus his own jealousy, or sense of racial inferiority, or whatever other rationalization we may wish to invent), then we partly free him from the charge of brutality, but only by convicting him of weakness and stupidity, so that he may claim our pity but not command our respect. Yet by virtue of Shakespeare's theatrical sleight of hand and hypnotic rhetoric, Othello is enabled to have it both ways and be a hero.

Robinson's reconciliation, however, is a matter of temperament rather than technique. At times, indeed, he seems to be unaware of the difficulty and to make no effort to avoid inconsistency. Those who fail are usually exempt from blame, while the fortunate are given credit.

The problem of freedom as it appears in Robinson's work is simplified by his rejection of a materialistic interpretation of the universe, for this rejection rules out the most obvious argument in support of determinism. Although this argument seems to be more than half accepted in the reference to the influence of "make-up" and "environment" upon a person's character and course of life, it is summarily dismissed in *The Man Against the Sky*:

> Are we no greater than the noise we make
> Along one blind atomic pilgrimage
> Whereon by crass chance billeted we go
> Because our brains and bones and cartilage
> Will have it so?

But the fact remains that man's freedom is limited by factors outside his conscious self—some of them apparently undiscoverable—to whose inscrutable workings the ancient poets gave the name of "Fate." In the rise and fall of civilizations, for instance, individual freedom counts for little. Whether or not King Arthur and King Jasper could have established enduring kingdoms, Robinson in his later years seems to have believed that Western civilization was heading inevitably for "a grand smash." Soon after World War I, when many people were still optimistic, he prophesied: "The whole western world is going to be blown to pieces, asphyxiated, and starved." [79] And at about the same time he spoke of having "comforted" his readers "with the assurance that, generally speaking, they haven't a damned thing to say about" what happens.[80]

Passing from such assertions about society as a whole to comments about more limited spheres of human existence, we find in *The Valley of the Shadow* a host of illustrations of the apparent helpless-

ness of men and women in general in the face of situations that are
common in ordinary life. There are those condemned to failure
through having been forced by parental pressure or led in other
ways into careers for which they had no taste or talent. There are
also girls driven (one infers) into loveless marriages by "the blast-
ing obligations of their birth," destined to be "Each an isolated item
in the family sacrifice." And to these and other innocent victims are
about to be added (the poem was published in 1920) the maimed
survivors of the war.

> So they were, and so they are; and as they came are coming others.
> And among them are the fearless and the meek and the unborn;
> And a question that has held us heretofore without an answer
> May abide without an answer until all have ceased to mourn.
> For the children of the dark are more to name than are the wretched,
> Or the broken, or the weary, or the baffled, or the shamed:
> There are builders of new mansions in the Valley of the Shadow,
> And among them are the dying and the blinded and the maimed.[81]

The question without an answer is simply "Why?" and it is asked
or implied again and again in Robinson's poems: poems about
the victims of poverty, illness, loneliness, and thwarted love.

Taking one more step, we arrive at the many particular persons
who are faced with unique conditions quite beyond their power to
alter or mitigate. One is John Evereldown, who loathes but cannot
escape the tyranny of sexual desire. Another is Tasker Norcross, for
whom (as far as we are told) it would have been impossible to be
other than he is—a human cipher, or nearly so, and damned to
be aware of his nothingness. What is there left for such a man to do
except to "live and die/ More quietly thereby"?

And finally (not to prolong the list unduly), there is Avon. Can
he be held responsible for the curse that destroys him? He did nothing to invite the leechlike attachment of his eventual nemesis. The
revulsion he felt was innate, unreasoning, quite beyond control. The
blow he struck was one for which a boy would normally be honored—as he was by his schoolfellows—and for which even a man
would hardly be blamed. He could not say he was sorry, because he
was not sorry and was not a hypocrite; and most readers will see

no reason why he should have either been sorry or pretended to be.
Yet as a result of these happenings, his life becomes a nightmare,
and his death is untimely and hideous. Perhaps after reaching matu-
rity he should have forgiven his persecutor. But forgiveness is not
merely a form of words. For Avon, at any rate, it is an

> "obligation
> That I have not the Christian revenue
> In me to pay."

Does he therefore deserve the damnation that comes to him? He
himself discusses the point calmly, as he waits for the final act of the
tragedy:

> "I'm at odds
> With conscience, even tonight, for good assurance
> That it was I, or chance and I together,
> Did all that sowing."

And he comes back to the question again as he nears the end of
what he has to tell.

> "Beware of hate, remorse, and fear,
> And listen. You are staring at the damned,
> But yet you are no more the one than he
> To say that it was he alone who planted
> The flower of death now growing in his garden.
> Was it enough, I wonder, that I struck him?
> I shall say nothing." [82]

At this point the reader may be ready to dismiss the statement
about man's "power to overcome whatever obstacles may be in his
way," and to write Robinson down as a complete fatalist. But there
is another side to the picture. If Avon sees no sin to explain the
horror that pursues him, Fernando Nash sees clearly that no one
but himself is responsible for the ruin of his life:

> "God was good
> To give my soul to me before I died
> Entirely, and He was no more than just
> In taking all the rest away from me.
> I had it, and I knew it; and I failed Him.
> I did not wait."

His friend tries to excuse him, but

> He would have none of it. He was to blame,
> And it was only right that he should lose
> What he had won too late.

Rembrandt to Rembrandt is another poem in which we see that even in the realm of art, where men have traditionally felt (as is suggested in the sonnets *Many Are Called* and *Caput Mortuum*) that their powers are given and not acquired, there is a place for freedom. Rembrandt may speak of himself as "but a living instrument/ Played on by powers that are invisible"; but the whole point of the poem is that Rembrandt, like Fernando Nash, has his temptation in the wilderness of doubt and loneliness, and chooses, unlike his fictional counterpart, to listen to God and not the Devil.

Again, turning to *Tristram*, Robinson's obsessive hatred of the "damned dose" and his vehemence against the lovers' being "turned into rabbits" can only be the reflection of a firm belief in the freedom of men and women to shape their own lives. It is his own "abject ineptitude" that Tristram curses as he listens to the wedding celebration of Isolt and Mark; and in the dialogue that follows, the lovers vie with each other in taking the blame for the sorry tangle in which they find themselves.

Robinson's treatment of the central story of the Arthurian legend is also significant. Tennyson's Arthur is a symbol of human perfection, so that the general theme of the *Idylls* becomes a cosmic struggle between good and evil, in which the latter always achieves a temporary, but never a permanent, victory, and in which the individual is of slight importance. But Robinson's Arthur is a man among men, sharing the strength and weakness of ordinary humanity; and his downfall comes from his having transgressed the code of purity and magnanimity that he himself embodies in the eyes of the world, and from his refusal to admit his guilt. And so Robinson's picture is of a world governed by moral law, from which the individual may expect neither more nor less than justice (though sometimes Grace may intervene); and of course justice implies freedom.[83]

In *Toussaint L'Ouverture* the picture is different. Here the hero is like Tennyson's Arthur, destroyed through no fault of his own. But the responsibility for the tragedy is not placed on fate, but on the callousness of some and the cowardice of others who ought to be the leaders of society:

> There are more slaves
> Than yet have felt or are to feel, and know it,
> An iron or a lash. This will go on
> Until more slaves like me, and more, and more,
> Throw off their shackles and make swords of them
> For those to feel who have not felt before,
> And will not see. It will go on as long
> As men capitulate who feel and see,
> And men who know say nothing.

In these late lines we find a resurrection of the youthful spirit of protest that flames out in the close of *Calvary*—which, again, is pointless unless men are presumed to be free.

Freedom is also implicit in many of the short dramatic poems. The seething scorn of *Bokardo* presupposes that its object has, or once had, some spark at least of manliness that he has chosen to drown in a flood of maudlin self-pity. On the other hand, Vanderberg, weak as he was, and perhaps partly deluded, is honored for his struggle:

> We grant him idle names enough
> To-day, but even while we frown
> The fight goes on, the triumph clings,
> And there is yet the unseen crown.

Other characters also find the will to surmount the general or particular ills that man is heir to—Cliff Klingenhagen, Old King Cole, Aunt Imogen, and the forgiving wife in *Ben Trovato*.

Finally, even the apparent failures, even the characters who seem to acknowledge by the act of self-destruction life's ultimate futility, are in that very act asserting their freedom: renouncing their allegiance to a world they never made; declaring their moral superiority to a ruling force that seems to them to outrage human ideals and trample on human values; or simply putting an end to an individual existence that seems no longer to have a purpose.

Whatever the motive, their action is, in their own eyes and in the eyes of their creator, a denial of determinism.

8

It is clear from the preceding analysis of Robinson's views on the issue of determinism versus freedom that the two conflicting tendencies in his thought—or perhaps rather in his feeling—cannot both be fitted into any systematic philosophy. But perhaps some further clarification of the whole matter is possible.

Without becoming too deeply involved in a problem that philosophers have fought about for centuries, we may say that, on the one hand, the concept of freedom is ultimately unintelligible, and that, on the other, a society in which it is not taken for granted is unimaginable. There is no evidence that Robinson ever troubled himself greatly with this particular difficulty; but it fits in with his view that the universe is basically nonrational, beyond the grasp of our finite faculties. We need not conclude that it is chaotic, but we must acknowledge that it is full of mysteries, many of which are painful. As Annandale says with unforeseeing irony,

> "God has been very good to him
> Whose end is not an asking why."

Robinson feels that there is a partial answer; but it is one that the individual must find for himself, if at all, and that cannot be put into words. Penn-Raven is clearly speaking for the poet when he says,

> "There are these things,
> And they are so—until we give them names,
> And harness them with words that have one meaning
> For no two men; and likelier none at all
> For one man—or one woman."

For those who are still troubled by the inconsistency, however, a partial solution is possible by distinguishing between events and actions on the one hand and states of mind on the other. Obviously a person is often involved in situations which he cannot control. Not to mention what the law calls "acts of God" (events always morally meaningless and usually calamitous), there are the wills of other persons, as we see in Robinson's many pictures of blasted romance and blighted marriage. But how a person responds to these situations, how they affect his character—this, one may feel, *is* within his power to determine.

Rembrandt cannot change the artistic taste of Holland, but he has his choice of yielding to it or defying it—or, like Fernando Nash, taking refuge in cynicism and debauchery. King Cole can do nothing about his sons' rascality, but he can prevent it from destroying his happiness. Captain Craig cannot postpone his death, but he can meet it—unlike Napoleon, for instance—with courage and a large humor. The Poor Relation can neither alter nor understand (nor can we understand) the cruelty of her destiny; but where another person might be crushed or embittered, she—without money, without friends, without health, without hope, without illusions—can muster a laugh and a song, however "slender."

And when there is a chance for action, people act differently, even when the circumstances are much the same. Llewellyn, caught in a marriage to a shrewish wife, breaks away; the husband in *The Unforgiven*, in a not dissimilar predicament, finds nothing to do but stay and suffer. Again, having each lost the woman he loves, Reuben Bright tears down his slaughterhouse, Vanderberg rededicates himself to his duty as a clergyman, the husband in *The Whip* kills himself.

Such instances are perhaps what lies behind the common saying —which our sense of justice and our self-respect make us wish to accept as true—that "character is fate." Coming back to what is perhaps the crucial example, we may conclude that Tristram and Isolt are not primarily the victims of an indifferent or malignant ruling Power. Another man and woman, placed in the same circumstances, would have had a different story. When Tristram indulges in an orgy of self-reproach, Isolt replies:

> "This thing has come
> For us, and you are not to see the end
> Through any such fog of honor and self-hate

As you may seek to throw around yourself
For being yourself.

.   .   .   .

We cannot say what either of us had been
Had we been something else."

Yet, after all, the argument against freedom is not disposed of. If the general pattern of a person's life is usually determined by character, is it not still *determined*? "Character" by definition is something more or less permanent, something that one can count on, something out of which action springs. Even if "character is fate," are not fate and freedom still at odds? Could Miniver Cheevy (we may ask) do anything else than drink and dream, and still be Miniver Cheevy? Does Robinson not imply in his remark about Levi in *The Field of Glory*—"just a poor devil, totally miscast, and without much in his head anyhow"—that for a person with such a character there can be little choice? Again, does not the poet himself think of Clavering as a musician compelled to play "a flawed instrument"? Is not Gabrielle in fact "a woman doomed never to live"—doomed not by what happens but by what she is, by her inability to share her husband's vision, to find one of her own, or to live without one? And what of John Evereldown with his despairing "God knows if I pray to be done with it all"?

And, turning to those who are more fortunate or more admirable, do we not find that their seeming choices are simply the inevitable consequences of what they are? Could not Rembrandt's decision be foretold by one familiar with his former life? Is not Aunt Imogen's response to her disappointment dictated by an unselfishness with which she has always been endowed? Have Isaac and Archibald really earned the tranquil old age that they enjoy, or are they simply gifted with a temperament that permits them to make the best of what life offers? Robinson acknowledged to an interviewer the presence in his poetry of "a deterministic, a fatalistic note" and added: "I suppose I do believe that we are pretty much what we are." [84]

Again, the difficulty cannot be wholly removed, but a partial solution is possible. Character, after all, is not entirely something that is given, but in a measure something that is made. Granting that a person's character becomes relatively fixed, it was not always so. A person's "choice is circumscribed," to be sure, "and man is, more surely than he likes to admit, the storehouse of his own destiny." But "there is a choice, yes." [85] Miniver Cheevy was not always a drunkard, surely; there was a point at which his addiction to alcohol began, and another point, later, at which he could still have conquered it. Likewise, Aaron Stark was not born a miser. And in the seldom noted but powerful sonnet *The New Tenants* we are shown a picture of a personality actually in the process of degenerating— one might almost say decomposing—under the assaults of long-tolerated vices.

So we see that people *do* change—that character is not dead bones but a living spiritual body. Nor does the change have to be for the worse. Robinson himself was for years, like Miniver Cheevy, an alcoholic, but finally broke the habit—as his friend in "The Dark House" will some day do. And many others of his characters, as they follow the call of the river or climb the hill to move against the sky, find the knowledge and strength to redirect their lives, while retaining their essential identity.

In Lorraine, for instance, the same impetuosity that led her to reject security and seek excitement still urges her upon the unknown adventure. But between times she has learned the fullness of the love she flouted and tasted the emptiness of the life she chose. In less absolute fashion, Llewellyn and Vanderberg free themselves from the clutch of circumstance and defy what might have seemed like destiny's decree. And in many of the long poems there are characters—Merlin perhaps, Lancelot and Guinevere certainly, Cavender, Nightingale, Matthias, and Talifer—who emerge as wiser and better persons from the prisons of ignorance or folly that they themselves once built.

9

And yet the mystery has not been banished, after all. How is it that some individuals are able to choose and change and gain salvation, while others find no choice except to suffer and die? And why should more be demanded of human beings than they have in them to give? Why should Avon die because he cannot conquer an involuntary hatred? Why should Gabrielle die, not because she will not, but because she cannot, see a reason for living? When a man is born blind, who has sinned? And why should Norcross be made to suffer under a double curse—a helpless awareness of a hopeless insufficiency as a human being? Why is it that to him that hath, shall be given, but from him that hath not, shall be taken away even that which he hath? Or, as Lorraine says:

> "Some creatures are born fortunate, and some
> Are born to be found out and overcome,—
> Born to be slaves, to let the rest go free."

Always the human mind struggles to reconcile the actual world with its own ideals—what is, with what ought to be—and always the effort ends in failure. Job's questions are never answered, but are simply brushed aside by the brute power of the universe. Why people are what they are, and why things happen as they do happen, are problems that the human mind can never wholly solve. This truth is part of Timberlake's dying message to Matthias:

> "Why are we as we are? We do not know.
> Why do we pay so heavily for so little?
> Or for so much? Or for whatever it is?
> We do not know. We only pay, and die."

One formulation of this mystery, which makes it more bearable by stressing its benevolent side, is the Christian doctrine of Grace. And, surprising as the fact may be to many readers, this doctrine—or something very like it—lies at the heart of Robinson's vision of the world. If some men seem to be born to be willing instruments of evil, like Modred and young Hebron, others are blessed with an innate and apparently incorruptible saintliness, like the Poor Relation and the gentle Oakes and Oliver. If some seem born to suffer and be betrayed, like Avon and Norcross and Gabrielle and Natalie, as if being punished for sins they have not committed, others are enabled as by divine intervention to gain a salvation for which their own unaided efforts would never have sufficed: Lancelot, by means of the Light; Roman Bartholow, by an imperfect instrument, Penn-Raven, of what nevertheless appears to be a supernatural power; or Fargo, by Amaranth, whose other name is Truth. And sometimes even those who have sinned or fallen short are forgiven, and receive not justice but mercy. Such are Malory and Matthias and, most of all, Fernando Nash. Even King Jasper, if he will look beyond the temporal catastrophe which nothing can avert, need not despair. Zoë counsels the dying king to

> "leave the rest to God.
> I don't say what God is, but it's a name
> That somehow answers us when we are driven
> To feel and think how little we have to do
> With what we are."

And for the religious mind—the mind aware of these heights and depths, these darknesses and illuminations—it is apparently natural to have faith that the grace and mercy that are only occasionally visible in life as we see it are always and everywhere busy at their unseen work. "The flame . . . must burn somehow for the best," the poet says in an early sonnet. And many years later he makes Garth's ghost tell the groping Matthias, "Nothing is wasted."

The danger is that this partial solution of the mystery may be taken as a whole one; that we may rush on to discard our own ideals, to surrender our individual judgment, to accept the actual world as being everywhere divinely ordered, to deny that evil is ever more than relative, to acclaim the principle that is in fact, no less than the crassest materialism, the negation of all human values: "Whatever is, is right." But from such a denial Robinson is saved by the Grace that caused him to be born with his skin inside out and that forbade his attention to be long diverted from the particular experiences of particular human souls.

chapter viii: VALUES

Such is Robinson's conception of what the world, including man, is like. The question that remains is, "What *ought* it to be like?" That is, what should man live *for*? What ideals should human beings try to realize, in their individual lives and in the life of society?

These questions presuppose acceptance of the principle that has just been analyzed: that man is to some extent free, and that in the operations of the universe certain conditions and events are contingent upon the choices that men make. In a deterministic system there can be no "ought" or "should." The question of whether anything might be better or worse is meaningless, even if it were not itself determined. The best of all possible worlds is neither good nor bad unless freedom is included among the factors that limit the possibilities; and then it ceases to be the best. All values depend on freedom.

As one would expect of an heir of the Puritans and Transcendentalists, Robinson's thinking about values always starts with the individual. His contemptuous statements about "the Race" have already been noted. He has little sympathy with crusades; he is suspicious of "movements" in literature and elsewhere; he looks askance, in fact, at almost any kind of group action. He admits in a letter to Percy Mackaye, "I'm well aware of my hopeless limitations when anything with 'Community' pasted on it rolls into sight." [1]

The first necessity, he feels, is for people to come to terms with life on their own account, to find some degree of peace and satisfaction within themselves. The ability to do so (as must already be clear) is Robinson's real yardstick for measuring success. And those who achieve such success do so, as a rule (the exception is Roman Bartholow), by themselves, without help from other persons. The great decisions are made, the great visions come, when men and women are alone. The tenant of any "Dark House" is not to be rescued from outside; he must liberate himself.

At times, indeed, Robinson seems almost to accept the doctrine quoted by Emerson from "the melancholy Pestalozzi": "that no man in God's wide earth is either willing or able to help any other man." "You cannot listen," says the old physician to Ponce de Leon,

> "To more than you may hear; you cannot measure
> More than is yours to comprehend."

This thought had already been expressed in the sonnet *Discovery*:

> That earth has not a school where we may go
> For wisdom, or for more than we may know.

Again, in *Roman Bartholow* Umfraville observes:

> "We cannot harvest evidence unseen
> As we do carrots, and we cannot buy it;
> Nor may we take it from the open hand
> Of love or friendship, merely wishing it."

And what one person cannot take, the other cannot give, because of (as the poet phrases it in *The Glory of the Nightingales*)

> the immeasurable distances
> That are between the nearest and most known
> Of loving and unfathomable strangers—

which is to say, in less cryptic language, that our closest friends are nevertheless complete strangers. "We all live in a world of our own," Robinson wrote to Smith from Harvard, "and wonder what it is to others." [2] In a similar vein, Matthias reflects, "No man has known another/ Since men were born." And Paul declares in *The Three Taverns*, "We are all alone." [3]

This is only one face of the coin, as will appear. In the meantime, something more needs to be said about what this essential inward peace involves. First of all, as must now be obvious, it does not involve material wealth, although the rich man fares somewhat better in Robinson's poems than in the Gospels. Roman Bartholow and Nightingale are able to salvage something from their lives (although Nightingale puts an end to his) despite the handicap of hereditary possessions. In Matthias's rather vague new career, he is apparently to be a captain of industry as he was before, but one with a conscience and a sense of obligation to his fellows. Wealth in itself, Robinson seems to say, is morally neutral; it becomes evil only when real values are sacrificed in its pursuit—a sacrifice, as he implies in *Cassandra* and *Dionysus in Doubt*, to which Americans are prone. "Dollars are convenient things to have," he wrote at the age of twenty-one to Smith, "but this diabolical, dirty race that men are running after them disgusts me. . . . Business be damned." [4] At Harvard he admired Charles Eliot Norton ("by all odds the greatest man in America")[5] for his sallies against American acquisitiveness. His lifelong attitude on the whole question, which presents itself so often in his work, is accurately summed up in a semihumorous outburst to the same friend seven years later: "The age is all right, material progress is all right, Herbert Spencer is all right, hell is all right. These things are temporal necessities, but they are damned uninteresting to one who can get a glimpse of the real light through the clouds of time. It is that glimpse that makes me wish to live and see it out." [6]

But if getting riches is the wrong vocation for any human being, there is a right vocation for every human being, which not to find and follow is to be so far a failure. It may be the exalted calling of preaching the word of God, like Paul and, in a way, Captain Craig; or it may be, as for Fargo, the seemingly inglorious one of making pumps. It may be the "long hazard" of art, which Robinson himself chose, or it may be a crusade to right some wrong or remove some evil from society, like that of Toussaint L'Ouverture and John Brown. It may be the weaving of fabulous romances for the delectation of innocent childhood, as with Uncle Ananias, or it may be that of being an exemplary husband and father, like Talifer in his later phase. It may be the saving of a nation, as with Lincoln (*The Master*), or it may be the attempt to raise artichokes, as with the gentle Oakes of *Two Gardens in Linndale*.

But whatever it may be, some calling (in the full sense of the word) a man must have if he would know the fullness of what life has to offer. Levi, Vickery, Briony, Norcross, Roman Bartholow before his regeneration—these and others offer melancholy examples of what lives are like to which is denied a commanding and fortifying purpose. Perhaps such orphans of destiny are in even sadder plight than the kindred souls—whom there is no need to name again—condemned to be called but never to be chosen, and so to wear out their lives fruitlessly in the wrong world. Such, Robinson felt, was the tragedy of his brother Dean, among others; and he must have wondered sometimes, as year followed year and recognition failed to come, whether such a fate had not also been decreed for him. In the end, his faith was justified. But suppose, we seem to hear him asking in *Amaranth*, this faith had been illusory? And how is one to distinguish, before it is too late, between illusion and truth?

The last question, like so many asked before, has no easy answer. And yet, Robinson feels, the distinction must be made by those who would be the masters of life and not its playthings. It is true that many of the latter are dealt with gently: Miniver Cheevy, Vickery, Bewick Finzer, and, most of all, the mother in *The Gift of God*. There is likewise no condemnation of those whose deceitful dreams have led them into the Valley of the Shadow, nor of Pink, Atlas, and Elaine Amelia Watchman. Amaranth even tries to persuade them to be satisfied with what they have. He tells Pink:

> "Dreams have a kindly way
> Sometimes, if they are not explored or shaken,
> Of lasting glamorously. Many have lasted
> All a man's life, sparing him, to the grave,
> His value and his magnitude. In this
> One sees, or feels, if so attuned and tempered,
> An ordered prudence, or an adumbration
> Of more than we arrange."

The same suggestion that human illusions may have a sort of divine sanction occurs in *Tasker Norcross*, where Ferguson comments on "men who are nothing" but who happily do not know it.

"God, you see,
Being sorry for them in their fashioning,
Indemnified them with a quaint esteem
Of self, and with illusions long as life.

. . . .

Blessed are they
That see themselves for what they never were
Or were to be."

These passages repeat a long-familiar theme, expressed in a letter to
Smith only a year after the publication of the first volume of poems.
"Nine tenths of the happiness in the world (if there is any) is due
to man's ignorance of his own disposition. The happy people are
they who never had time to think it over." [7]

Yet it is clear that all these apologies for illusion are intended
to apply only to the weak. Those who are content to keep their
agreeable misbeliefs are essentially comic figures, even the mother
in *The Gift of God*. If people are to be taken seriously, they must
want to know the truth. And if they want to know it, apparently,
they get their wish. Pink and Atlas and Watchman are destroyed by
what they learn, but we respect them for looking into Amaranth's
eyes. They are moved, to be sure, by self-distrust and a sort of fear;
but these motives, viewed from a different angle, turn out to be a
desire for truth and the courage to face it. They do not, however,
find the courage to go on facing it; and so they are unlike the truly
tragic figure of Tasker Norcross.

It is not a mere paradox to say that this character is in a
sense the most heroic of all Robinson's creations. For in the other
poems, those persons who are stripped of their illusions either suffer
dumbly and uncomprehendingly, like Levi or the wife in *Eros
Turannos*; or find some relief in passionate protest, as in *London
Bridge* and *An Evangelist's Wife*; or seek refuge in death, like Pink
and Atlas and Gabrielle and Natalie; or find that the truth is really
more satisfying in the end, like Matthias and Talifer. But Norcross,
although to him truth is a Gorgon whom he is forced to behold without a mirror, is not blinded, does not go mad, does not find the
face grow gracious, and yet does not kill himself but waits for death
to release him.[8]

And it seems clear that what Robinson here asks of his readers is not pity but respect, sprung from the perception that, whatever the cost in earthly happiness, it is better to live without illusions than with them. "You mustn't forget the redemption, even if you don't see it." In some other life, for which his endurance here may have prepared him, Norcross, like Levi, "reborn may be as great as any," destined to find self-knowledge change from a curse to a blessing and lead him to such a world as is described by Amaranth in his farewell to Fargo,

> "Where, far from this miasma of delusion
> They know the best there is for man to know;
> They know the peace of reason."

And of course "reason" here is not that of modern "Science" but of what Socrates calls "science"—the ultimate wisdom of which human beings are capable, the "right reason" of the great Renaissance humanists.

From all this it would appear that the greatest virtue, as far as an individual life is concerned, is fortitude. And this conclusion is stated by the poet himself in a letter written to Richard Watson Gilder to thank him for a volume of poems: "I admire most your willingness to look life in the face without resorting to the nauseating evasions of the uncompromising 'optimist.' The predominance of this willingness to be honest, with never the suggestion of surrender—or even of weariness—is to my mind the most admirable thing in life or in art." [9]

Robinson's innate temperament, his New England background, his admiration of the great Victorians, in most of whom there is so strong a Stoic trend, his own long wanderings in the Valley of the Shadow—all these led him to the conclusion that for most men and women the only way to the good life is through fortitude. What sets him apart from more severe moralists, what makes him, in fact, almost a unique representative of the Puritan tradition, is his compassion for those whom destiny seems to have given much to endure, with but little capacity for endurance. The words of Lawyer Figg at the grave of Atlas might have been Robinson's own in regard to any seeming failure:

"I have no reproach,
Or verdict, or vain censure for this man,
And none for Pink. I have not lived their lives.
I have not shared their pangs or felt their terrors
On their awakening here in the wrong world
That unassayed ambition said was right."

2

In another way, also, Robinson differs from the extreme type of Puritanism (from which, it may be noted, many Puritans also differed); namely, that in the good life he finds a place for beauty, the beauty that is known through the senses. A minor but touching instance is given by Hagedorn, who records Robinson's pleasure, when *Tristram* had brought him a measure of affluence, in the purchase of fine clothes, in the indulgence of "his hunger for things satisfying to the eye and the hand," [10] which now, at fifty-eight, no longer financially dependent on the kindness of his friends, he was willing for the first time to permit himself.

His appreciation of natural beauty has already been mentioned. In his youth, as far as the evidence goes, he seems to have taken it more or less for granted. At any rate, he resented the sentimental exploitation of it by popular poetasters, for he wrote of *The Torrent and The Night Before* to Gledhill: "You won't find much in the way of natural description. There is very little tinkling water, and there is not a red-bellied robin in the whole collection. When it comes to 'nightingales and roses' I am not 'in it' nor have I the smallest desire to be." [11] Yet in this volume, *Luke Havergal, The Wilderness,* and *The Torrent* all contain evidence of an authentic and personal awareness of natural beauty; and the same awareness is present in succeeding volumes. No one who is himself familiar with such a scene can read the first part of *Pasa Thalassa Thalassa* without recalling the nostalgic and foreboding pang that comes with the falling of a late summer dusk upon some well loved spot. The poem invites and sustains comparison with two of the great English lyrics of the nineteenth century, Swinburne's *A Forsaken Garden* and Tennyson's *Tears, Idle Tears.*

In later life, after Peterborough became a part of his existence, nature took a stronger hold on him. His letters during his first summer there are full of references—with an undercurrent almost of incredulity—to the beauty of the surroundings. All his later writing was done there. The muse that had been so often a reluctant visitor in the human wilderness of New York seemed wholly at home amid the serenity of New England's woods and hills. What these meant to him appears in *Hillcrest*:

> Between the sunlight and the shade
> A man may learn till he forgets
> The roaring of a world remade,
> And all his ruins and regrets . . .

But it was the human world, after all, that was to him most real and most absorbing. "Doctor Johnson was right," he wrote from London in 1923,[12] recalling the passage in which Boswell records the preference of the Great Lexicographer, though not blind to the beauties of the English countryside, for the life of London. And accordingly, the beauty that Robinson feels to be the most intimate and essential to human existence is that which human beings have created.

It is not the lightest part of the curse placed on Tasker Norcross that to him the world of art—literature, music, sculpture—is a desert:

> "Towers of sound
> And flowers of sense are but a waste of heaven
> Where there is none to know them from the rocks
> And sand-grass of his own monotony
> That makes earth less than earth. He could see that,
> And he could see no more."

In these lines, clearly, the poet is trying to picture the desolation that would have reigned in his own life without an appreciation of the arts.

He had, to be sure, his own blind spots. "For painting or sculpture," says Hagedorn, "he seemed to have neither natural liking nor acquired understanding. . . . 'I simply don't get anything from pictures and I can't understand how anyone else does.' "[13] This confession may at first surprise readers of *Rembrandt to Rem-*

brandt; but reflection will show that what interests the poet is the moral problem that Rembrandt faces, and, to a less extent, the general nature of the artist's inspiration.

What surprises us more, perhaps, considering Robinson's introspective bent, is his passion for the theater, which began in his Harvard days and lasted throughout his life. When Julia Marlowe visited Boston in 1892, he saw her in four Shakespearean plays and wrote of them lyrically to Smith.[14] The frustration of his own intense desire to be a successful playwright did not diminish his enjoyment of the plays of others.[15]

But it was in music that he found most complete release from the tensions of daily existence. Here, too, his real education apparently began during the awakening and liberating years at Harvard. He confided to Gledhill during his second year: "Symphonies & grand operas are a perfect revelation to me and I am cursing myself for letting so many go by last year."[16] Thereafter music came to play an ever greater part in his life; became, in fact, a passion second only to poetry, although he composed nothing except occasional simple tunes for other men's verses, and did not persist in his early attempts to master the clarinet and violin.

But wherever he was—in the Richards home in Gardiner, listening to one of the daughters playing the piano; in New York, spending the money that he had been saving to buy a badly needed pair of trousers on a ticket to *Tristan und Isolde*; in Peterborough, during evenings devoted to music, when "with his hands resting upon his cane he would sit, motionless, listening, like some sculptor's conception of reverie, carved in stone";[17] in New York again, now able to indulge, with less strain on his pocketbook and his conscience, his insatiable passion for (especially) Wagner and Gilbert and Sullivan—music always had the power to lift him into a different world. It even made him almost ready, sometimes, to retract his prophecies of the doom of Western civilization, as when he wrote to Mrs. Ledoux after hearing a performance of *Tristan* in 1921: "For a few hours I fancied that our so-called civilization might not be going after all—though of course it is."[18]

This passionate love of music does not obviously dominate his poetry, where there are no more musicians than painters among the characters, and no more references to music than to the other arts, or to science, or to politics. It does stand forth, however, in *The Man Who Died Twice*, in which not only is the protagonist a composer of genius but the verbal rendition of the great symphony that he was never to write may be thought by some readers to be the most stirring passage of blank verse that Robinson ever created— stirring because of the masterful rhythm, the sonorous tones, the visionary splendor of the imagery, the pervasive reverberant associations with the deepest beliefs and highest aspirations of the Western world; and because of the aptness and richness of the symbolism—surpassing that of *Twilight Song*, *The Town Down the River*, even *The Man Against the Sky*—in which is mirrored the spiritual pilgrimage of man from sunlit innocence through the shadow of guilt and shame to the final redemption.[19]

Here, then, are the elements that seem to compose the "good life" as Robinson conceived it, as far as it can be realized by the individual apart from others: freedom from dependence on material possessions, a calling suited to his native gifts, the fortitude to face the world without illusions and accept without bitterness life's inevitable afflictions, and the capacity and opportunity to enjoy the beauty of nature and of art.

3

But of course no human being really lives in isolation from his fellows. The individual by himself is an unimaginable abstraction. We *are* members of a society; we *are* bound to other persons. "We are all alone," says Paul,

> "And yet we are all parcelled of one order—
> Jew, Gentile, or barbarian in the dark
> Of wildernesses that are not so much
> As names yet in a book."

"Anything with 'community' pasted on it," Robinson rejects; but leave aside the labels, the slogans, and the sermons, and no more staunch believer in human brotherhood will anywhere be found.

The battered, shapeless, soiled, and speechless wreckage of a man cast up from unknown depths to die upon a stranger's threshold in *Alma Mater* is a symbol of the mysterious and indissoluble bonds that hold human beings together. The marchers in *Twilight Song* "have shared the day's load." The Watcher by the Way must in the end give up his isolation and join the general pilgrimage to the Town Down the River. "Whatever the dark road" the Man Against the Sky may have taken, "His way was even as ours."

This truth is part of Timberlake's dying message to Matthias: "We are like stairs/ For one another's climbing." Not to have understood this fact and its implications was one of the shortcomings mainly responsible for bringing tragedy into Matthias's life. But in this failure he is not different from the majority. Penn-Raven observes to Gabrielle

> "That we are all at work on one another
> Not knowing how or when, nor, as a rule,
> Much caring."

Captain Craig, however, is less cynical. In the urgency of his words to his young friends is implied the belief that if men know better, they will do better.

> "But there is this to be remembered always:
> Whatever be the altitude you reach,
> You do not rise alone; nor do you fall
> But you drag others down to more or less
> Than your preferred abasement."

The Captain has already instanced the life of a certain soldier, who, dying in battle and being soon forgotten by most, lives on in the memory and in the very existence of a person who as a child had been saved by the soldier's kindness from despair and perhaps death.

That this is Robinson's own feeling is confirmed by many passages in his letters, some of which were quoted in the first chapter of this study, which show the intensity of his desire, through his poetry, to do some benefit to his fellows. In the letters to Smith he himself finally becomes conscious of what a frequent theme it has been. "The fact that I have done a little spiritual good in the world is what keeps me going now. How many times have I said this, I wonder?" [20] The same sense of fellowship, especially with those whom life seems to have treated harshly, appears in the many poems already mentioned in which he draws his characters from among the poor, the weak, and the lonely, from the ranks of the downtrodden and defeated. If he really meant what he said in writing to Smith of "the dismal truth that the majority of mankind interest me only as studies," [21] either he was thinking of the respectable middle-class people who perhaps formed a majority of Gardiner's inhabitants, or he was expressing a feeling which he later outgrew.

At any rate, his personal life as well as his poetry revealed a consideration for others that was unfailing and generous far beyond the call of duty. When in the years of fame he became subject to all sorts of financial importunities, and his inability to resist an appeal drew a remonstrance from his friend Lewis Isaacs, Robinson replied, "You've never walked the streets of New York without a nickel in your pocket." [22] Even when he lay dying in the hospital, the same compassion, the same sense of identity with struggling and suffering humanity, prevailed. "When Torrence spoke of the beauty of the view from his window, he said that he did not dare look out. 'I found that, when I did, I could see the corner of Welfare Island and I couldn't stand it. Think of the old men down there, think of what is going on, the suffering, the crowded, dingy quarters, the loneliness. And here I am, getting the utmost that can be given!' " [23] Fame and affluence had not turned or toughened his skin.

Fitting into the same pattern is the tenacity with which he clung to friends. Torrence is right in saying that he "actually made a cult of friendship," [24] and Mrs. Richards also stresses his "extraordinary *genius for friendship*." [25] His remark to Smith, "I suppose I can stand more letting alone than any man who ever breathed," [26] is something less than a half-truth. In fact, he had previously written to the same correspondent that "this living alone is bad business; and I have had more than my share of it." [27] What made the years at Gardiner High School so golden in his memory was that for the first time he realized the meaning of friendship, through his asso-

ciation with Smith, Gledhill, and Moore. Perhaps the greatest of
Harvard's many gifts was the intimacy with men of widely differing temper and background, whom he nevertheless felt to be in
some sense kindred spirits—Saben, Burnham, Butler, and others—
of whom he spoke later as "the friends of my life." [28] The harshness of the early years in New York was made more bearable by
the companionship of Burnham, Betts, Coan, and Torrence. His
letters to Miss Peabody and Mrs. Richards reveal unobtrusively
his sense of how much he owed them for their loyal confidence and
affection.

Although the circle of friends widened in later years, the new ties
were not less strong. And when some of the old inevitably weakened, the change always brought regret—how poignant we may
read in *The Long Race* and *Reunion*:

> By some derision of wild circumstance
> Not then our pleasure somehow to perceive,
> Last night we fell together to achieve
> A light eclipse of years. But the pale chance
> Of youth resumed was lost. Time gave a glance
> At each of us, and there was no reprieve.

On the other hand, what most exalts the character of Clavering, in
one of the most heartfelt of Robinson's many pictures of seeming failures, is the undemanding, all-forgiving, never failing loyalty
to his friends, sketched with the customary irony by which the poet
veils the feelings that are "too deep for tears":

> He clung to phantoms and to friends,
> And never came to anything.

We are therefore not surprised to read Robinson's confession to
Esther Bates that the seeming remoteness and reserve that were
almost always present in his manner were not merely due to native
shyness but were in part an armor deliberately worn to hide the
outgoing tendency of his affections. "It is because I am too completely at the mercy of people that I find I have to keep away from
them." [29] His is a different motive from that of the "frozen brothers,
who have yet," as Captain Craig declares,

"Profoundly and severely to find out
That there is more of unpermitted love
In most men's reticence than most men think."

The Captain himself reflects regretfully, remembering "some faces
I have known—/ Sad faces, hungry faces,"

"that had I not been mute
And actionless, I might have made them bright
Somehow, though only for the moment."

Perhaps it was some similar memory of the poet's own that made
him return to the theme in *The Corridor*.

But if so, there were other times when he felt happier, and could
write to Miss Peabody, speaking first of her career as a poet: "I
cannot, in the nature of things, help you to any great extent; but as I
look back on thirty years of somewhat ridiculous existence, I find
that I have helped others, and sometimes (which is the real thing,
[*sic*] without their knowing it. And this discovery is, it seems to
me, the only thing which really counts." [30] The role of the man
Flammonde in healing the enmities and ending the estrangements
of Tilbury Townspeople was one that Robinson himself was happy
to play in fact, when the opportunity came, as well as in imagination. Telling Smith the story of how two of his Harvard friends who
were "at swords' points" had by chance dropped into his room at
the same time and, thanks in part to the tact of the host, had become before leaving "as good friends as they were before the difficulty," he continues: "a few words at the right time and in the
right place might destroy hundreds of petty 'spats' every day. I am
not setting myself up for a professional peace-maker, but I honestly
think that in this case I was the indirect means of bringing two
people together who might have otherwise hated each other to the
end of their lives." That he felt "a kind of un-christian pleasure" at
seeing them recognize their folly is not inconsistent with genuine
satisfaction at their renewed friendship.[31] The same theme and the
same ironical attitude recur in a late sonnet called *Glass Houses*,
where, after warning his friends against trying to learn what other
friends say about them, he concludes dryly, "and you may slowly
have inferred/ That you may not be here a thousand years."

This poem provides a transition to another main article in Robinson's code of courtesy, already stated by implication in the discussion of his attitude toward the people in his poems: a scrupulous respect for the privacy even of one's friends, a rocklike support of the principle that every human being has the right to live his own life, so long as he does no injury to another. A happy illustration is to be found in the delicate whimsy of *Two Gardens in Linndale*, which caused Theodore Roosevelt to comment, after reading it and another poem in manuscript: "What a queer, mystical creature he is! I did not understand one of them—that about the gardens." [32] This failure to understand was not unnatural, for along with the President's generosity there seems to have gone the confidence that he knew what was best for those who were its recipients; whereas the moral of the poem is that tranquillity and happiness lie in permitting people to do what they wish. In a way the poem is complementary to Frost's *Mending Wall*. The brothers Oakes and Oliver put up a fence to separate their shares of the land inherited from their father, and the former devotes himself to what the latter is sure will be the fruitless undertaking of raising artichokes. "But anyhow," says Oliver,

> " 'Tis here we are, 'tis here we live,
> With each to take and each to give:
> There's no room for a quarrel now."
>
> .   .   .   .   .
>
> Year after year 'twas all the same:
> With none to envy, none to blame,
> They lived along in innocence,
> And never once forgot the fence,
> Till on a day the Stranger came.

The Stranger is Death, and Oliver is left alone, comforted by the thought that he and Oakes had never quarreled. Thus among the needs to which Christian charity in its fullness ministers is the need of every soul to preserve its own identity—a need perhaps less often recognized than many others.

In the end, Robinson's notions of how human beings would treat each other in an ideal society come down to the simple old-fashioned virtue of unselfishness. "I fear I haven't the stamina to be a Christian," he wrote to Gledhill in 1896, "accepting Christ as either human or divine. Selfishness hangs to a man like a lobster and is the thing that keeps humanity where it is, I know that, but at present I am pretty much a human being, though I see a glimmer of the light once in a while and then meditate on possibilities." [33] A similar thought underlies the words of Timberlake to Matthias:

> "There is no cure for self;
> There's only an occasional revelation,
> Arriving not infrequently too late."

"Self" cannot be cured; it can only be transcended. This is a lesson that Malory also learns in *The Glory of the Nightingales*:

> There was time
> For living in himself and on himself,
> Like a thought-eating worm, and dying of it
> Unthought of, or for life larger than that,
> Larger than self, and one that was not death.
> There was avengingly not time for both.

What Robinson is evidently condemning in these passages is not merely selfishness in regard to material possessions, like the avarice of Aaron Stark, but a kind of self-centeredness that makes people insensitive or indifferent to the feelings of those about them, whose existence they take for granted as part of a general economy designed for their own convenience, and whose failure to accept this role arouses their resentment. "This utter lack of consideration for others goes far towards making this life of ours the rat-trap that it is." [34] It may appear as self-pity, in Bokardo, or as self-importance, in Matthias. It may take the form of the parental tyranny that is glanced at in *The Valley of the Shadow*, or of the small-town smugness that dismisses as "The Rat" a person who has failed to meet its standard of respectability. It is manifest in Gawaine's relatively harmless resolve to live on the surface of life, and in Modred's deadly aim of rule or ruin, and in the unconsidered marriage choices of Arthur and Mark. It may take the shape of religious fanaticism, either in the hideous extremity of an action like Jael's, or in Caiaphas's more common but not less damn-

able way of doing the Devil's work. Most often, in Robinson's poems, it appears as the factor destructive of happiness in the relation
between a man and a woman.

4

This relation, the most intimate of all that exist among human
beings, seems to be taken by Robinson as a type of all human relations, and as the form of experience in which is most clearly revealed, on the one hand, the fatal effects of "self"—of what many
people mean when they speak of "love" between men and women;
and, on the other, the saving grace of self-transcendence, which is
part of what "love" has meant to the prophets and poets who have
given a voice to human dreams of a life unscarred by the despair
and hate inevitably bred by the worship of "self."

Much has been written about Robinson's general view of the
sexes—about the likenesses and differences between male and female in the realm of the intellect and the emotions. Some critics have
felt that his attitude toward women, his conception of their essential nature, and his view of the role which they do or ought to
play in the human drama, are radically different from those which
he holds in regard to men. A masculine reviewer of the *Collected
Poems* in 1929 qualified his high praise by declaring the poet
to be "apparently interested in men only; in the dramatis per-
sonae of his poems, no woman is accorded a principal part." [35]
And a feminine reader in 1933 went even further, concluding
that "his women are in fact not real at all, but are projections of
some need in man. They are therefore a little tiresome. . . . They
seem to keep men from spiritual research, to tame men's leaping
imaginations and intellects. They are absolutely worthless as fine
critics of life, as commentators upon the deeper significance of
living." [36]

In such comments there is perhaps a grain of truth. Robinson's
women are not artists, they are not philosophers, they are not re-

formers. Shakespeare and Rembrandt have no feminine counterparts in his poems, as they have none in history.[37] Nor does the
poet, any more than history, give us any female philosophers or
seers (since Zoë never quite ceases to be a symbol) like Merlin
and Captain Craig. And, unlike history, his poems contain no
Joan of Arc or Florence Nightingale to stand beside John Brown
and Toussaint L'Ouverture.

But this is not to say that his feminine characters are vague or
weak or unconvincing. As a rule, indeed, they seem to be more
three-dimensional than his men, and to have a firmer grasp on the
realities of day-to-day existence. They may not see so far, but
they see more clearly, are not so easily deceived by remote mirages, do not so eagerly (except perhaps when particular persons are
involved) embrace illusions. The critic (male) is mainly right who
says that the "Robinson heroines throughout speak more directly
than the heroes. The men fumble about; are haunted by doubts
and dreads; still cling to illusion; are immature compared with the
woman." [38] This is not always true in the shorter poems, although
we may recall Lorraine, Aunt Imogen, and (at an all but unimaginable remove) Jael. But it is true to a certain extent of Merlin and
Vivian; it is obviously true of Lancelot and Guinevere, of Tristram
and the two Isolts; it is true of Roman Bartholow and Gabrielle,
of Matthias and Natalie, of Talifer and Althea. And although perhaps not everyone will unreservedly accept the verdict of the critic
(feminine this time) who says that "he is perhaps at his best in the
portrayal of feminine character," [39] no serious reader can say that
he is not interested in women or that he does not treat them as persons in their own right. That they differ from men does not make
them less human, or less important in "the Scheme."

It is true that the poet does sometimes seem to feel that women's
role in life involves an undue share of the suffering of humanity as
a whole. Somehow the cards are stacked against them. It is for them
to suffer, like Gabrielle and Natalie and Laramie Cavender, that
men may be saved.[40] But it is one thing to describe such a situation,
and another to approve it.

On the other hand, Robinson does not sentimentalize women by making them always the victims in life's accidents and conflicts. Mark can suffer and forgive; Morgan can hate and betray. Priscilla is only involuntarily responsible for whatever salvation it is that Llewellyn gains. Men and women are capable of equal folly, equal cruelty, equal selfishness. The callous husband of *Eros Turannos* is matched by the vindictive wife in *The Unforgiven*. The husband's infidelity in *The Clinging Vine* is more than matched by the wife's infidelity, envenomed by hatred, in *The Whip*. The stubborn pride of John Gorham is not more repellent than the obsessive devotion of Avenel Gray, in *Mortmain*, to a brother's ghost. In fact, it sometimes seems as if women were more calculating in their cruelty, like the wife in *If the Lord Would Make Windows in Heaven,* who pretends in public to honor the husband whom at home she torments by systematic and sadistic disparagement; whereas men's cruelty to the other sex seems in general to be more simply selfish, arising mainly from lack of feeling or of imagination.

At the same time women seem capable of more exalted devotion to the person beloved. No man in Robinson's poems makes a sacrifice comparable to that of the wife in *Ben Trovato*. Likewise, one feels, it is the greater insight and devotion of "the wife of Palissy" (Robinson's first and more informative title for *Partnership*)[41] that redeems and restores a long-tried love before it is ended by her death:

> But the clashing is all past,
> And the gift is yours at last.
> Lift it—hold it high again! . . .
> Did I doubt you now and then?
> Well, we are not men.

The tender irony of the last line of this stanza occurs again in the closing line of *As a World Would Have It,* when Alcestis asks the husband whom she has at last persuaded to forgive her for having placed him so hopelessly in her debt by offering her life for his: "And was it very strange?"

Ideally, however, the partnership of a man and a woman in love is equal and tranquil. The love that is pictured in two of Robinson's most perfect sonnets, *Firelight* and *Vain Gratuities,* is not less deep for being less dramatic than that presented in some other pieces, nor less true for being less severely tried.

It is clear from this analysis that Robinson's view of love between the sexes differs widely from that which has generally prevailed in twentieth century literature, especially fiction and drama. By a majority of the writers who have been taken most seriously, love has been treated as primarily a biological or psychic drive, according to the behaviorist or Freudian leanings of the author. It may be made repulsive, as among Huxley's sophisticates; glamorous, as among Hemingway's adolescents of all ages; grimy, as among Caldwell's primitives; or grotesque, as among Faulkner's eccentrics. But it is in any case irrational and self-centered, uncompromisingly hostile alike to the practical demands of daily life, to intellectual or artistic creation, to social responsibilities, to religious aspirations— in short, to almost everything that gives life interest or value for civilized persons.

In Robinson's work, however, in line with the great tradition of Western culture, the biological or instinctual basis of love is accepted without ado and assigned to its place among the other natural conditions, such as those that have just been mentioned, of existence in a human society. Sex is a physical fact, essential to the propagation of the race; but otherwise, like other physical facts, of no importance except in relation to reason, will, and affection.[42]

This calm acceptance perhaps explains why Robinson is so unexpectedly tolerant of sexual intimacy unsanctioned by marriage. Lorraine is not censured by her creator for (as most of the world would have it) "going to the devil." The poet clearly does not join with Roman Bartholow in reproaching Gabrielle for her affair with Penn-Raven. Whether Laramie was or was not guilty of infidelity to Cavender is treated as of little consequence. Prince Jasper and Zoë live together without benefit of matrimony, and even Honoria finally ceases to blame them (though these facts may somehow be involved in the allegory). The Church does not bless the union of Merlin and Vivian, concerning whose story the poet remarked dryly, "The thing seems to me . . . on the whole, entirely moral." [43]

Likewise, the fact that Lancelot and Guinevere, and Tristram and Isolt, are guilty of what is called adultery is apparently considered irrelevant to the world of spiritual values with which the poet is concerned. "Adultery" is a word in a legal code, standing for an act that man-made law may punish; but Arthur's sentencing of Guinevere to be burned, although legal, is an act far more immoral than any committed by her. It is the act of a person still ruled by "self," the same self that the lovers gradually learn to subdue.

From these instances it is evident that, like the man whom he could not accept as Christ, Robinson sees that morality and legality are different things. It is the inside of the cup that needs most to be kept clean. Actions in themselves do not defile a person, or cleanse him. It is the motive that counts—and of course the ultimate effect upon the character and inner life of himself and others.

One further comment may be made in this connection upon the story of Tristram and Isolt. They do not die until they have learned that love is more than passion and possession; until their feeling for each other has been disciplined and humanized by a long separation and then a period of almost domestic life together; until each has so far transcended "self" as to think of the other first (perhaps Isolt always did so), and even to spare a thought for Mark and the other Isolt.

There is, however, a wider life and a higher wisdom still, were they but able to achieve it—to pass from the love of individual persons to the love of God and then back to a more inclusive love of the human beings who share His nature. It is this wider life and higher wisdom that are given a symbol in "the light that Galahad found"; that Lancelot, having seen but once, and dimly, can never forget; and that Merlin says shall one day light the world. It is really the same experience, although expressed in terms of a "non-theological religion" (which is not merely humanitarian, either), that enables Malory and Matthias to reconstruct their lives. It is perhaps the same goal to which the unheroic Vanderberg painfully gropes his way. But it is a goal beyond the reach of Tristram and Isolt; and therefore they die. "There was no more for them," as Mark perceives, although perhaps without fully perceiving why.[44]

The two full-length pictures that Robinson gives us of almost completely satisfying love are that of Damaris and Annandale (as told in *Annandale Again*) before the latter's tragic death, and that of Althea and Talifer. In these, perhaps surprisingly, the happiness is tranquil and almost—if not quite—domestic. The affection is tender and humorous rather than exalted or passionate, lighted by laughter that need not ask to be forgiven, and anchored with forbearance that there is no desire to dramatize. No doubt this is to some extent the inevitable quality of a love that lasts, and that is lived among people—not under the visible shadow of imminent destruction, nor on some enchanted island. And we must remember Robinson's lifelong emphasis on "the romance of the commonplace." On the other hand, those readers who feel that the poet slipped unawares into commonplace romance (as perhaps he really did in some parts of *Tristram*) should not forget that almost certainly the poet is as keenly aware as they are of the limitations and surrenders involved in such a life. Neither Althea nor Talifer is intended to be heroic; and *Annandale Again*, despite its bewildering and painful conclusion, obviously pokes fun at the fervor of the lovers' courtship.[45]

The really surprising thing, however, in view of Robinson's profound sense of human solidarity, of universal brotherhood, is not the homely quality of the love that is described in these narratives, but the fact that it is no less exclusive of the world in general than is the romantic passion of the Arthurian lovers. To a college teacher it may even suggest the common tragicomic surrender, by eager and intelligent and sensitive minds, of the world of ideas and mature responsibilities in exchange for a world of formulas and thermometers and books on child psychology. Putting aside this depressing reflection, one still pauses to ponder the "gratefulness" of husband and wife, in these poems as in *Firelight*, "For love's obliteration of the crowd."

Of course, these are human dramas, concerned with the lives of particular people living in the world we know—on which, despite his doubts of its substantiality, Robinson usually keeps a firm grasp. His is not the soaring idealism of Dante or Spenser or Shelley. Nevertheless, he *is* an idealist; and when he is illustrating his philosophy, instead of dramatizing a unique situation, he finds for the love between the sexes a role in the general human drama that is more than merely romantic or domestic.

This role is perhaps most definitely suggested in Merlin's words to Dagonet, as they look for the last time upon the doomed city of Camelot, the capital of what soon must be

> "a wrecked empire, lighted by the torch
> Of woman, who, together with the light
> That Galahad found, is yet to light the world."

The light of the Grail leads us to look beyond the world of time and matter, the world of passions and actions and things, to the ultimate good that poets have dreamed of but never been able to describe in "time-born words." "Woman," on the other hand—or perhaps more properly, "man's love for woman" [46]—teaches that earthly existence also has a meaning; as the closest relation with another person that most human beings ever know, it puts the body to use in the service of the soul, it exalts and purifies, it reveals (to those who are ready for the revelation) the need and the capacity for union with another soul and hence with other souls, and it opens the way to the conquest, if not the cure, of "self."

All this, to be sure, is perhaps only for the initiated. The wisdom that Merlin gains from his love for Vivian is one that she herself cannot yet share:

> "She knows not yet the name
> Of what she is, for now there is no name;
> Some day there shall be." [47]

The thought of these lines is not very far from what Paul says in *The Three Taverns*, though in a very different context: "The world is here for what is not yet here/ For more than are a few." For Paul himself no second light is needed; yet as he says elsewhere,

> The fire that smites
> A few on highways, changing all at once,
> Is not for all.

And in an age where this fire descends still more rarely, a poet may feel that the love between a man and a woman, rightly known, may be a way for more persons to find what the world is here for.

Nor should we forget, finally, that in *King Jasper* the saving principle of knowledge, which survives each wreck of man's renewed attempt to build a civilization, and derives from each something with which to serve the next, is personified in the radiant Zoë, whom it was surely no part of the poet's intention to make so bodiless as she seems to be. The Prince is not in love with an abstraction, and the Queen's initial jealousy is not of a symbol but of a woman. Nor is it merely as an idea that the King finds her presence so desirable and disturbing. Here, again, "woman" lights the way to wisdom, which is not wasted, though it seems to come too late.[48]

5

So far we have considered the values that exist, for Robinson, in relation to the individual human being and his unique destiny; and those that exist in relation to his association with other individuals, both in the physical world and in a spiritual community. It remains to consider a third set of values, existing in relation to his life as a member of an organized society. Even if we grant that all values originate in the individual and in relations between individuals, we must ask the question, "In what kind of possible society can these values best be realized?"

This question, it is true, is one that some modern poets have chosen not to face. Some, like Pink, have retreated to a private world where they amuse themselves with abracadabra arrangements of words and letters and punctuation marks. Others have struck out in blind fury against a society that refuses to conform to their personal prejudices; like the person in *Hillcrest* who "reads a planet out of tune/ For cause of his jarred harmony."

For such an attitude Robinson has no sympathy. He has prejudices of his own, but he also has a Puritan conscience, so aggressive that once it even led him to fall foul of Thoreau, with whom he obviously has so much in common. "I stretched out yesterday and read *Walking*," he wrote in 1899 to Daniel Gregory Mason, "but did not quite relish what seemed to me a sort of glorified Thoreau cowardice all through the thing. For God's sake, says the sage, let me get away into the wilderness where I shall not have a single human responsibility or the first symptoms of social discipline, let me be a pickerel or a skunk cabbage, anything that will not have to meet the realities of civilization." [49]

After this outburst, we need not be too greatly surprised, despite his admonitions against mixing poetry and propaganda, to find him assuming the role of Cassandra during the early years of World War I, summoning Dionysus to his aid in a sally against Prohibition, and ending his work, as the great depression dragged grimly through its fifth year, with an allegorical "treatise on economics." Although in later life he often expressed Spenglerian forebodings about the impending destruction of civilization, he might have said what he makes Paul say in a different connection:

> I do not see myself as one who says
> To man that he shall sit with folded hands
> Against the Coming.

It is natural to wonder what Robinson would have said about Thoreau if he had read *Civil Disobedience* after the passage of "a certain much to be damned amendment" [50] to the Constitution. At any rate, what strikes one first in regard to his social thinking is his conception, in the tradition of nineteenth century liberalism, of government as a necessary evil against whose encroachments on individual liberty men must be always on guard. Moreover, like most of the great Victorian liberals, he felt that the danger was no longer from the few but from the many—from the will of an uninformed and undisciplined electorate.

What shocked him into public protest and warning (and into private anathemas) was the adoption of the Eighteenth Amendment to the Constitution in 1918. At this time he was not drinking—although he started again, "almost as a matter of principle." [51] He saw Prohibition as an indefensible invasion of personal liberty, setting a precedent for more dangerous, although not more offensive, future invasions. "I don't see the independence of an alleged democracy that will accept the eighteenth amendment without general secession or civil war. The worst feature of it all is that the people don't seem to see that such a thing is fundamentally evil and arbitrary, and therefore cannot work for good." [52]

It is not, of course, that he dislikes "the masses," but that he distrusts their judgment. "I'm a democrat in that I'm as likely to form a lifelong friendship with a coal-heaver as with a millionaire (rather more so, in fact), but there my democracy ends." [53] Especially he fears their susceptibility to propaganda, their willingness to be used to serve the purposes of one or a few powerful and determined men. That these men may be sincere is irrelevant. "Oh no, I don't want the world drunk," he wrote to Mrs. Richards, who appears to have tried to defend Prohibition. "On the other hand, I don't want a world tyrannized by Henry Fords, W. J. Bryans, and Charles W. Eliots—which appears to be on the way." [54]

What he fears most in such movements is the tendency, as the god puts it in *Dionysus in Doubt*, "To moronize a million for a few," to turn human beings into faceless counters in games that they do not understand, played for stakes that they have not set. As Dionysus observes:

"An ultimate uniformity enthroned
May trim your vision very well;
And the poor cringing self, disowned,
May call it freedom and efficiency.
Others would somewhat rather call it hell."

The same sort of innate absurdity that seems to Robinson to be present in materialistic metaphysics appears to him to exist in all proposals to produce happiness wholesale,

"To perpetrate complacency and joy
Of uniform size and strength."

The ultimate evil triumphs when the conformity that may at first have been merely incidental becomes itself the end, when collectivism becomes a dogma, and individualism is labeled treason. This is the position of Demos in *Demos and Dionysus*:

"We have had too much
Of the insurgent individual
With his free fancy and free this and that,
And his ingenuous right to be himself.
What right has anyone now to be himself . . . ?"

What Robinson is attacking in these poems, of course, is not democracy but totalitarianism. What he dislikes in democracy is simply the tendencies that might make it cease to be democracy; and he would see no point in curing the disease by killing the patient. And what he asserts is what no responsible believer in democracy has denied—that a free society cannot survive without the leadership provided by "an aristocracy of virtue and talent." When the speaker in the sonnets called *Demos* declares that

the few shall save
The many, or the many are to fall—
Still to be wrangling in a noisy grave,

he is not libeling "the masses" but stating the verdict of history. And when Dionysus insists,

"There are too many sleepers in your land,
And in too many places
Defeat, indifference, and forsworn command
Are like a mask upon too many faces,"

he is not calling for a *Fuehrer* nor urging abandonment of popular elections but declaring that the persons who are most highly gifted should be less careless of the common good.

6

One of the ends that Robinson saw men being eagerly enslaved to serve was nationalism. In fact, his earliest attacks on regimentation were inspired by German militarism in the 1890's. His friend Smith, studying in Germany, had apparently acquired a taste for military parades, and Robinson wrote:

I could never kindle any enthusiasm for the military spirit which is so rampant with the German people. The whole thing always went against the grain with me and always seemed in complete opposition with all human and spiritual progress. The result of it in Germany is not far to seek. It breeds, almost in infancy, an unnatural recognition of authority which is really nothing but an unwarrantable despotism softened a little by tradition.[55]

Later, commenting on Smith's remarks about American tourists, he comes back to the same theme:

I don't know why it is that the average American has to be such a damned fool, but I suppose it is because he is young. Independence and ignorance make a most unhappy combination to a critical observer, but I prefer it to servility and ignorance, for all that. I wonder how much longer the German people are going to sacrifice the best years of their life to the army and Divine (!) right? The whole thing makes me fairly gag when I allow myself to think of it.[56]

Nor, apparently, was Germany the only state whose autocratic government he condemned. We find him writing a year or two later, in 1898: "From my present 'jaundiced' point of view it looks as if the whole so-called civilized world would have to go back and get a new start. If it buries 'divine right' and three or four priest-ridden, rotten monarchies in the process, perhaps it will be worth while."[57] There is no evidence that he ever changed his views on this subject, any more than on most others. It is true that in a letter written in 1919 he remarked: "Sometimes I wonder if it would take much to set me yelling for an absolute monarchy in this country—assuming that we haven't got one."[58] But the general tenor of his writings indicates that it would have taken a great deal.

Robinson has also enough comments on the American brand of nationalism, regardless of forms of government, to show that *Cassandra* expresses no temporary mood. Twenty years before this poem appeared, he had told Smith that "Harvard College . . . is the object of almost the only patriotism I possess";[59] and neither then nor later does he seem to have felt any particular personal attachment to America as a whole. Much less was he capable of what "patriotism" apparently means in today's mad world—the arrogant assumption and the blatant proclamation that one's own country is faultless (except for a minority who are "un-American" or "non-Aryan" or "deviationist"), and that all other countries ought to acknowledge its absolute and predestined superiority. From an awareness of this evil force springs Althea's reflection in *Talifer* that the world might "behave" better "if jungle-minded knaves/ And patriots were not always playing with it."

If, however, patriotism has a place for "a decent respect to the opinion of mankind," for an honest appraisal of the merits and defects of one's country as measured against the unchallenged ideals of Western culture, and for the desire to make one's country *worthy* of the world's respect, then Robinson possesses it. From this point of view it is the blindly loyal who are the real traitors; and the real patriot is he who tells his countrymen unpleasant truths. Accordingly, Robinson does not hesitate to voice his anger and foreboding at America's dedication to greed and pride.

> "What unrecorded overthrow
>   Of all the world has ever known,
> Or ever been, has made itself
>   So plain to you, and you alone?
>
> .   .   .   .   .   .
>
> "The power is yours, but not the sight;
>   You see not upon what you tread;
> You have the ages for your guide,
>   But not the wisdom to be led."

A similar attitude is implied in a sardonic reference, in a letter written to Mason in 1900, to "the right of our incomparable republic to make a game preserve of the Philippines." [60] A more restrained comment is one to Witter Bynner in 1921. (The first part of the quotation is not really irrelevant.) "I am pretty well satisfied that free verse, prohibition, and moving pictures are a triumvirate from hell, armed with the devil's instructions to abolish civilization —which, by the way, has not yet existed, and cannot exist until the human brain undergoes many changes. A brain, for example, that is 100% American cannot in the nature of things have many percent left over." [61] Two years later, just back from England, with the Republicans in power and clamoring for the payment of "war debts" while raising tariffs to unprecedented heights, Robinson remarked that "it is easy to be a prophet and to say that all this chatter about peace will continue to be an imbecility so long as there are custom houses in the world." [62]

The last quotation suggests that as he grew older, Robinson began to turn from general denunciation of materialism in its form of

American dollar-worship to an analysis of the economic organization of Western society. His conclusions may be studied in *King Jasper*, which in substance is mainly a critique of traditional capitalism.

In approaching this question, Robinson was drawn in opposite directions. His liking for order, his respect for individual achievement, his enjoyment of cultural luxuries, such as symphonies and operas, that the American system seemed generously to provide, and his native skepticism in regard to social theories, arising out of his conviction that evil has its origin mainly in people rather than in institutions, all tended to make him prefer capitalism with its acknowledged faults to some alternative system with its theoretical virtues. Working against such an acceptance were his lifelong disgust at the "diabolical, dirty race for dollars"; his appreciation of the meaning of poverty and his unwillingness to accept the capitalist assumption that the people at the bottom of the economic scale —as well as those at the top—are where they deserve to be; and his perception that economic competition between nations (in which, until the Russian Revolution, private capitalism was always involved) was one of the causes of war.

The last point seems to have been in his mind when he commented that in *Merlin* and *Lancelot*, Lancelot "may be taken as a rather distant symbol of Germany, though the reader will do well not to make too much of this or to carry it too far." [63] "The world has paid enough for Camelot" would therefore seem to imply that Robinson regarded World War I as the death struggle of economic nationalism. It does *not* imply that he followed the party line of Germany's apologists and blamed "British imperialism" for the war. His letters, early and late, show that he had no love for Germany; and he wrote in 1923 that England might have been "perfidious in its own way, perhaps, in the past, but it is the best thing that we have now." [64] So the evil must have been at least partly in the economic system according to which the world was organized. "Your reign was more a system than a sin," Honoria tells her husband, who appears in general to represent capitalism as a whole.

King Jasper seems especially, however, to be a symbol of Amer-

ican big business. As such, he is a not unattractive but far from flaw-
less character. His basic guilt is in his having dealt unjustly with his
partner Hebron, who possessed inventive genius but not Jasper's
ability to exploit his inventions. He would, in fact, as Jasper alleges
in self-defense, have been a hindrance in this exploitation:

> "If you had lived,
> Your freaks of caution, and your hesitations,
>
> .   .   .   .
>
>   . . . would have been clogs
> And obstacles that would have maddened me."

There was nothing malicious in Jasper's duplicity; it was not even
motivated by greed, but rather by a lust for power, a "demon of
ambition," a drive to do big things. And so, seeing success for himself and death for Hebron only a little way ahead, he held out no
hope, but left his friend "To starve on lies and perish."

As for the years of his reign, they were not particularly stained
with evil. So far as he is hated by the populace, it is because of his
success, and not because of how he achieved it:

> When told the king was ill, a few were sorry,
> More were indifferent, and the rest, rejoicing,
> Prayed for the worst because he was a king,
> And therefore better dead.

His private life is marked neither by avarice nor by conspicuous
waste. He has, and on the whole deserves, the love of his wife, who
seems to symbolize the courtesy, the taste, the self-respecting dignity, the accepted obligation to uphold time-tested values, of true
aristocracy. He is tolerant of what must seem to him the inexplicable caprices of the Prince (whose engaging grace and freedom may
represent the ingenuous and openminded enthusiasm for sheer living that Robinson apparently saw and liked in the "younger generation," but which he felt to be undisciplined and irresponsible).
And he is sensitive enough to see that something is missing in his
life and to recognize the personification of it in Zoë when she comes.

Despite his virtues, however, Jasper's kingdom rests (as kingdoms
in Robinson's poems have a way of doing) on a rotten foundation
—the selfish betrayal of a friend, a failure in humanity. Hebron the

elder apparently stands for the multitude of human beings that cap-
tains of industry have seen fit to use and throw away—or, to change
the figure, to feed to the "dragon" that seems to symbolize (as does
his master in a different way) the capitalist system itself, which
Robinson, as he watches the depression continue with no end in
sight, believes to be dying. In *Captain Craig*, long before, he had
warned society's fortunate few to remember that

> "Down yonder where the clouded millions go,
> Your bloody-knuckled scullions are not slaves,"

but the warning had gone unheeded.

For young Hebron, naturally, the poet has no sympathy. His lust
for power is as unbridled as Jasper's has been, and it is made infinitely more abhorrent by its alloy of ignorance, arrogance, sensu-
ality, and vengefulness. In him are personified all the evils of violent revolution, whether in the form of Nazism, Communism, or
any similar "ism," when power is seized by those unfit to wield it,
who exploit for their own fanatical ends the innate viciousness that
exists in human nature on every social level, as well as the legitimate
grievances of "the masses." Perhaps Robinson is thinking more of
Nazism than Communism, since he wrote early in 1934, when *King
Jasper* was taking shape in his mind: "Today I have been thinking
of Hitler, and of what one neurotic fanatic may yet do to us and
drag us into. It's all right to say it can't happen, but unfortunately
it can." [65]

Yet even a neurotic fanatic, if the allegory holds, cannot gain the
followers needed to bring him to power except when they have real
grievances. It is the injury to his father that obviously motivates
young Hebron's assault upon the established order (although there
are hints of innate and causeless evil, since he was a "dark" child,
like his mysterious mother, and unlike his father). At any rate,
Jasper has always known that injustices existed, while trying to hide
the knowledge from himself. The Hebron who torments him in his
nightmare is the creature of his own conscience; and the knife with
which Zoë stabs him at the dream's end is the recognition, no longer
to be evaded, of the wrong involved in his whole career. He does not
deny Honoria's assertion with reference to the "false gods" whose

temples his "chimneys" have been: "You knew from the beginning
of your ascent/ How false they were." It is therefore only just to
describe as "retribution" what happens to him and his kingdom.
And this retribution has become, whether justly or not, "a world's
infection"; the cure of which—to apply the allegory—is the great
social problem of the twentieth century.

7

Obviously, such ruinous uprisings as young Hebron's, however
natural, solve no problems. He has no program except hate, which
his prototypes in real life have shown to be a more effective "opiate
of the people" than is religion. How is he to be forestalled or defeated, or, if neither of these is now possible, how is reconstruction
to proceed when his reign of terror is over?

A preliminary observation is that Robinson's attitude is essentially forward-looking. Repelled as he is by many aspects of twentieth century America, sure as he is that its vaunted "progress" is in
most ways an illusion, he has no inclination to turn back the clock
or to embrace the opposite illusion of "the good old days." He may
warn in *Modernities*, after granting to the present age achievements
surpassing those of "our fathers,"

> Yet we shall have our darkness, even as they,
> And there shall be another tale to tell;

and he may tell Mrs. Richards, "The more I try to make a picture
of this world for the next hundred years, the more I don't like it,
and the gladder I am that I shall be out of it";[66] but whatever he may
think of the future, he deprecates nostalgic gropings toward the
past. One of the early *Octaves* meets the issue squarely:

> We lack the courage to be where we are:—
> We love too much to travel on old roads,
> To triumph on old fields; we love too much
> To consecrate the magic of dead things,
> And yieldingly to linger by long walls
> Of ruin, where the ruinous moonlight
> That sheds a lying glory on old stones
> Befriends us with a wizard's enmity.

He comes back to the theme in *The Wandering Jew*, a portrait of the perennial disbeliever in the goodness of his own time.[67] The wanderer's vision of "new lions ramping in his path" leads the poet to comment:

> The old were dead and had no fangs,
> Wherefore he loved them—seeing not
> They were the same that in their time
> Had eaten everything they caught.

And *The Old King's New Jester*, published just after the Armistice in 1918, and addressed to those who would like to escape from the difficult present into the dusty past, rings the changes again:

> You that in vain would front the coming order
> With eyes that meet forlornly what they must,
> And only with a furtive recognition
> See dust where there is dust,—
> Be sure you like it always in your faces,
> Obscuring your best graces,
> Blinding your speech and sight,
> Before you seek again your dusty places
> Where the old wrong seems right.

He is willing to face the worst, and does so near the end of *Lancelot*:

> "A played-out world,
> Although that world be ours, had best be dead,"
> Said Lancelot: "There are worlds enough to follow."

But despite his forebodings, he never quite concedes that his own world is played out, although he has no program for its salvation except a rather vague hope of gradually increasing enlightenment and altruism, apparently beginning at the top with men like Malory and Matthias. As far as America was concerned, Robinson hoped for a time that the nation had found its leader in Theodore Roosevelt. *The Revealer* was not written out of personal gratitude. In Roosevelt's assaults on the evils of big business—which earned him almost as much enmity as was later accorded to Franklin Roosevelt, and for which he has been given credit perhaps somewhat too grudgingly by admirers of the latter—Robinson saw reflected his own disgust at the dirty race for dollars.[68] He is not merely play-

ing with metaphors in describing the results of the first Roosevelt's
efforts:

> And ills that were concealed are seen;
> The combs of long-defended hives
> Now drip dishonored and unclean.

But the poet realizes that one man's power is limited. The evils having been brought to light, it is for the citizens themselves to continue the cleansing:

> What You and I and Anderson
> Are still to do is his reward;
> If we go back when he is gone—
> There is an Angel with a Sword.

We did go back, of course; and some would say that the Sword fell.

There are other grounds for hope, however, besides the appearance from time to time of gifted leaders. There is, indirectly, encouragement in the very recalcitrance and stubbornness of human
nature which foil the hopes of so many reformers and make human
progress so slow. If, as Dionysus says, "when a sphere is hammered
square/ All that was hammered is still there"; and if King Jasper's
judgment is sound when he says to those

> "Who'd see this world turned neatly upside down,
> I fear that you might find the same absurd
> And abused atom that was here before";

then those who would hammer human nature into new shapes for
obscene uses, and those who would turn society upside down for
evil ends, are also destined finally to be foiled. And the particular
nightmare of a world where

> all would be alike—
> A thought so monstrous that King Jasper shivered
> As long as it was in him—

will never take shape in reality. As Dionysus prophesies, all those
are doomed to failure who would

> "Conspire somehow by law to wring the neck
> Of nature, not seeing how large a neck it is
> That your beneficent severities
> Would humble and subdue."

Nor does Robinson pin his faith merely on the negative force of inertia. At heart he believes, as his life and poetry show, that despite all appearances to the contrary, human beings in general are fundamentally decent and right-minded. Young Hebron only represents humanity at its worst. Zoë tells the King: "There are two Hebrons, and there always will be." The Demos who would put society in a strait-jacket is an impostor, as Dionysus knows:

> "There *is* a Demos, and you know his name
> By force of easy stealing; yet his face
> Would be one of a melancholy stranger
> To you if he saw yours."

It is this other Demos, the genuine, essential, better nature of humanity as a whole, who speaks in the sonnets called by that name, warning men not to sell their birthright of potential achievement for an advertised "equality" that will turn out to be the same old tyranny, or worse. And there is hope that the warning will be heeded; for Dionysus, surveying American democracy, perceives that

> "Also intelligence is hidden there—
> Much as a tree's unguessed immensities
> Are hidden in a seed"—

even though it is currently overshadowed by "hypocrisy, timidity, and sloth."

A still more inclusive, even if vague, assurance speaks in a letter to Miss Peabody written before the struggle between Dionysus and the false Demos had become so sharply defined in the poet's thought. His correspondent had apparently been inspired by the scenery of Scotland to revive the Romantic contrast between the beauty of nature and the deformity of human nature, and Robinson replies:

I don't think I quite agree with you in your relative estimation of human beings and heather, and I will even go so far as to believe that this same heather will send you home thinking rather more than ever before of the previously despised who are trotting all over the earth and apparently to no great purpose. There is something in them, or they wouldn't keep on trotting so long.[69]

Besides this hope for humanity in general, Robinson has, surprisingly, a special hope for America, though it will hardly coincide

with the idolatry of "America First." Organized patriotism, as has
been seen, he simply despised. (What he would have thought of
"loyalty oaths" may be guessed.) Pride in the magnitude of the
country's natural endowment and physical achievements, which it
is hard for even rational Americans not to feel, passed him by. He
never went outside New England and the New York metropolitan
area. "The rest of the country . . . means nothing to me, and I
wouldn't give ten cents to see it. The Grand Canyon is no doubt
a grand piece of work, but I know just about how it looks." [70]

But despite all this, he had a more imaginative as well as a saner
vision of his country's destiny than the flag wavers and orators and
apostles of muscular Americanism. "I am just beginning fully to
realize," he wrote to Smith in 1896, "that America [is] the hopper
through which the whole civilization of the world is to be ground
—consciously or otherwise. I am not much of an American, either—
in a popular way; but I am glad to feel an inkling as to what the
western continent was made for." [71] The same vision inspires the
lines in Captain Craig in which the Captain tells of a man

> "Who dreamed that he was Æschylus, reborn
> To clutch, combine, compensate, and adjust
> The plunging and unfathomable chorus
> Wherein we catch, like a bacchanale through thunder,
> The chanting of the new Eumenides,
> Implacable, renascent, farcical,
> Triumphant, and American."

"If I was 'interpreting' anything in Captain Craig," Robinson
wrote to Charles Eliot Norton, "it was America, I should say,
rather than life. I do not mean to leave a final impression of anything more than hope, more or less obfuscated, may be, but still
good-natured and real." [72] He himself does not share the Æschylean
dream; yet he does not dismiss it, either, but leaves it in the distance, resplendent and not impossible, while he looks with good-
natured hope upon the nearer scene. Even partisan politics and
public hysteria in times of crisis did not unduly depress him.
"America is proving its crudeness and craziness just now," he told
Smith in 1898, "but things will right themselves—even in Congress
and the White House." [73] It was not in the nature of things that

quite this measure of confidence should long survive; yet thirty-six years later, with Hitler on the rise, and the "wave of the future" beginning to agitate some erstwhile believers in democracy, he declared in much the same spirit: "There is a lot of untried resource and vitality in this country that will require a lot of smothering before we hear its death-squeak." [74]

In verse, again, *The White Lights* implies a hope for America that includes far more than a dramatic renaissance. And that this hope was not wholly destroyed by the First World War is shown by the powerful vision in *The Old King's New Jester*:

> Farther away than feet shall ever travel
> Are the vague towers of our unbuilded State;
> But there are mightier things than we to lead us,
> That will not let us wait.

What underlies this sort of optimism about America is his old conception of life as "a spiritual exercise," for the individual and for humanity. On the one hand, "the world is a hell of a place"; on the other, "the universe is a great thing." To accept life without surrendering to it; to permit no glamorous illusions about the past and to put one's faith in no "moonshine millennium" [75] of the future; to confront the picture, painted in one of the *Octaves*, of "The onslaught that awaits this idiot world/ Where blood pays blood for nothing," without flinching and without giving up the quiet hope that "something better will come sometime . . . in spite of human stupidity" [76]—this is what human beings must learn to do; it is apparently what they are here for. From such a discipline, America with its youthful energy and courage has much to hope.

And if our generation is "going forward into darkness" faster and farther than we would wish, the darkness will not last forever.

> "Today the devil is more than God. Tomorrow
> He will be more, and more. Out of it all
> He'll come with crutches, and not the devil he was."

This must be Robinson's view, for it is Zoë who is speaking, and we have his own word that "Zoë is knowledge." She is "the child of King Jasper, who is ignorance"; "without ignorance, there can be no knowledge." [77] Jasper's kingdom—the world that we have known

—goes down in ruins, but it is not wasted. "A world has died," the voice of Lancelot's vision tells him, "For you that a world may live." From past failure men will learn to build on a firmer foundation. And if the new structure falls—as it must—knowledge will still survive, and those who rebuild will again know a little more than their predecessors. Thus we see why Zoë must always "go alone." Knowledge is never absolutely possessed by man; but neither is it ever destroyed.

A last word on Robinson's last poem is that Zoë is clearly, in the poet's intention, not only knowledge but also beauty and love. Perhaps the main reason why she fails to convince us of her human-ness is not merely that she is a symbol but that she symbolizes so much—everything, in fact, that justifies and ennobles human life. She embodies the synthesis that poets have always dreamed of, in which reason, affection, and the sense of beauty are combined, and in which man may achieve complete self-realization, casting out the devils of ignorance, hatred, and disintegration which are always finding a new but always a temporary incarnation, as in young Hebron. In such a synthesis there is no place for "self," with its ser-vile attendants of fear, envy, and greed. From such a synthesis will emerge an all-inclusive community of free spirits, joined in the ful-fillment of a purpose that finite human beings, without being able to put it into words, can know and trust and help to realize.

This realization will of course never be complete in the world of Time; yet it will never be even partially achieved in any other. Time and matter present us with both an illusion and an opportu-nity; in short, with a spiritual kindergarten where we are to learn our lessons as well as we can, however painful the process, trusting thereby to prepare ourselves (to change the metaphor) for the next "scene in the big show." [78] If sometimes we are tempted to despair, there is a Word to hearten us and a Light to guide us, and we have, if we will, the power to understand and the strength to go forward.

Such is Robinson's vision, first and last. What he says in one of the *Octaves* is what he continued to affirm throughout his life.

> Forebodings are the fiends of Recreance;
> The master of the moment, the clean seer

Of ages, too securely scans what is,
Ever to be appalled at what is not;
He sees beyond the groaning borough lines
Of Hell, God's highways gleaming, and he knows
That Love's complete communion is the end
Of anguish to the liberated man.

Notes

In the first reference to a work, all the essential bibliographical data are given. In subsequent references the work is identified simply by the author's name or, in a few instances, by the title, either abbreviated or in full. When there is so long an interval between references that the reader may have forgotten the original one, the location of that original is indicated. For example, in Note 2, Chapter III, the notation "Kilmer [I, 15]" tells the reader that full information about the work is given in Note 15, Chapter I.

foreword

[1] William Stanley Braithwaite, "America's Foremost Poet," Boston *Evening Transcript*, May 28, 1913, p. 21.

[2] *Selected Letters of Edwin Arlington Robinson*, ed. Ridgely Torrence (New York, Macmillan, 1940), p. 112. (This volume will be referred to hereafter as *Letters*.)

[3] Yvor Winters, *Edwin Arlington Robinson* (Norfolk, Conn., New Directions, 1946), p. 48.

[4] Emery Neff, *Edwin Arlington Robinson* (New York, Sloane Associates, 1948), p. 259.

chapter i

[1] Quoted by Hermann Hagedorn, *Edwin Arlington Robinson* (New York, Macmillan, 1938), p. 89.

[2] He wrote to his friend Craven Langstroth Betts, after Theodore Roosevelt had appointed him to a position in the New York Customs House: "Sometimes I think the funniest thing in my whole life, and pretty much all of it is funny, is my staying alive since 1903—I mean since 1902" (Neff, p. 141).

[3] Nancy Evans, "Edwin Arlington Robinson," *Bookman*, LXXXV, 676 (Nov., 1932).

[4] *Letters*, p. 9.

[5] Hagedorn, p. 118.

[6] *Untriangulated Stars: Letters of Edwin Arlington Robinson to Harry de Forest Smith, 1890–1905*, ed. Denham Sutcliffe (Harvard University Press, 1947), p. 297.

[7] Hagedorn, p. 311. He also said late in life to another friend: "It's all I could have done, write poetry. I can't do anything else; I never could. And I have to write the kind of stuff I do write" (Esther Willard Bates, *Edwin Arlington Robinson and His Manuscripts* [Waterville, Me., Colby College Library, 1944], p. 32).

[8] Hagedorn, p. 215.

[9] For instance, *Shiras*, which he at first thought one of "the best things in the book" (*Letters*, p. 48) that was to have as its title poem *Captain Craig*, was discarded before publication. It was with such experiences in mind that Robinson remarked of another poem, "Personally I should call the woman and wife affair the best I have ever done or am likely to do, but next year I may throw it away" (*ibid.*, p. 50). (He did not, however.) And years later he wrote to Louis Ledoux with reference to his current work: "Some of it seems rather good, but I never know until I have pondered over it, and pronounced it rotten and then changed my mind" (unpublished letter, dated July 22, 1913, in Houghton Library). In this connection, Mr. Neff seems to say (p. 87) that *The Night Before* was not included in *The Children of the Night*, whereas it was kept until the *Collected Poems* of 1921. Since Robinson's early volumes are extremely rare, the following bibliographical note may be helpful. *The Children of the Night* reprints all but two—*For Calderon*, a melodramatic poem in the manner of Browning, and the satirical *A Poem for Max Nordau*—of the pieces in *The Torrent and The Night Before*. It includes the following additional poems: *Two Men, Richard Cory, Calvary, The Story of the Ashes and the Flame, Amaryllis, The Pity of the Leaves, Cliff Klingenhagen, Charles Carville's Eyes, Fleming Helphenstine, Reuben Bright, The Tavern, Octaves* (I–XXV), *Two Octaves, Two Quatrains, Romance, L'Envoi*. The following poems in *The Children of the Night* were omitted from *Collected Poems: The Children of the Night, The Night Before, The Ballade of Dead Friends, Ballade of the White Ship, For a Book by Thomas Hardy, For Some Poems by Matthew Arnold, Walt Whitman, Kosmos, The Miracle, The World, Romance, Two Octaves*, and two of the *Octaves* (I and III). (It is worth noting that all but the last three items are from the first volume. Even in a year Robinson's taste had matured greatly.) In addition, *Boston* was reduced from a sonnet to its present 8-line form.

[10] *Letters*, p. 54.

[11] *Ibid.*, p. 172.

[12] Unpublished letter to Mrs. Lionel Marks (Josephine Preston Peabody), dated Nov. 17, 1919, in Houghton Library.

[13] Karl Schriftgiesser, "An American Poet Speaks His Mind," Boston *Evening Transcript*, Nov. 4, 1933, Book Section, p. 1. Robinson continued: "I write these long poems of mine because they come to me and have to be written." The same was true, he declared, of such "young poems" as *John Evereldown* and *Luke Havergal*, "written when he was twenty-three. 'I don't know where they came from. They just came, out of the air'" (p. 2). Many additional quotations showing Robinson's belief in "inspiration" are assembled by Edwin S. Fussell, *The Early Poetry of Edwin Arlington Robinson* (unpublished doctoral dissertation, Harvard University, 1949), pp. 312–317. Mr. Fussell, whose thorough and penetrating study I did not discover until my own work was largely completed,

arrives at a number of the same conclusions that I have stated in the present chapter.

[14] *Letters*, p. 103.

[15] Robinson told Joyce Kilmer that poetry has two attributes: it is "undefinable" and it is "eventually unmistakable" (*Literature in the Making* [New York, Harper, 1917], p. 266). He had previously said the same thing to Braithwaite.

[16] *Letters*, p. 63.

[17] *Untriangulated Stars*, p. 1

[18] *Ibid.*, p. 236.

[19] *Letters*, p. 103.

[20] Edwin Arlington Robinson, "The First Seven Years," *Colophon*, Dec., 1930 (71st page—pages bear no numbers). This passage is quoted by Hagedorn, pp. 31–32, with "signification" for "significance" in the first sentence (an unusual error, since Mr. Hagedorn's transcriptions are almost always accurate).

[21] In the last seven years of his life, Robinson published a volume a year, containing on the average about 2,200 lines each. Why he wrote so much is not entirely clear. Mr. Hagedorn suggests as a motive his ineradicable fear of renewed financial dependence, and quotes a comment made to a friend during his last illness (p. 376). But on almost every other occasion Robinson described these poems as resulting from an inner compulsion. He said this not only to Esther Bates and Karl Schriftgiesser (see above, Notes 7 and 13), but to Rollo Walter Brown and Mrs. Laura E. Richards; and in unpublished letters to Betts he repeats it with reference to practically every one of the long poems. Often, at the same time, he expresses a preference for writing shorter pieces and regrets his inability to do so. Miss Bates records: "Once, during his later years, he said sadly, 'People ask me why I do not do the short poems any more. I can't. They don't come any more'" (p. 22). And he wrote to Betts in 1925: "I came down here with every intention of writing some short things for a new book, but our old friend Tristram, whom I have been fighting off for some five years, got me finally by the throat and refused to let go. . . . When he is disposed of—if he doesn't dispose of me—I hope to give the rest of my life to shorter pieces" (letter dated June 10, 1925, in Houghton Library; first sentence quoted by Hagedorn, p. 340).

[22] *Letters*, p. 98.

[23] *Ibid.*, p. 147.

[24] Bates, p. 20.

[25] For example, *Another Dark Lady*, written in "twenty minutes as a joke" (*Letters*, p. 103), and *The Children of the Night*, of which he said, "I was painting the front fence, when the thing came so fast that I had to go into the house and write it down" (Hagedorn, p. 101). Of this piece he later came to have a low opinion, explaining that he had omitted it from *Collected Poems* "because it seemed to me a rather naïve and juvenile sort of metrical exercise, and because I said the same thing again in the latter part of The Man Against the Sky" (unpublished letter, dated Jan. 17, 1922, in Houghton Library). Whether or not this judgment is too severe, there is one poem of similar origin that has remained among his most famous and highly praised. This is *Flammonde*, which came to him one night when he "was sitting in a movie theatre: 'Suddenly I saw Flammonde and I could hear the poem quite clearly. All the lines were there and I only had to write them down'" (Evans, p. 677).

In writing the long poems, he judged that what came most easily and rapidly was best. To Rollo Walter Brown he talked "about the inevitable good stretches that got themselves down on paper without much trouble. 'And they usually require less tinkering, too. The big job is bringing the rest up to the level of those good spots. It can't be done, of course" (*Next Door to a Poet* [New York, Appleton-Century, 1937], p. 73). He told the same friend that his greatest quantitative achievement in one day was 110 lines in the latter part of *Tristram* (*ibid.*, p. 74); but this was exceptional.

In fact, his deliberation and scrupulousness became a legend at Peterborough. One story told of him was that a friend, noting his increasingly wan and haggard appearance, inquired if he were ill; to which Robinson replied: "For two weeks I've gone to my studio every morning after breakfast, and stayed there till five o'clock. For two weeks I've searched for one word—and I haven't found it yet" (Frederika Beatty, "Edward Arlington Robinson As I Knew Him," *South Atlantic Quarterly*, XLIII, 379 [Oct., 1944]). Another tale told by Miss Beatty, which I have heard in the following more elaborate version, concerns two young colonists who one evening were speaking complacently of their own extensive creation during the day, while Robinson listened with customary inexpressiveness, until one of them inquired, "And what did *you* do today, Mr. Robinson?" "This morning," answered the poet, "I took the hyphen out of 'hell-hound'; and this afternoon I put it back."

Probably the real reason why Robinson produced so much poetry during the last twenty years of his life is simply that he worked so hard at it. He enjoyed writing poetry; he had no family to distract him; he had no other work; he had no hobby (unless it were music); he did not travel. For four months or more every summer he worked eight hours a day writing poetry. (Until about 1921 or 1922 he also worked during the winter; thereafter he spent the winter revising and reading proof.) This is all the explanation that is needed. His inspiration may have weakened; his craftsman's conscience did not.

²⁶ *Letters*, p. 102.
²⁷ *Ibid.*, p. 79.
²⁸ *Ibid.*, p. 40.
²⁹ *Ibid.*, pp. 93–94.
³⁰ *Ibid.*, p. 95.
³¹ Evans, p. 679.
³² *Ibid.*, p. 676.
³³ *Letters*, pp. 95–96.
³⁴ *Ibid.*, p. 90.
³⁵ *Ibid.*, p. 81.
³⁶ *Ibid.*, p. 82.
³⁷ Hagedorn, p. 285. Robinson made the same statement to Karl Schriftgiesser in 1932: "Sociology—whatever the word means—usually kills poetry, art of any kind. All propaganda that is permissible in art has got to be pretty thoroughly disguised" (p. 1).
³⁸ Braithwaite, quoted by Hagedorn, with some commas added, p. 286. The implications of the last part of this statement will be discussed in a later chapter. The statement can become confusing if we try to analyze it too minutely; but what Robinson seems to be saying, in general, is that human beings are basically much alike, and that most of the differences between them, upon which society places so much stress, are due merely to accident.
³⁹ *Hagedorn*, p. 198.
⁴⁰ *Letters*, p. 121.

[41] *Untriangulated Stars*, p. 247.

[42] *Letters*, p. 123. Poets far more pessimistic than Robinson have offered a similar justification of their work; for instance, James Thomson in the "Proem" to *The City of Dreadful Night*, and A. E. Housman in the last two poems of *A Shropshire Lad* and in the introductory verses of *More Poems*. The reason is, of course, that a sense of unity with his fellows is among the things that make a man a poet; and one is tempted to add that no man can be a poet of importance who does not have it.

[43] *Ibid.*, p. 92.

[44] Robinson wrote to Mrs. Richards concerning this poem, "I'm sorry that you find destruction in it, for I was aiming at just the other thing" (unpublished letter, dated Sept. 30, 1924, in Houghton Library).

[45] The *method* in these last two poems is obviously—to some readers, it may be, annoyingly or discouragingly—indirect; but it is equally obvious that a definite "message" is intended, whatever obstacles are placed in the way of our getting at it.

[46] Bates, p. 9. Mr. Seymour Betsky, in an unpublished doctoral dissertation entitled *Some Aspects of the Philosophy of Edwin Arlington Robinson: Self-knowledge, Self-acceptance, and Conscience* (Harvard University, 1942), shows how much stress Robinson places on the importance of "self-knowledge."

chapter ii

[1] Brown (I, 25), p. 19.

[2] Hagedorn, p. 101.

[3] *Letters*, p. 67, where "am" is erroneously printed for "was" in the first sentence. This volume has many misreadings, some of them important, which even Robinson's handwriting cannot excuse.

[4] Hagedorn, p. 178.

[5] *Letters*, p. 158.

[6] Hagedorn, p. 298.

[7] *Letters*, p. 105.

[8] Hagedorn, p. 325.

[9] *Ibid.*, p. 297.

[10] Daniel Gregory Mason, *Music in My Time* (New York, Macmillan, 1938), p. 125.

[11] Hagedorn, p. 196.

[12] *Ibid.*, p. 198.

[13] *Letters*, p. 161. This apparently refers to Amy Lowell's identification of "The House" as the Gardiner mansion in Robinson's home town. Mr. Neff, similarly specific, finds in the poem "a contemporary local tragedy—the forsaking of the East for the broader lands and wider opportunities of the West" (p. 53). But, as the same critic points out, Robinson was not at that time much interested in social problems, at least as themes for poems. The poet's own comment, beyond which there is no reason to go, is simply that it "is a little mystical perhaps and is an attempt to show the poetry of the commonplace" (*Untriangulated Stars*, p. 132).

[14] *Letters*, p. 103.

[15] *Ibid.*, p. 102.

[16] Hagedorn, p. 169.

[17] *Ibid.*

[18] *Letters,* p. 111.

[19] Bates (I, 7), p. 28.

[20] Theodore Maynard, *Our Best Poets* (New York, Holt, 1922), p. 158.

[21] Kilmer (I, 15), p. 269.

[22] *Untriangulated Stars,* pp. 166–167.

[23] Mr. Winters, who declares of *Flammonde* that "the substance as a whole and phrase by phrase is repulsively sentimental," excoriates particularly the third and fourth lines of this stanza as "reminiscent of the worst sentimentalism of the nineties" (p. 51). Amy Lowell, however, who finds the style "straight, severe, and quiet . . . also admirable," comments that " 'a long-faded scarlet fringe' is not only imaginative, it has something of Flammonde's own forgiving tenderness" (*Tendencies in Modern American Poetry* [New York, Macmillan, 1917], pp. 59–60). In general, *Flammonde* has received much more critical praise than censure. My own feeling is that some passages (including the one that Mr. Winters dislikes the most) show Robinson at his best, while others do not rise much above mediocrity.

[24] Critics are almost unanimous in praising *Eros Turannos,* but it seems to me that some of them are confused about the story that it tells. According to Professor Cestre, "An ill-mated woman, full of resentment for the missed happiness, reflects that it will be a lesser evil for her to nurse the feeble gleam of affection she still feels than moodily to break off the marriage tie" (*An Introduction to Edwin Arlington Robinson* [New York, Macmillan, 1930], p. 14). And Mr. Neff seems to agree with him: "A woman . . . holds to her Judas husband out of pride and out of fear of lonely old age. The stanza imagining her winters shut with him in their house in a small sea-coast town is big with tension" (p. 181); and he then quotes:

> And home, where passion lived and died,
> Becomes a place where she can hide,
> While all the town . . .

It has always seemed to me, however, that the story is brought to a climax by the husband's desertion of the wife. Stanza 3 suggests that he has been a footloose character whom "tradition" (and the flattering passion shown for him by an intelligent, cultured, and presumably wealthy woman) "beguiles" into accepting marriage and respectability, but who, after the novelty has worn off, becomes bored and moves on. Furthermore, only some such dramatic happening would make the town "vibrate" with excited gossip; and "hide" suggests (to me) a refuge where she can be *alone.* Besides, the wife neither "reflects" nor "holds to" anything; she is simply "driven," "blind" and helpless, to accept what "Love the King" decrees. The critics have been misled, I think, by two lines in the second stanza:

> And Love, that will not let him be
> The Judas that she found him,

not observing that this is the situation *before* the marriage.

[25] Robinson, according to Esther Bates, always *did* have a dictionary on his desk, "which he read literally and advised me to read" (pp. 29–30). Beside it was a Bible.

[26] The list includes *Lazarus, The Three Taverns, Sisera, Young Gideon,*

Nicodemus, and *The Prodigal Son*, besides *Calvary* and *A Christmas Sonnet*, two meditations on the Crucifixion.

[27] Belshazzar is referred to in *Sonnet* ("When we can all so excellently give") in *The Children of the Night*.

[28] The same words of Job's wife are referred to in *Avon's Harvest*.

[29] Robinson's ties with the literature of Greece and Rome are well summarized by Henry R. Fairclough, *The Classics and Our Twentieth Century Poets* (Stanford University Press, 1927). It is also treated, along with the contribution made by the Bible and by American, British, and Continental literature, by Mr. Fussell (I, 13), Chap. II. This is a thorough and levelheaded treatment of Robinson's literary backgrounds, and ought to be published. Mr. Fussell notes a gradual decrease in classical allusions after the *Captain Craig* volume, and a corresponding increase in biblical allusions, until "the last three long poems," in which "there is a falling off of allusions of all kinds" (p. 287). This is especially true of *Amaranth* and *King Jasper*, and it fits in with what is said later in this study (p. 82) of the greater simplicity of style in these poems. As for Robinson's imagery, no systematic study has yet been made, and perhaps none is needed. The counting and classifying of figures of speech, despite its current vogue, seems to me a singularly unrewarding approach to poetry.

[30] Concerning the general interpretation, see below, Note 43. "Having died," I think, is not to be taken literally, but figuratively, as expressing the agony involved in escaping from the "Demon" of alcoholism (to which Robinson was no stranger). In the play *Van Zorn*, Lucas, after giving up drinking, speaks of having been "born again." A passage in Hagedorn's biography is also relevant: "A number of Robinson's friends recognized that he was destroying himself, and beset Burnham to exercise a deterring influence. Burnham, serene and patient, refused. 'I know Robinson,' he would say. 'When the time comes, he will see the necessity and do the right thing' " (p. 206).

[31] See below, Note 38.

[32] Mr. Hagedorn says that the poem was written in memory of his brother Herman (p. 249).

[33] According to Mr. Winters, who declares this sonnet to be "among the greatest" of Robinson's poems, the sailor "is made a symbol of the immeasurable antiquity of the sea and of its ruins." This seems to me correct as far as it goes. But he then adds: "The poem is wholly admirable, but the skill with which the sailor's illegitimate birth, mentioned, as it is, at the very end, is made to imply the amoral and archaic nature of the sea, is something which can scarcely be too long pondered or too greatly admired" (p. 39). Here, I think, most readers will feel that the critic has (in the vernacular, which is singularly appropriate) gone off the deep end.

[34] This judgment apparently runs counter to most critical opinion, for Ben Ray Redman denounces *Her Eyes* as "nearly as bad as it could be" (*Edwin Arlington Robinson* [New York, McBride, 1926], p. 11); and Mr. Fussell, equally severe, calls it imitative of Browning and Swinburne, speaks of the "maudlin paradox" of the two lines quoted near the end of Section 4 of this chapter ("With a gleam of heaven," etc.), and wonders why Robinson kept it in his *Collected Poems* (pp. 218, 482). I can only report that I see no significant influence of Browning or Swinburne (although it seems a little reminiscent of Kipling's *The Light That Failed*), that I like the poem as a whole, and that I especially like the two lines which Mr. Fussell condemns.

[35] Such is Amy Lowell's interpretation: the piece is a fragment, she says, "not of a poem, but of a man's life" (p. 62). Mr. Neff (p. 179) and others speak of Briony's "neurosis," but this rather evades than faces the issue.

[36] Hagedorn, p. 218.

[37] Letters, p. 30.

[38] Untriangulated Stars, p. 238. Mr. Fussell, whose comments always deserve respect, has a different interpretation. "The dark ('western gate,' 'crimson vines,' 'western glooms,' 'twilight') is to be taken as the confrontation and stoic acceptance of tragic experience . . . there is only one way ('acceptance') to 'her' ('her' on this level apparently relates to the more customary symbol of the 'light')" (pp. 473–474). But this seems to me quite out of keeping with the sound, the rhythm, and the imagery, all of which are suggestive of death, as well as with Robinson's use of the adjective "uncomfortable" and noun "degeneration." For another possibility, see below, Chap. III, Note 16.

[39] Letters, p. 160. See also pp. 112–113.

[40] Ibid., pp. 164–165.

[41] Ibid., p. 172.

[42] Hagedorn, p. 369.

[43] Perhaps at this point a warning is in order against reading Robinson's dramatic poems as accounts of actual persons and events. Robinson himself says, "I do not recall anything of mine that is a direct transcription of experience" (Letters, p. 103); and he never modifies this statement except in regard to Captain Craig (ibid., p. 151, and elsewhere) and John Evereldown (ibid., pp. 50–51). Even in regard to the first and most personal of his books, he warns Smith that the " 'I' is not always 'me' " (Untriangulated Stars, p. 269).

Of course, everything that a poet writes is in some sense an *indirect* transcription of experience; and no doubt many of Robinson's poems were *suggested* by particular personal experiences, as he is "half inclined to think" that Captain Craig was "suggested" by the ostentation of a certain funeral parade in Gardiner (ibid., p. 306). What the incautious reader may forget in meeting, for example, Mr. Hagedorn's comments that the "Demon" in The Dark House is alcohol (p. 274), that in Calverly's he "enshrined the romance of the fellowship of his early years in New York with Burnham and Betts and Coan and Louis," and that "he 'spoofed' himself in 'Miniver Cheevy' " (p. 238), is that these statements, although they are very likely true and certainly have human interest, are essentially irrelevant to the understanding and enjoyment of the poems as poems. They may even, for literal-minded persons, obscure the general human significance which is all that is finally important. Even in Captain Craig it does not really matter that the central figure had a living model.

I should like, however, in connection with Captain Craig, to establish one personal identification which will correct the misleading statement by Mr. Neff that in this poem, as part of his attack on various aspects of American culture, Robinson "had taken the offensive to pillory the poetaster Killigrew" (p. 154). To me the portrait of Killigrew has always seemed an affectionate one; and as a matter of fact Killigrew is drawn from the man whom of all his friends Robinson perhaps cherished most tenderly and tenaciously, Seth Ellis Pope. In a letter to Miss Peabody, speaking of a scene in which Killigrew appears, he says, "That particular part of Killigrew [i.e., the part for which Pope furnished the model] is now in the Library School at Albany," where Pope *was*, as we learn from a later letter (Letters, pp. 32, 40). This identification is also suggested by Mrs. Laura E. Richards (E. A. R. [Harvard University Press, 1936], pp. 31-33); and it is also implied in a passage of *Captain Craig* that was omitted from *Collected Poems*, where the narrator, referring to his farewell to Killigrew on leaving the city, speaks of "the spirit of the friend who cared the most." For Robinson's relations with Pope, see Hagedorn, pp. 322-323.

Furthermore, Killigrew's *Ballad of Ladies* is not, as is sometimes said, a mere parody. I have always felt that it had real beauty of a sort; and a letter to Miss Peabody suggests that Robinson felt the same way: "I wish you would tell me just what you think of Killigrew's *Ballad of Ladies*. I made it some ten years ago as an experiment in mechanism and threw it away; but it has stayed with me somehow and has forced itself into its present position. I don't know whether it will go or not" (unpublished letter, dated Oct. 29, 1900, in Houghton Library).

It is possible that Morgan, with his fiddle, and the "learned Plunkett" may likewise be identified to some extent with the other two members of a group of friends in Gardiner known as "the Quadruped": Arthur Blair (who played the violin) and Linville Robbins (the "scientist").

[44] Cestre, p. 14.
[45] Hagedorn, p. 360.
[46] *Ibid.*, p. 293.
[47] Cestre, pp. 13-14.
[48] Mabel Dodge Luhan, *Movers and Shakers* (New York, Harcourt, Brace, 1936), p. 139.
[49] *Letters*, p. 104. Italics added.
[50] Somewhat similar comments have been made by Mark Van Doren, *Edwin Arlington Robinson* (Garden City, N.Y., The Literary Guild, 1927), p. 37; and by Mr. Fussell, p. 586.
[51] Robinson's own comment is that "Flammonde is the man who sees but cannot do for himself, 'others he saved,' etc." (*Letters*, p. 104).
[52] *Van Zorn* (New York, Macmillan, 1914), p. 54.

chapter iii

[1] Robinson was an early and permanent admirer of Hardy's novels (mainly, as Mr. Fussell shows, for their artistry and not their philosophy), although his later praise is not unqualified. As to poetry, Robinson's own verse began to appear before Hardy's, and there seems little question of any "influence." Henry James's earlier works he read with pleasure, but the last novels—to which his own long poems have sometimes been compared—were apparently too demanding. Of Mark Twain he says relatively little, but a comment to Miss Peabody may be recorded: "Did I ask you in my last letter if you had read Huckleberry Finn? If you have not, get it at once—this is a command, not a request—and absorb it" (unpublished letter, dated Jan. 30, 1901, in Houghton Library).

[2] Robinson commented in 1916: "Within his limits, I believe that A. E. Housman is the most authentic poet now writing in England. But, of course, his limits are very sharply drawn" (Kilmer [I, 15], p. 270). As for Yeats, no comment on his poetry by Robinson (so far as I know) is on record.

[3] Brown (I, 25), p. 66. This is a rare instance of overstatement by Robinson. *The Torrent and The Night Before* was at least mentioned in *Poet-lore*, the *Bookman*, the *Outlook*, the *Dial*, the *Sewanee Review*, and several less well known publications; and the comments were generally not unfavorable. *The*

Children of the Night and *Captain Craig*, it is true, had a decidedly lukewarm reception, but were not entirely ignored. (See Hagedorn, pp. 139–140, 190–191; also Charles Beecher Hogan, *A Bibliography of Edwin Arlington Robinson* [Yale University Press, 1936], pp. 136–138.) Editors more than reviewers must bear the blame for Robinson's remaining so long unknown. As Mr. Neff points out, "Between 1896 and 1905 Robinson's verse appeared in no commercial periodical" (p. 129).

⁴ "The notion of 'sweating blood' in the beginning is all right to me, but I suppose I shall have to take it out in order to keep my friends" (unpublished letter to Miss Peabody dated June 4 [1901?], in Houghton Library).

⁵ Hagedorn, p. 190.

⁶ Allen Tate says that "*Luke Havergal*, a poem in which the hard images glow with a fierce intensity of light, is one of the great lyrics of modern times" (*Reactionary Essays* [New York, Scribner's, 1936], p. 197).

⁷ Professor Cestre (II, 24) accurately describes these two kinds of writing as Robinson's "stripped language" and his "sumptuous language" (p. 24). Other critics have described the first kind as "dry," "bare," "abstract"—implying by the last term the relative absence of imagery, the use of direct factual statement, by which many of his poems are marked. Often the two styles occur in different parts of the same poem, even a short one like *Mr. Flood's Party*, where "sumptuous language" dominates the second stanza and "stripped language" the last. And often, of course, the two merge, as perhaps in *Richard Cory*.

⁸ *Letters*, p. 49.

⁹ *Untriangulated Stars*, p. 214.

¹⁰ *Ibid.*, p. 108.

¹¹ Hagedorn, pp. 165–166.

¹² Evans (I, 3), p. 676.

¹³ *Letters*, p. 82.

¹⁴ Robinson seems to have had something of Dickens's inventiveness in names, though one feels that he worked harder to find them. Even in the Arthurian poems he exercised what little choice was possible, as we see from a letter to Mrs. Richards (who apparently preferred "Iseult" for Tristram's beloved), in which he explains his "allegiance to Isolt, which for some reason is darker; and I have always seen a dark-haired Isolt . . . Iseult sounds yellow, and as if it might scratch. Something like a tortoise-shell cat" (unpublished letter, dated July 24, 1926, in Houghton Library).

¹⁵ Robert Frost, who ought to be a good judge, exclaims: "What imagination for speech in 'John Gorham'! He is at his height between quotation marks" ("Introduction" to *King Jasper* [New York, Macmillan, 1935], p. xiii). But this imagination is not the kind that distinguishes the speakers from each other. In regard to the people in the long narratives, Alfred Kreymborg remarks with some reason: "The blank verse they talk is a perfect instrument in the hands of the poet, but one longs to put it in the mouths of the characters" (*Our Singing Strength* [New York, Coward-McCann, 1929], p. 313). Of course, one may ask how many writers of drama and fiction, especially in verse, *do* possess the power to differentiate their characters through the quality of their speech—vocabulary, imagery, tempo, and stress. To me, for instance, different characters in a play by Shakespeare often *sound* exactly alike when speaking in blank verse. As for prose drama, it is notorious (Mr. Kreymborg makes the comparison) that Shaw's plays almost invariably have at least one character who talks exactly like Shaw—and sometimes *all* the characters seem to! Returning

to Robinson, I think he *does* do in his plays, to some extent, what he fails to do, in his verse. Van Zorn, for instance, speaks with weight and deliberation, as befits the instrument of destiny; whereas Larry Scammon, in *The Porcupine*, speaks with the quickness and buoyancy of one who has yet to learn that he is not the master of circumstances and of other people's wills.

[16] These poems may show the influence of the French Symbolists, whose aim (as I understand it) was to increase the proportion, in a poem's total effect, of the direct, irrational, emotive element at the expense of the proportion derived from the "meaning"; that is, to bring poetry closer to music. Robinson knew their work, at least to some extent, as is shown by his sonnet to Verlaine and by two references to Villiers de l'Isle-Adam in the letters to Smith. It is possible that *Luke Havergal* is primarily a Symbolist poem, "without a great deal of specific meaning" (Richard Crowder, *Explicator*, VII, 15 [Nov., 1948]); but this is a conclusion that I hesitate to accept. Of course, we should always remember that, as Mr. Crowder implies, we do not have to make an "either-or" choice.

[17] On this point, see above, Chap. I, Note 21.

[18] Robinson's favorite rhyme scheme for the sestet, among the fifteen combinations that occur in *Collected Poems*, is *c d e c d e*. This occurs twenty-six times.

[19] Contrasting treatments of similar themes can also be found in *The Garden* and *The Garden of the Nations*, and in *Sonnet* ("Oh for a poet") and *Many Are Called*.

[20] These, it is interesting to discover, are nearly the same in number as his sonnets. Counting each of the eleven *Variations on Greek Themes* as one, and counting as one the three rhymed stanzas in *The March of the Cameron Men*, there are ninety-five rhymed pieces in *Collected Poems*.

[21] Some critics have made much of Robinson's debt to W. M. Praed, which the late Professor Hoyt H. Hudson attempted to establish in "Robinson and Praed," *Poetry*, LXI, 612–620 (Feb., 1943). The theory is based entirely on internal evidence, consisting of: (1) similarity of tone and meter between Praed's *Quince* and *The Vicar* and Robinson's *Old King Cole*, and (2) use of similar themes and names. Praed has a character called Clavering in *The Eve of Battle*; one of his poems states "the main theme of *Miniver Cheevy*"; both "wrote poems entitled *Cassandra*; both wrote tributes to George Crabbe. Robinson wrote a sonnet to Thomas Hood; Praed imitated Hood. Praed wrote of Captain Craven and Reuben Nott; Robinson, of Captain Craig and Reuben Bright." This sounds impressive. But the chief stylistic resemblance is the use of iambic tetrameter lines, with occasional feminine endings and consequent double rhymes, for which Robinson certainly did not need to go to Praed. Praed's Clavering is apparently modeled on Zimri in Dryden's *Absalom and Achitophel* and has nothing in common with Robinson's; and Robinson could as well have got the name from Trollope's novel *The Claverings* or from Thackeray's character Frank Clavering in *Pendennis*. The theme of *Miniver Cheevy* is not rare; nobody has a copyright on the name "Cassandra"; Captain Craig's surname came to Robinson (presumably when he was working in the Harvard office) from "the application of a Divinity School man who gloried in the name of Louis Craig Cornish" (unpublished letter to William Vaughan Moody, dated May 10, 1900, in Houghton Library). People have read and liked Crabbe and Hood without reading Praed. Robinson very likely read Praed and remembered a name or two. (Esther Bates says, "He was amazingly

familiar with English poetry, especially that of the nineteenth century" [p. 30].) But Praed is verbose and sentimental, a careless stylist with a superficial grasp of character; he represents neoclassicism gone to seed. Any contribution to Robinson's achievement is negligible.

²² Miss Louise Dauner, in her *Studies in Edwin Arlington Robinson* (State University of Iowa doctoral dissertation, 1944; this part unpublished), gives a detailed analysis of the effects sought and achieved by the poet in his choice of meters and rhyme schemes. Many of her comments about Robinson's adjustment of form to content—"restraining," "intensifying," or "lightening" the intrinsic tendency of the subject matter—are thoughtful and suggestive. But I cannot accept her view that the six poems just mentioned (whose meter she treats as "pæonic tetrameter"—that is, having a line of four feet, each foot composed of one stressed and three unstressed syllables—and discusses along with the 8-syllable tetrameter that Robinson uses much more frequently) reveal a "consistent personal rhythm" which gives fullest scope to his gift for creating "musical" and "emotional" poetry; whereas pentameter is reserved for verse in which the appeal is more "intellectual," "rational," or "philosophic" (Chap. V, pp. 70–71). The evidence does not seem to me to support this thesis. *Luke Havergal* and *Mr. Flood's Party*, written in pentameter (except for the refrain in the former), are nothing if not musical and emotional; *Cassandra* and *Hillcrest*, written in tetrameter, are among Robinson's most notable "philosophic" pieces. Furthermore, the long lines used in *John Gorham* and the other poems mentioned produce an effect altogether different from that of the 8-syllable line; and, in fact, they vary among themselves so widely that the meter cannot be precisely defined. Finally, in my judgment only *John Gorham* and *Leonora*, in this group, are really distinguished in style. It seems to me impossible to establish a consistent relation between a particular verse form and a particular purpose or subject matter.

²³ Robert Frost, in his "Introduction," tells of his and Ezra Pound's uncontrollable mirth in reading *Miniver Cheevy* together. (However abhorrent Mr. Pound's political aberrations, one ought not to forget that in happier and saner years he was among the first to champion the work of Robinson and Frost.)

²⁴ Mr. Winters says that this poem "describes an old woman" (p. 34); but surely much of the pathos depends on the assumption that the traditional afflictions of old age have come upon her while still relatively young. It is true that she tells her friends that "it is wholly wrong/ Of her to stay alive so long"; and the poet tells the reader that her former rivals "Have lost her laughter for so long / That none would care enough to fear it." But there is certainly irony, either conscious or unconscious, in her words; and the persons mentioned in the second passage would naturally have short memories. Besides, she still has "beauty," which is only "blanched with pain," not age; she remembers "Her power of youth, so *early* taken" (italics added); her friends can still talk without patent absurdity of "roses that are still to blow" beside her path; and if she were really old, there would be no need at the end to speak of a "cage/ From which there will be no more flying." Her life has not been long; but the latter part of it has *seemed* long.

²⁵ This achievement has been noted by Robert Frost, among others, who says, "Robinson could make lyric talk like drama" ("Introduction," p. xiii).

²⁶ Theodore Maynard (II, 20) has made an enlightening distinction between lyric *form*, of which Robinson often shows his mastery, and lyric *quality*, which is rare in his work (p. 161).

[27] See, for example, Hagedorn, pp. 237, 238, 249; and for *The White Lights*, see below, Chap. IV, Note 13.

[28] This poem had been in his mind since 1894. See *Untriangulated Stars*, p. 170.

[29] Mr. Neff stresses Robinson's early reading of Wordsworth's *Ode on Intimations of Immortality*, which "in due time" "would inspire Robinson to a great ode of his own" (p. 60). Despite a vague similarity of theme and form, I find the poems so different in tone, movement, and structure that it would never have occurred to me to compare them, to say nothing of conjecturing that Robinson's poem was "inspired" by Wordsworth's. Robinson wrote to Amy Lowell, on Nov. 26, 1915, of "my latest intimations of mortality" (*Letters*, p. 89); but which side of the argument this supports—if either—I am not sure.

[30] *As a World Would Have It* might be included here, since the trimeter line that ends each stanza, following three lines of blank verse, has a suggestion of classic form; and the arrangement seems to me not ineffective. *The Night Before*, written in unrhymed, somewhat irregular tetrameter verse, unlike anything with which I am familiar, should also be mentioned.

[31] He told Mrs. Marks that the poem was written in two days (unpublished letter, dated Aug. 28, 1918, in Houghton Library).

[32] This poem has been otherwise interpreted. Mr. Fussell (I, 13) feels that in both it and *The Wilderness* the poet emphasizes the pioneers' "desperate loneliness and homesickness" (p. 470); and Miss Dauner says that in it "he indicts a world" for its greed ("Vox Clamantis: Edwin Arlington Robinson As a Critic of American Democracy," *New England Quarterly*, XV, 408 [Sept., 1942]).

[33] Hagedorn, p. 237.

[34] An interesting blank-verse variant occurs at the beginning of each of the six sections of *The Glory of the Nightingales*, where the opening line has an extra unstressed syllable both at the beginning and at the end; and in all but the first and third sections the extra initial syllable is repeated through at least four lines. The following are the opening lines of Section II:

> With a wealth beyond a mortal estimation,
> And not heavy, though it had the weight of doom,
> He had come from other cities there to Sharon,
> Where a woman had been left too long alone.

[35] Ludwig Lewisohn, *The Story of American Literature* (New York, Harper, 1932), p. 558.

[36] In my judgment Robinson's most difficult poem, as far as style is concerned, is *Roman Bartholow*, published in 1923. This does not mean that it does not contain beautiful and moving passages.

chapter iv

[1] The phrasing varies, but the same elements usually occur. The only one missing in the present instance is "foam" or "foaming." See *Collected Poems*, pp. 603, 621, 623, 637, 665, 669, 673.

[2] Several critics find this poem unsatisfying, and Mr. Fussell, with his usual insight, puts his finger on what is probably the main difficulty: that in what purports to be a "realistic, psychological dramatic poem," the book (which can only be "a symbolic suggestion" that the lovers were "destined for each other from the beginning") becomes "nonsense" (p. 534). But perhaps the book is

not so much a symbol that they were destined *for each other* (the face of Annandale's vision is a "lineless, indistinguishable face" that he only later associates with Damaris) as a symbol of life's onward surge, its refusal to be bound by mere conventions, its compulsion on men and women to change or die. (That it was written while Miriam was still alive apparently symbolizes an otherwise unformulated realization that his marriage with her had no possibilities for change or growth.) This is a constant theme in Robinson's poetry, and it is especially strong in the *Captain Craig* volume. I agree that "the book" is obtrusive and confusing; but the poem is in many ways superb, both in style and insight. Robinson's own comment is typical: "I don't know who will read it, but I shall put it out and trust to somebody's finding music and a few ideas in it" (unpublished letter to Miss Peabody, dated June 4 [1901?], in Houghton Library).

³ Other symbolic houses are "The Dark House" and "Cavender's House," both symbolic of imprisoning obsessions; and perhaps the houses of Briony and Tasker Norcross, as well as that to which the wife retreats in *Eros Turannos* ("As if the story of a house / Were told, or ever could be").

⁴ Mr. Neff considers that Bartholow's "cure is incomplete, for he has transferred his habit of idealizing from his wife to Penn-Raven . . . and has not completely broken the bonds of convention" (p. 211). This is plausible, but is nowhere clearly indicated by the poet. The same critic comments that Gabrielle is "one of the most repellently negative and destructive minds in American verse" (p. 214); but I can find nothing in the poem to support so extreme a statement. In fact, she is the one person in the story for whom I am able to summon much sympathy. I also find unconvincing Mr. Neff's argument that in the general treatment of the story, as well as in the style, Robinson owes "a great debt" to Meredith (p. 212).

⁵ Mr. Winters objects violently to the central symbolism of "the door," which he says is "a pure fraud" (p. 115); declaring that there is no "justification on the realistic level for it to exert the extraordinary attraction which it exerts for the characters. It is not, so far as one can discern, a real tomb or ruin; it is apparently an accidental rock formation in New England. To expect people in real life to be drawn as in this poem to commit suicide in such a place is ridiculous" (p. 118). Mr. Neff, with more urbanity, agrees: "the means of his [Matthias's] chastening—the successive suicides of two friends and his wife in the same spot—hovers between symbol and realistic impossibility to a degree that somehow escaped the author's vigilant sense of humor" (p. 235).

These criticisms are as puzzling to me as Robinson's poem appears to be to the critics. Such a rock formation might well exist in the more rugged regions of New England, and would be quite as appropriate a place for suicide as would any "real tomb or ruin." Garth says to Matthias: "Here is a place I like. I live in the dark, / And for a year have done so." Why should he not come back to this familiar place, which is the property of the man whose "success" he both despises and envies, to do what he has long been thinking of doing? By his act, as Timberlake says, he "tore a few farewell holes" in Matthias's complacency; and such no doubt was his intention.

After this, the rest is equally plausible. It is not in the least surprising that Timberlake and Natalie (and Matthias) should each be drawn, on the day following the death of a man who in various ways had meant so much to them, to the place where he had died; nor is it unnatural that Natalie, under the stress of what has happened, should finally surrender to her long-suppressed love for Timberlake. And, with these added associations, it becomes all but inevitable that when she finally decides that death is preferable to life, she should seek it here. (Timberlake, by the way, does *not* commit suicide.)

The symbolism also seems to me natural and satisfactory. The philosophical point of the poem is that death *is* a door, though a "dark" one, to something else (a belief that in all our minds is associated with the tombs of Egyptian kings—hence the "dark *Egyptian* door"); but that life on earth also has a purpose (not the same, in detail, for every person), and that a man may not die until this purpose has been fulfilled.

In all this I see nothing ridiculous or fraudulent. *Matthias at the Door* seems to me to have a better planned and more plausible story, more credible and interesting characters, and a more effective narrative technique than any other of the long poems dealing with love in a modern setting. My only serious objection is to the length of the concluding exposition by Garth's ghost.

⁶ In connection with his early melodramatic monologue *The Night Before*, Robinson wrote to Smith: "The success of the poem will depend wholly upon the success of this intensity [of the murderer's confession], which ought to increase from the start and end with a grand smash" (*Untriangulated Stars*, p. 162). Mr. Winters thinks that *Richard Cory* "builds up deliberately to a very cheap surprise ending" (p. 52); and Mr. Redman (II, 34) considers that it displays a "kind of easy trickery" (p. 37) which makes it not worth reading more than once. Mr. Fussell answers such objections by observing justly that "not surprise but paradox and irony provide the structure of the poem" (p. 477). In general, the critics have shared the popular liking for this piece. Robinson told Karl Schriftgiesser (I, 13): "I am a little tired of hearing of *Richard Cory*"; adding, "I suppose it is because it is concise and clear and has a sharp conclusion that people like it and remember it." His comment perhaps does not so much deprecate the popularity of this poem as hint a wish that others less simple might be equally popular.

⁷ As in many other poems, Robinson did not intend the story to be so obscure as it is. In the first edition, after the attack in Asher's cabin, a knife was found lying with its point at Avon's throat. "I supposed," Robinson wrote to Carl Van Doren, "that the knife would be enough to show that the other fellow was not drowned but chose merely to let Avon think so. Maybe I had better add a few lines to the collected edition to make this entirely clear" (*Three Worlds* [New York, Harper, 1936], p. 161). The most crucial of these additions includes what are now lines 3–6 on p. 571 of *Collected Poems*:

> Through all those evil years before my respite—
> Which now I knew and recognized at last
> As only his more venomous preparation
> For the vile end of a deceiving peace—

These lines make clear that Avon's enemy was physically present in Asher's cabin. But Robinson obscured the situation again by deciding to "take out the material knife and leave the whole thing psychological" (*Letters of E. A. Robinson to Howard G. Schmitt*, ed. Carl J. Weber [Waterville, Me., Colby College Library, 1943], p. 29). He also omitted the lines in which Avon, after finishing his story and before bidding his friend good night, gives the latter the knife and asks him to take it home with him. But the poet left (not inadvertently, since he changed it, but for no reason that I can see) a later reference to the knife in the line "The part that I had taken home with me," which is now meaningless. As for the final episode, Avon's enemy this time was not actually in the room, but outside—Avon having the power, as shown previously in London and at Asher's cabin, of detecting his enemy's presence by (apparently) "extrasensory" means; and this presence by itself is now sufficient to induce a fatal stroke.

David Brown argues that despite the other changes, Robinson's decision to leave out the knife removes the enemy entirely as a physical agent in the last two scenes of the tragedy: "Thus, in the revised version there is no question that the experience of Avon by the Maine lake was a hallucination; or, if there is, the question is irrelevant, since the effect is the same, and the reader is not thrown off the center of interest, which is Avon's mind and not a world of clues and evidences like knives. It now becomes clear that, while Avon *thought* the man had actually returned, the reader need not think so, since there is no external clue to prove that he did" ("A Note on *Avon's Harvest*," *American Literature*, IX, 348 [Nov., 1937]). But this raises a new difficulty, for it leaves us without the slightest hint as to *why* Avon's obsession returns *at this particular time*, after he has apparently escaped from it for good. He has been perfectly certain that the man was drowned in the sinking of the *Titanic*. What makes him change his mind? For further discussion, see Chap. VII, Note 82.

⁸ Winters, p. 133. The critic refers to *The Book of Annandale*, but he dislikes other poems, such as *Cavender's House*, even more.

⁹ See pp. 48–50. Mr. Winters would undoubtedly say that this argument is based on what he calls "the fallacy of imitative form." The example that he gives of this "fallacy" is Arthur's incoherent and all but hysterical speech in *Lancelot*, when he thinks that Guinevere is being burned at the stake; whereas such a state of mind, when dealt with in poetry, should be *suggested* by the speaker's words, but not *exposed*. The portrayal of Napoleon in *An Island* is another (and I think better) example. Extending the application, we meet (and find unsound) the common argument that contemporary art of all kinds must abandon traditional forms in order to represent the disordered state of current society. I am inclined to think that Mr. Winters's notion has some validity but certainly not the absolute validity that he seems to claim for it. What would become of some of the most famous speeches in Shakespeare's tragedies?

¹⁰ Redman, p. 41. He suggests comparison with Conrad; and Henry James also uses the method—as, indeed, many great storytellers have done, though not always with entire success (nor does anyone claim that Robinson is always successful).

¹¹ Although Mr. Fussell finds *Llewellyn* "long and loose and undeniably tedious" (p. 631), I think John Drinkwater is nearer right in calling it "a poem of perfect dramatic proportions" (*The Muse in Council* [Boston, Houghton Mifflin, 1925], p. 260). Adherents of the New Criticism evidently feel that "tension" should be maintained throughout a poem; whereas Robinson, except in his very briefest pieces, likes to relax it at times by adopting an informal and even colloquial tone. This is not carelessness, of course, but an essential quality of his art, reflecting both his firm grasp on "real life" and his perception of the irony that often rules it—the irony, that is, between the drama of individual lives, which seems to those involved to be of unique and overwhelming importance, and the uninterrupted flow of the life of the community. (The "irony" insisted on by the New Critics seems to be artful rather than natural, to be rather a poetic device than a reflection of "reality.")

[12] The story of King Jasper has a number of striking parallels with that of King Arthur as told in *Merlin* and *Lancelot*. There is at least one difference, however. Jasper recognizes his guilt and is prepared for the consequences of it.

[13] Mr. Hagedorn says (p. 242) that the poem celebrates the brilliant Broadway success of William Vaughan Moody's play *The Great Divide* in the fall of 1906. But Mr. Fussell notes (p. 563) that Robinson had described the poem in a letter to Miss Peabody dated July 4, 1906. This letter is in Houghton Library.

[14] *Letters*, p. 104.

[15] There is a parallel here with the theme of A. E. Housman's *Epilogue* ("Terence, this is stupid stuff") in *A Shropshire Lad*.

[16] *Letters*, p. 112.

[17] *Ibid.*, p. 113.

[18] *Ibid.*

[19] *Ibid.*

chapter v

[1] For a brief account of this romantic personage, Alfred H. Louis, see Hagedorn, pp. 132–136; and, for practically all the known facts, Denham Sutcliffe, "The Original of Robinson's Captain Craig," *New England Quarterly*, XVI, 407–431 (Sept., 1943).

[2] Nancy Evans (I, 3) gives the following classification of the failures among Robinson's characters: "Sometimes, like Timberlake in *Matthias at the Door*, they are rich in the gold that is 'not negotiable,' sometimes they fail as Merlin did when he left Camelot for Vivian, sometimes they are afraid, and again, as with Matthias, they are not yet born" (pp. 677–678). It is not clear whether this classification is hers or Robinson's.

[3] For a quotation more or less summing up his character, see p. 87.

[4] Other characters who closely resemble Norcross in being outwardly secure and inwardly cursed are Briony and Avon, although their stories are less clear.

[5] Robinson wrote to Arthur Davison Ficke, "Of course I didn't expect anyone to take the thing very seriously as a reconstruction of Shakespeare, but I hope it makes fairly interesting reading" (unpublished letter, dated Dec. 30, 1915, in Houghton Library).

[6] Robinson described Levi as "just a poor devil, totally miscast, and with not much in his head anyhow" (*Letters*, p. 80).

[7] Mr. Neff says, "Among the failures Robinson counts himself, under the thin disguise of Clavering" (p. 155). I find this interpretation incredible. Equally off the mark, I think, is his comment that Robinson "smiles . . . at the Broadway lightweight in 'Bon Voyage'" (p. 154). But I believe he is correct in speaking of "the imitative mediocrity of Atherton" (p. 154).

[8] *Letters*, p. 104. In July, 1910, the month when *Vickery's Mountain* was published, Robinson wrote from Chocorua, New Hampshire, to a friend in New York: "I have a mountain here entirely of my own—so far as I can make out—and it comforts me in many ways. Also, it convinces me that Vickery's psychology is sound—a point on which one or two have differed" (*Letters*, pp. 66–67. I have corrected, from the original in Houghton Library, the erroneous reading of "comes over" for "convinces.") Many years later a fellow colonist at Peterborough recorded: "When one of the lesser poets told him that she liked to sit and contemplate Monadnock, he answered cryptically, 'Don't look too long'" (Beatty [I, 25], p. 380).

[9] *Letters*, p. 104.

[10] Hagedorn, p. 237.

[11] *Ibid.*, p. 249.

[12] Robinson told Esther Bates, "Sentimentality is far worse than death" (p. 19).

[13] Mrs. Richards (II, 43) says, on the authority of Robinson's niece, that he told his sister-in-law that "in 'Aunt Imogen' it was himself that he was revealing —or concealing, as you will" (p. 59); and Mr. Hagedorn (pp. 143-145) associates it with a particular experience and reads it as a personal confession of pain at realizing that domestic happiness was not to be his. It was written "in the rough" in 1898 and revised in 1900, when he wrote to his friend Mason (II, 10): "I am wearing poetical petticoats and making a regular analysis of an Old Maid" (p. 125). To Miss Peabody he wrote of the poem's main character that "she was inspired somehow . . . by a millpond. Great is association"; and later, "Perhaps the most valuable thing I have is the MS. of the Old Maid, which I value at $1.75" (unpublished letters, dated Oct. 8 and 23, 1900, in Houghton Library). The joking tone of these comments may be intended to conceal the personal significance of the poem; but it seems evident, at least, that the original emotion is being recollected in tranquillity. See also Chap. II, Note 43.

[14] Critics agree, with a rare approach to unanimity, that this is one of Robinson's finest short poems.

[15] All the poems mentioned in this paragraph have been given varying interpretations, but *The Whip* is notorious. Most people agree that the story is about a man pursuing a woman (presumably, though not necessarily, his wife) whom he loves and who is eloping with another man. But exactly what happens has been much disputed. Professor Cestre thinks that all three drown and that the "welt" on the face of the dead man whom the speaker is addressing was *not* from "a physical blow" (p. 52). Mr. Winters says: "The three are in some fashion tipped out from a boat in a river. . . . As the three are about to emerge to safety, the wife turns and strikes her husband across the face; and . . . he chooses to sink rather than save himself and face his tragedy" (p. 46). William Rose Benét pictures the three as approaching the river on horseback, the husband "but a neck behind" (this would also account for the whip); and although Mr. Winters is unconvinced (for the exchange of opinions, see *Saturday Review of Literature*, XXX, Jan. 18, 1947, p. 32, and March 8, 1947, p. 48), this seems to me plausible. The fleeing pair escape "to find/ Their own way to the brink" of *eventual* death; the husband chooses "to plunge and sink" to immediate death. Robinson himself wrote to Carl J. Weber: "I hardly know what to say about 'The Whip,' except that it is supposed to be a literal and not a figurative instrument. In this poem—not to mention a few others—I may have gone a little too far and given the reader too much to carry. If he refuses to carry it, perhaps I have only myself to blame. I am inclined to believe that this particular poem is not altogether satisfactory or very important" (*ibid.*, XXVI, April 17, 1943, p. 54). For a hilarious parody of esoteric interpretations of the poem, by Ben Ray Redman, see *ibid.*, Feb. 20, 1943, pp. 18-19.

[16] *Letters*, p. 50.

[17] The main theme of this sonnet, I think, is not, as has been sometimes said, the "triumph of time" in rendering finally futile all human ambition and effort, but rather the artificiality of all conventional standards of "success"—the fact that (in theological terms) "there is no distinction of persons with God."

[18] Robinson may (not that it matters) have taken a hint, consciously or un-

consciously, from Crabbe's *Arabella*, in which the central figure is a similarly learned female:

> But (though her young companions felt the shock)
> She studied Berkeley, Bacon, Hobbes, and Locke.

Her story, however, is very different from Karen's.

[19] Miss Bates records that Robinson got the idea of this poem from Ellen Key's biography *Rahel Varnhagen*. "But he said he did not take his character from Ellen Key's book, nor did he draw directly from life in any of his poems" (p. 5). The second statement is one that the poet regularly insisted on, although he usually excepted *Captain Craig*.

[20] This interpretation of a rather obscure story is shared by Mr. Neff, who speaks of "a *Scarlet Letter* situation," in which there is an "apparent reversal of Dimmesdale's experience in Hawthorne's novel" (p. 122). Robinson described the poem to Miss Peabody as "about a clergyman who had a hard time, but came out—according to his own ideas, all right." (Here again is the suggestion that *nobody* knows the truth.) Later he wrote to her: "You are the first person . . . who has found anything vague in Sainte-Nitouche. I don't think I agree with you in regard to the unanswered questions, for they seem to me to answer themselves." (The first of these two letters in Houghton Library is undated, the second is dated "June 4." The year is probably 1901.)

[21] This is the interpretation of Mr. Neff, who considers Leonora to be one whom "death saves from an inevitable path of shame," observing that "the tripping of hexameter and the idyllic description of the grave do their best to soften and disguise her somber story" (p. 155); and some other critics agree. But Miss Dauner (III, 22) sees no hint of shame, describing the theme as "really an appraisal and a balancing of values for the living and the dead" (Chap. V, p. 11); and this is the interpretation that I originally inclined to, during a long period of puzzlement (not yet ended—though I think Mr. Neff *may* be right). There appear to be three crucial passages. One is the line, "Better kept and longer valued than by ways that would have been." This may mean simply that we have more effective methods of embalming, and are inclined to remember the dead longer, than people in earlier and more "primitive" societies; and if this interpretation seems somewhat banal, we may remember Robinson's habitual irony. The other view is that the line means that it is better for her to be dead than to undergo the physical and moral degeneration of "a life of shame." In this case, "better kept" would have a somewhat macabre connotation, even for a poet who does not dodge life's grimmest realities. The second key line is, "There'll be lilies that are liars, and the rose will have its own." Here the lilies may be (as traditionally) a symbol of purity, and the rose a symbol of passion; or, as Miss Dauner evidently assumes, the former may be a symbol of death and the latter a symbol of life (after death)—a somewhat less usual but not at all impossible meaning. Finally, there are the concluding lines:

> But the builders, looking forward into time, could only see
> Darker nights for Leonora than to-night shall ever be.

Here the builders (of the house, i.e., the coffin) may have been her fellow townsmen, who (not knowing that their work was to be for her) anticipated for her a life of shame (did the town "vibrate" with her affairs?); or they may, as materialists, have regarded death as final, whereas the poet insists on some sort of life after death. Thus the poem would provide a dramatic contrast with *For a Dead Lady*, in the same volume, which implies (though it does not assert) the finality of death. (The other interpretation would provide a dramatic contrast of a different kind.) The reader may take his choice of these interpretations—or perhaps find another.

²² Mr. Fussell says that "the close of the poem suggests that the artist has forgotten and thrown away more than he has won" (p. 642), and this is probably correct. Mr. Redman also thinks the theme is "the failure of success" (p. 70).

chapter vi

¹ "What he wanted to know was the inclusive story behind the appearances—the story behind this man's or that woman's conduct. When the story was not obvious, he would shake his head and say, 'There must be something there'" (Rollo Brown [I, 25], p. 52). The following lines from *Fortunatus* will also apply:

> You will not see the drama of dead lives
> That are behind calm faces and closed doors.

(This poem, never published except in a limited edition [Reno, Slide Mountain Press; copyright 1928 by James Raye Wells], is a 24-line address to the type of person—the second of the five types described in *The Man Against the Sky*, and one often referred to by Robinson—to whom belongs the agreeable destiny of "seeing all things for the best.")

² Akin to this is his love of subtlety and indirection. "I'm not a playwright," he told Nancy Evans. "A play must be *direct*—there is no chance for a movement of light and shade" (p. 677).

³ Robinson told Esther Bates: " 'You know this sort of thing happens every day,' and to my look of inquiry he added, 'I mean people love the way Tristram and Isolt were supposed to'" (p. 19).

⁴ For the quotations in context, see *Letters*, p. 145, where "robots" is printed for "rabbits," the unmistakable word in the original.

⁵ Bates, p. 19.

⁶ Mr. Winters comments on this general topic that in "the original story" "the theme was the power of physical passion," which Robinson "suppressed"; "and what he had left was a popular love story" (p. 86). Mr. Kreymborg (III, 15), also, comments that Robinson's love scenes lack "sensual elements" and "passionate drive." "Even when lovers are swept into each other's arms, they are swept there by a series of beautifully cadenced speeches" (p. 313).

⁷ Carl Van Doren (IV, 7) explains how *Tristram* happened to become the choice of the Literary Guild, a choice which was of course important. But, as he goes on to say, this only helped give the poem a *chance* to be popular.

⁸ At the same time, as he told Miss Evans, "The romantic framework enabled me to use my idiom more freely" (p. 676).

⁹ For other comments on this poem, see above, Chap. IV, Note 7, and below, Chap. VII, Note 82. Professor Cestre finds the origin of the piece in the impression made upon the poet by accounts of the visionary "hellish horrors that used to appal the early Puritans" (p. 144); and many readers will feel that the ambiguity of this and other poems is strongly reminiscent of Hawthorne.

[10] Robinson's own comment is: "What I tried to do . . . was to create an extension or projection of Cavender's own mind that could stand off and examine him without mercy—and without ordinary hate" (Rollo Brown, pp. 79-80).

[11] Robinson has no studies of out-and-out insanity with which Avon's case may be compared, except the sonnet *En Passant*. This sonnet has been so impenetrable to many readers (including me) that I quote in full what I believe to be the correct interpretation, offered by Earl F. Walbridge in the *Saturday Review of Literature*, XXX, March 8, 1947, p. 48: "The He of the poem is mad, or an Ancient Mariner type ('a soul accurst'). He has 'famished eyes . . . lit with a wrong light.' He has been watching highways and now intends to watch the sea, for some person, probably an enemy, whom he is expecting. Everyone he sees may be this enemy, and has to be stopped and interrogated. Fortunately the narrator of the poem *did* stop that afternoon (he was 'a gentleman' who did 'come when called,' 'with deference always due to souls accurst'), otherwise he would have been shot by the madman. He 'came out of his own grave—and not too soon,' *i. e.*, if he had ignored the madman when the latter spoke to him he would have been instantly killed."

[12] This line was not in the first edition. It was added later to clarify the general situation (*Letters to Howard G. Schmitt* [IV, 7], p. 29). Some sort of conception of the poem seems to have been in Robinson's mind as early as 1912, when he wrote to Hagedorn, after using the phrase "the Valley of the Shadow": "I shall still reserve my likes to a Valley of my own which will be very queer, and rather long, and will have a tendency to make people sit up, if it is done as it should be done. It is in the distance now, but I know it is there for I can see it. It will be as cheerful as hell (which it is, or was) and there will be a foggy sunrise at the end with the fog gradually disappearing from a land of joy and song and grasshoppers" (*Letters*, p. 75).

[13] What Ipswich and the grave-diggers stand for is not altogether clear. The former's magic potion might be taken almost literally as alcohol or opium, but Robinson is rarely so direct in his dealings, and the particular quality of the fanaticism that is evident in Ipswich and his followers suggests that the drink is a spiritual drug—perhaps some sort of extreme religious revivalism. Of course the two interpretations come to much the same thing in the end—the attempt to escape from failure in the world of consequences and responsibilities by embracing a delusion. The grave-diggers on one level seem to represent simply the process of physical decay, for Amaranth calls them "necessary vermin." But clearly they are more than this, since Fargo, as Amaranth repeatedly warns him, is in spiritual peril from them. Possibly they represent what was for Robinson the logical end of a materialistic interpretation of the world—the denial of meaning and value to life on any level; an end from which Dr. Styx, a tentative materialist, is perhaps to be saved by his unusual humility and humanity. Mr. Winters remarks, apparently with a straight face, that they "doubtless represent the generality of critics and reviewers, who are incapable of perception or of judgment, but who live in the manner of scavengers by destroying or trying to destroy whatever they encounter" (p. 121).

[14] Possibly Robinson was influenced here by George Crabbe, who, while he does not lay much stress on appearance, often uses direct exposition in presenting his characters, as in the following lines from *The Brothers* (the poem in *Tales*, not the one with the same title in *Tales of the Hall*):

George was a bold, intrepid, careless lad,
With just the failings that his father had;
Isaac was weak, attentive, slow, exact,
With just the virtues that his father lacked.

If there *is* any influence, of course, it is one that Robinson quickly outgrew.

[15] This preoccupation also appears in *Her Eyes; Charles Carville's Eyes;* Amaranth's eyes, through which he exercises the power of revealing people to themselves; the eyes of Penn-Raven in *Roman Bartholow,* in which shone "A nameless light whereon but few could look/ Long without flinching"; and the eyes of Avon's enemy with their "weird gleam" of "sorrow" and "vengeance."

[16] Unpublished letter to Mrs. Richards, dated Jan. 17, 1922, in Houghton Library. Robinson concludes characteristically, "but it ends happily"; earlier in the same letter he calls it "a formidable piece of optimism."

[17] Comment should perhaps be made on a recent interpretation of this poem by Mr. R. H. Super in the *Explicator,* V, 60 (June, 1947): the lady (although not entirely without good qualities) is "frivolous and unsympathetic," she is a "flirt," "she refuses to be serious," "she demands the praise of her companions." This view seems to have been partially accepted by Mr. Neff, whose comment is: "For all her worldliness Robinson cannot restrain regret for the passing of so perfect a work of nature and of art" (p. 155). This appears to me to verge on travesty: to dull (at least) what I should say is clearly the point of the poem, which is the apparent triumph of absolute nonbeing over life in its absolute fullness (as in Wordsworth's "A Slumber Did My Spirit Steal"), and thereby to transform what seems to me to be indisputably one of the supreme lyrics of the language into not much more than a brilliant exercise in rhetoric. Mr. Hagedorn suggests that the poem contains "memories of his mother" (p. 238); but I cannot feel (here I agree with Mr. Super) that the love and admiration expressed are precisely filial.

[18] Bates, p. 3. Harriet Monroe comments: "Robinson's method is . . . akin to that of the psychoanalyst who encourages confessional monologue, or uses dialogue, as a probe to strike through the poison of lies and appearances and reveal the truth" (*Poets and Their Art* [New York, Macmillan, 1926], p. 5). Mr. T. K. Whipple also has a point, though he overstates it, in saying that Robinson's gift "is less for creation than for dissection; he does not embody or make men so much as take them apart" (*Spokesmen* [New York, Appleton, 1928], p. 63).

[19] Other sonnets include some speech: *Amaryllis, The Long Race, Recalled, Why He Was There,* and *En Passant.* But in none of these is character the main interest.

[20] I judge that critics are more nearly unanimous in their approval of this poem than of any other medium-length piece in Robinson's work.

[21] The "I" in these poems may remind one of Marlow in some of Conrad's stories. Though the idiom is of course entirely different, his relation to the main character on the one hand and the author (for whom he is by no means a mere mask or mouthpiece) on the other is much the same.

[22] For the quotation, see p. 46.

[23] *Letters,* p. 104.

[24] For further comment on this point, see pp. 20–23.

[25] *Letters,* p. 121.

[26] Aldous Huxley, in *Eyeless in Gaza,* pp. 184–185.

[27] The twelve are Luke Havergal (probably), Richard Cory, Lorraine, the unnamed men in *Bon Voyage* and *The Whip*, the miller and his wife in *The Mill*, Nightingale, Gabrielle in *Roman Bartholow*, Garth and Natalie in *Matthias at the Door*, and Honoria in *King Jasper*.

[28] *Letters*, p. 127. The word "little" is added from the original letter.

[29] In this discussion no attempt is made to distinguish between "comedy" and "humor." Historically, as far as I can see, the words have been used interchangeably in recent centuries.

[30] Hagedorn, p. 169.

[31] Matthias does eventually become willing to accept the view of his own character held by his wife and friends, and the end is not tragic for him. But in the meantime Natalie has been driven to suicide. There is as a rule much suffering in the stories that Robinson tells, but rarely do they leave the reader with a sense of total waste. Whether or not they should be called tragic is a matter of definition.

[32] Mr. Fussell feels that the mother faces "a future that can only bring bitter disillusion, the more galling for being so totally unexpected" (p. 611). But to me the poem has always seemed essentially and tenderly comic, and I can find no suggestion of future catastrophe.

[33] Mr. Winters takes this poem to be "an expression of pity for old prostitutes" (p. 33), but this is to overlook the obviously whimsical tone. Robinson's theme is the traditional one—treated with unique lightness and forbearance—of the superannuated flirt. The point is discussed in detail by Laurence Perrine in the *Explicator*, VI, 13 (Nov., 1947).

chapter vii

[1] *Letters*, pp. 19-20; *Untriangulated Stars*, p. 274.

[2] *Letters*, p. 166.

[3] Schriftgiesser (I, 13), p. 1.

[4] Compare the comments on propaganda in poetry quoted on p. 19. In line with the passage from *Amaranth* just quoted is (I think) the powerful but obscure sonnet called *The Laggards*.

[5] *Untriangulated Stars*, p. 273.

[6] *Letters*, p. 165.

[7] *Ibid.*, p. 160.

[8] Recent advances in physics have made "materialism" inadequate as a term for what is here in question. Robinson himself in *Annandale Again* makes Annandale remark, "You doctors, who have found so much/ In matter that it's hardly there." But "naturalism," the usual replacement, may be still more confusing. The first term still seems the best, despite its Victorian overtones.

[9] *Untriangulated Stars*, p. 12.

[10] See p. 118. The widening application of Robinson's basic beliefs has led some critics to find in his work a development that is not really there. Robinson matured late, but he matured quickly. *The Children of the Night* contains a number of pieces that are juvenile in both style and substance, but the poet realized this almost immediately. He wrote to Mason in 1900: "I am the only man on earth who knows how sorry I am now for some of the stuff in a small book for which I was responsible" (Daniel Gregory Mason, "Early Letters of Edwin Arlington Robinson," *Virginia Quarterly Review*, XIII, 226 [Spring, 1937]); and an even more explicit statement occurs in an unpublished letter to

Miss Peabody dated Jan. 30, 1901 (in Houghton Library). By the time of the *Captain Craig* volume, he knew where he stood, and he did not thereafter change his position, either as artist or thinker. His philosophical beliefs remained firmly anchored, and he remained "an incurable preacher" of them (though not often in his own person). His concern for the individual in himself and for the "universal" significance of the individual's experience is present from *Cliff Klingenhagen* to *King Jasper*. The problem of the individual's relation to society is explored in *Captain Craig*. In its general theme and materials, even in its method, *The Book of Annandale* anticipates *Matthias at the Door* and *Talifer*. And before the appearance of *The Town Down the River*, Robinson had perfected all his verse techniques—though, as already noted, the later blank verse differs somewhat from the earlier. In my judgment, no significant, consistent development of any kind can be found in Robinson's work after 1902—though age brought an inevitable loss of buoyancy and lyricism.

[11] *Letters*, pp. 163–165. Compare the discussion of *The Flying Dutchman* on p. 116, and these lines from *Matthias at the Door*:

"Science that blinds its eyes incessantly
With a new light that fades and leaves them aching."

[12] Arnold seems to have been Robinson's favorite poet during his early twenties. See *Untriangulated Stars*, Index.

[13] *Letters*, p. 80.

[14] See pp. 78–79 and 114–115.

[15] *Letters*, p. 164.

[16] Rollo Brown, pp. 56–57.

[17] Bates, p. 14.

[18] Hagedorn, p. 111.

[19] *Letters*, p. 165.

[20] Of such periods there seem to have been three. The first included the years in Gardiner (June, 1893 to Dec., 1896) after he left Harvard, when separation from his friends, an apparent disappointment in love, the seeming hopelessness of a poetic career, and, at the end, the emotional aftermath of his mother's death, made life almost unbearable. His sufferings are recorded (though even here one must read between the lines) in the letters to Smith and Gledhill, especially some of those to the latter that remain unpublished. What lifted him out of this depression was the thrill of publication and the exhilaration of his first contacts with New York. The second was from about 1901 to 1905, when he was oppressed by his long failure to find a publisher for *Captain Craig*, the indifference of critics and public after it finally appeared, and the absolute destitution that compelled him to accept the job in the subway. From this he was rescued by Theodore Roosevelt. The third period followed the failure of *The Town Down the River* to win attention, in 1910, and included the final collapse of his hope to be a popular playwright or novelist. He was also tortured by the struggle to give up drinking, and haunted by the old specter of poverty. Early in 1914, as he later told Rollo Brown, "I was on my uppers—absolutely. . . . It was the one time in my life when there seemed to be nothing ahead" (pp. 66–67). This time it was an unexpected bequest following the death of his old friend and benefactor John Hays Gardiner that saved him. "Somehow, I was always able to keep going after that. It almost makes a man feel that maybe there is somebody somewhere who makes it [*sic*] a business of looking out for people" (*ibid.*).

[21] Mason (II, 10), p. 127.
[22] See especially Van Wyck Brooks, *New England Indian Summer* (New York, Dutton, 1940), and T. K. Whipple, *Spokesmen* (New York, Appleton, 1928); also Bruce Weirick, *From Whitman to Sandburg in American Poetry* (New York, Macmillan, 1924); Clement Wood, *The Poets of America* (New York, Dutton, 1925); and Gorham B. Munson, *Destinations* (New York, J. H. Sears, 1928).
[23] Richards (II, 43), p. 8.
[24] *Ibid.*, p. 31.
[25] *Ibid.*, p. 28.
[26] *Ibid.*, p. 30. Such recollections, after the subject has become famous, are notoriously colored by his later career. The striking thing here is that the recollections are so at variance with what seems to have been (and seems still to be) the generally accepted picture. Mrs. Richards herself is somewhat inconsistent, for she says elsewhere: "His schoolmates had known him as a bookish boy, quiet and retiring" (*Stepping Westward* [New York, Appleton-Century, 1931], p. 381). This is an earlier opinion, however, and further inquiries may have modified it.
[27] Richards (II, 43), pp. 13–14.
[28] Carl Van Doren (IV, 7), pp. 161, 165.
[29] Rollo Brown, p. 89.
[30] Schriftgiesser, p. 1.
[31] *Ibid.* He had said almost exactly the same thing to Carty Ranck a year earlier. See "Edwin Arlington Robinson," *Boston Herald*, Dec. 14, 1930, Magazine Feature Section, p. 2.
[32] Bates, p. 18.
[33] *Early Letters*, p. 230.
[34] *Letters*, pp. 80–81.
[35] *Ibid.*, p. 160.
[36] *Ibid.*, pp. 165–166. Compare a comment to Mrs. Richards: "I . . . can only say again that life means everything, or it means nothing. If it means nothing, we are caught in a sorry trap. . . . I have to believe that there is a little more to it than we see now—but what it is I can't tell you" (unpublished letter, dated Aug. 20, 1926, in Houghton Library).
[37] *Letters*, p. 97.
[38] *Untriangulated Stars*, p. 263.
[39] *Ibid.*
[40] *Ibid.*, p. 264.
[41] Hagedorn, p. 91.
[42] *Ibid.*, p. 286.
[43] Mason (II, 10), p. 127. My impression is that the following three years were still more trying—but equally without effect on his basic attitude. Compare the following comment in a letter to Mrs. Ledoux in 1916: "O Lord, what a world! But I doubt if I could make one that would be any better, or half as interesting" (unpublished letter, postmarked Feb. 21, 1916, in Houghton Library).
[44] *Letters*, p. 93.
[45] *Ibid.*, p. 92.
[46] *Ibid.*, p. 168.
[47] See above, p. 179.
[48] Lloyd Morris, *The Poetry of Edwin Arlington Robinson* (New York, George H. Doran, 1923), p. 71.

⁴⁹ After writing this paragraph, I was gratified to discover that it is practically a paraphrase of a passage in Henry W. Wells's *New Poets from Old* (Columbia University Press, 1940), p. 318. The same general point of view is presented by Floyd Stovall, "The Optimism Behind Robinson's Tragedies," *American Literature*, X, 1–23 (March, 1938). Robinson himself always insisted (with seriousness underlying the surface irony) that the long poems are not pessimistic. He wrote to Miss Peabody (Feb. 11, 1922) and to Mrs. Richards (Jan. 17, 1922) that *Roman Bartholow* "ends happily," and in the first letter he called it "my Pollyanna tragedy"; and to Betts (July 13, 1921) he characterized it as "rotten with optimism." He also told Betts (May 5, 1929) that *Cavender's House* is "a cheerful book and ought to make a lot of people happy." Of *Tristram* he wrote to Mrs. Richards (July 24, 1926): "it seems to me that I'm making it pretty cheerful"; and of *Matthias at the Door* (letter undated, apparently July or August, 1931) that it "has a happy ending." (All these letters are in Houghton Library.) To Miss Bates he wrote of *The Glory of the Nightingales*: "It is full of sunshine and ends happily—with only one suicide—and should make those who read it feel warm and pleasant all over" (p. 18).

⁵⁰ *Untriangulated Stars*, p. 247. He adds with habitual self-consciousness, "All this, no doubt, will make you grin."

⁵¹ Some critics, especially those with anti-Romantic leanings, have wished to derive the third of these from the second. Such a view, in my judgment, is mistaken.

⁵² Hagedorn, p. 371. Robinson said the same thing to Rollo Brown (p. 95).

⁵³ *Letters*, p. 177.

⁵⁴ *Untriangulated Stars*, p. 260.

⁵⁵ *Ibid.*, p. 270.

⁵⁶ *Letters*, p. 169. The reason for Robinson's severity toward the Methodists does not appear.

⁵⁷ How far Robinson is to be identified with Captain Craig has been a matter of argument. Mr. Winters sees "no reason to believe that Craig is offered as a genuine embodiment of wisdom" (p. 98); but this is because he judges (correctly) that the Captain is an "Emersonian philosopher," and he wishes to minimize the likeness between Robinson, whom he admires, and Emerson, to whom he is notoriously allergic. It can hardly be imagined, however, that Robinson would have written so long a poem, and given the Captain so many lengthy speeches, merely for the sake of an objective sketch of a character somewhat comparable to Mr. Flood. He told Mrs. Richards that a projected poem was, "somewhat unlike C. C., almost wholly objective"; and he added, "I hope . . . you will not mislike him for his theory that it is possible to apply good natured common sense even to the so-called serious events in life" (*Letters*, pp. 50–51). The bearing of his comment to Miss Peabody—"I'm afraid that you take him . . . too seriously. I think you put more of my own shortcomings into him than are there" (*ibid.*, p. 31)—is not entirely clear to me. On Mr. Winters's side, seemingly, is a statement in a letter to Smith (containing other interesting comments on the poem): "There is not very much of myself [in it], but there are pages of what certain people take to be myself" (*Untriangulated Stars*, p. 306); and so, perhaps, is his remark to Mason that the Captain "is something of a scholar but not 'me'" (*Letters*, p. 20). But here we must distinguish between personal character and philosophy. The Captain's loquacity, assurance, and boisterous humor are certainly not Robinson's. But most of his *ideas* (I should say) just as certainly *are*. I submit that: (*a*) the *tone*

of many passages suggests that the poet himself is speaking; and (b) the ideas expressed here are in harmony with those expressed by the poet in other works, especially during this period of his life. The *Octaves*, for instance, in *The Children of the Night*, offer a number of convincing parallels.

⁵⁸ See above, Chap. VI, Note 13.

⁵⁹ *Untriangulated Stars*, p. 280.

⁶⁰ *Letters*, p. 162.

⁶¹ *Ibid.*, pp. 170–171.

⁶² *Untriangulated Stars*, p. 131.

⁶³ *Ibid.*, p. 264. *Kosmos* is a sonnet in *The Torrent and The Night Before*, omitted from *Collected Poems*.

⁶⁴ *Letters*, p. 142.

⁶⁵ *Ibid.*

⁶⁶ William T. Walsh, "Some Recollections of E. A. Robinson," *Catholic World*, CLV, 711 (Sept., 1942). Mr. Walsh expresses only regret for Robinson's inability to accept a more definite form of faith; but there is a noticeable tendency among contemporary critics to speak with disparagement of the "vagueness" of the poet's religious beliefs. Mr. Winters dislikes the *Octaves* and the early reflective sonnets (as he does almost all of Robinson's "philosophical" poems), declaring that they are "carelessly thought" and "indicate a belief in the discovery of God through pure intuition" (p. 50)—not stating what the legitimate method is. Malcolm Cowley similarly complains that Robinson opposes to "materialism" only "a sort of Buddho-Christianity too vague to be intellectually respectable" ("Edwin Arlington Robinson: Defeat and Triumph," *New Republic*, CXIX, Dec. 6, 1948, p. 30); although he, like Mr. Winters, has high praise for some other aspects of Robinson's work. These particular adverse criticisms are unintelligible to me. I do not see that the faith of St. Thomas Aquinas (whom "intuition" eventually led to abandon his great rationalization of Christian belief) is more "respectable" than that of St. Francis of Assisi, nor that a person is to be reprehended for failing to give his faith a verbal formulation that seems to him not only unnecessary but impossible. It is one thing to say that because of this failure Robinson's work is "inadequate" to the religious needs of many of his readers (see Fussell, p. 84). This is to raise a legitimate issue; and if the statement is true, as perhaps it is, then the fact is to be deplored, and Robinson is (I should say) that much less great as a poet. But to dismiss as "carelessly thought" or not "respectable" a religious position with which one does not happen personally to sympathize is a critical procedure impossible to justify.

⁶⁷ *Untriangulated Stars*, p. 280.

⁶⁸ *Ibid.*, p. 252.

⁶⁹ Hagedorn, p. 112. In 1932 Robinson told Nancy Evans (I, 3), "with a fond sort of disapproval, 'I was young then, and it was a smart thing to say'" (p. 680). Presumably his disapproval was not of the substance but of the "smartness" of the phrasing.

⁷⁰ Such speculations recall at once Hardy's conception of the Immanent Will in *The Dynasts*. But whereas Hardy sees the world as a sort of embodiment of a chaotic cosmic dream, with only a tenuous hope of ultimate conscious control, Robinson sees the "eternal will" as being at all times purposeful.

⁷¹ *Untriangulated Stars*, pp. 246, 285, 286.

⁷² *Letters*, p. 115. He had made the same statement to Mrs. Marks exactly four years earlier: "I still stick to my theory that the world is a Hell of a

Place, and that it should be one if it means anything" (unpublished letter dated March 12, 1915, in Houghton Library). He also wrote to Hagedorn in 1915: "The world has been made what it is by upheavals, whether we like them or not. I've always told you it's a hell of a place. That's why I insist that it must mean something. My July work was a poem on this theme and I call it 'The Man Against the Sky' " (Hagedorn, p. 302).

[73] For the former attitude, see *Untriangulated Stars*, pp. 142, 263; for the latter, *Letters*, p. 160.

[74] Unpublished letter to Betts, dated March 19, 1932, in Houghton Library.

[75] Unpublished letter, dated April 5, 1931, in Houghton Library. This general philosophy is implicit in much of the work of Robert Frost, and is made explicit in a remark in *The Masque of Reason* (copyright 1945 by Henry Holt) that "Earth" "would be meaningless" to man "Except as a hard place to save his soul in" (p. 16).

[76] For a discussion of character changes in the long poems, see pp. 108–110.

[77] See also p. 20.

[78] *Untriangulated Stars*, p. 279.

[79] *Letters*, p. 124.

[80] *Ibid.*, p. 123.

[81] It seems to have been one of Robinson's eccentricities to insist that some of his most somber or depressing poems were really amusing. Concerning *The Valley of the Shadow* he declared that it "is not in all ways what its name suggests. In some ways it's as cheerful as a Cheshire Cat" (*Letters*, p. 111). He wrote to Smith just before the appearance of *The Torrent and The Night Before*, "My book . . . is one of the funniest things ever written by a mortal man" (*Untriangulated Stars*, p. 254). And he called *The Klondike* "a pretty amusing piece of literature . . . even if it isn't very good poetry" (Hagedorn, p. 178).

[82] *Avon's Harvest* seems to me the most baffling of Robinson's longer poems; not because we do not know, finally, what happens, but because we do not know *why* it happens. Some critics have tried to find a psychological explanation (e.g., Neff, p. 198, and Mark Van Doren [II, 50], p. 59); but Mr. Winters is right in saying that if the poem is "to be regarded as a serious study in abnormal psychology . . . we do not know enough about the actual facts of the case to understand it" (p. 102). In this connection, Robinson told Miss Evans that he was not "interested in the exploration of pathological extremes" (p. 677). A second class of critics have attempted a moral interpretation (e.g., Cestre, p. 144, and Louise Dauner, "Avon and Cavender: Two Children of the Night," *American Literature*, XIV, 55–65 [March, 1942]). But Avon has done nothing wrong, and he feels no guilt; if his tormentor had really been drowned, he would, by every indication, have lived happily ever after. In the eyes of the narrator (whose point of view in such poems is always the one the poet wants his readers to accept), Avon is a thoroughly decent and (except for his one obsession) completely sane person. His fate simply cannot be rationalized. And therefore I suggest that the poem deals with the intrusion into human life of evil that is uncaused, inexplicable. Avon himself suggests the comparison with Job, and it is valid. Critics should beware of assuming the office of Job's comforters. For many reasons we do not wish to admit that such evil can exist. But it can. It does.

[83] This general contrast between Tennyson's and Robinson's treatment of the story is touched on by Mr. Winters, pp. 64ff.

[84] Schriftgiesser, p. 1.

[85] Evans, p. 678. Robinson added: "But it's difficult to discuss these ideas. We're getting metaphysical and our terminology may mean such different things."

chapter viii

[1] *Letters*, p. 121.

[2] *Untriangulated Stars*, p. 61.

[3] No doubt Robinson remembered Arnold's formulation of this thought in *To Marguerite*:

> Yes: in the sea of life enisled,
> With echoing straits between us thrown,
> Dotting the shoreless watery wild,
> We mortal millions live alone.

But he did not need Arnold or anybody else to tell him about the experience itself.

[4] *Untriangulated Stars*, p. 4.

[5] *Ibid.*, p. 76.

[6] *Ibid.*, pp. 278–279. Here may be quoted Robinson's comment to Nancy Evans with reference to the lines in *Lancelot* where the hero says:

> "The Vison shattered, a man's love of living
> Becomes at last a trap and a sad habit."

The poet explained: "This Vision is not only the cosmic vision; it is the personal vision, the inner truth of his own nature which is the persuasion by which a man lives" (p. 678).

[7] *Untriangulated Stars*, p. 285. Compare, in *The Night Before*, the statement that "a happy man is a man forgetful/ Of all the torturing ills around him."

[8] Professor Cestre's suggestion (p. 126) that Robinson got the idea of this poem—though only "a mere hint"—from Hawthorne's story *The Christmas Banquet* has been accepted by some other scholars. But although Robinson apparently knew Hawthorne well, and may have known this story, the actual connection (as almost always with Robinson's alleged sources) is extremely tenuous.

[9] *Letters*, p. 65. He adds, "provided always that the artist has the faculty of being interesting."

[10] Hagedorn, p. 346.

[11] *Letters*, pp. 12–13. Compare the comment to John Hays Gardiner with reference to *The Book of Annandale*: "Six hundred lines of blank verse without any bumblebees and sunsets is a pretty stiff dose, I fancy" (unpublished letter, dated Dec. 8, 1901, in Houghton Library). The poem has, nevertheless, some brilliant bits of nature description, as on p. 208 of *Collected Poems*.

[12] *Letters*, p. 131.

[13] Hagedorn, p. 300.

[14] *Untriangulated Stars*, p. 54. See also Index under "Theatre."

[15] "The playwright died hard in him. Once he said, 'When I die, they ought to put D. D.—Defeated Dramatist—on my tombstone'" (Bates, p. 9). And see Hagedorn, pp. 243–244, 272–273, 331.

[16] *Letters*, p. 8.

[17] Hagedorn, pp. 370–371.

[18] *Letters*, p. 124.

[19] For some brief and inadequate quotations, see pp. 60–61. For other comments on this poem, and on Robinson's feeling about music in general, see Lewis M. Isaacs, "E. A. Robinson Speaks of Music," *New England Quarterly*, XXII, 499–510 (Dec., 1949). Of special interest are the poet's views on the relation between verbal and tonal music, "his feeling that to put most good verse to music was like 'sticking a pin through a butterfly and fastening it down forever.' If the lyric was good enough it didn't need the addition of music" (p. 503). Isaacs was a gifted amateur musician. For further comment, by a friend who was a professional composer, see Mabel Daniels, "Robinson's Interest in Music," *Mark Twain Quarterly*, Vol. II, No. 3 (Spring, 1938), pp. 15, 24. (This entire number is devoted to Robinson.)

[20] *Untriangulated Stars*, p. 286.

[21] *Ibid.*, p. 135.

[22] Hagedorn, p. 347.

[23] *Ibid.*, pp. 374–375.

[24] *Letters*, p. viii.

[25] Richards (II, 43), p. 26.

[26] *Untriangulated Stars*, p. 249.

[27] *Ibid.*, p. 24. Compare also the following passage from a letter to Betts in 1917: "This living outside the hive may look easy from the inside, but in reality it's a damned poor kind of life. If I were to know that I were not making some sort of contribution to 'Igh Art (and very likely I am not) I should be tempted to hang myself as a matter of principle" (Hagedorn, p. 322; here slightly corrected from the original in Houghton Library).

[28] Hagedorn, p. 83.

[29] *Ibid.*, p. 351.

[30] Unpublished letter, dated Sept. 14, 1900, in Houghton Library.

[31] *Untriangulated Stars*, p. 65.

[32] Hagedorn, p. 223.

[33] *Letters*, p. 13.

[34] Letter to Miss Peabody, dated March 27, 1904, quoted by Neff, pp. 132–133. He adds, "With the world so beautiful and life itself so hideous, I don't wonder that [the] closing choruses of the Greek tragedies were all alike."

[35] Henry Morton Robinson, "No Epitaph," *Commonweal*, XI, 60 (Nov. 13, 1929).

[36] Eda Lou Walton, "Robinson's Women," *Nation*, CXXXVII, 415 (Oct. 11, 1933).

[37] Robinson wrote to Miss Peabody: "For some unhappy [?] reason nearly all the time that women have spent in writing plays since the world began— Eve wrote five or six—has been more or less lost. If . . . you can make a man who doesn't talk like a woman or an archangel, you can do something that you were never intended to do" (unpublished letter, dated Sept. 7, 1903, in Houghton Library).

[38] Kreymborg (III, 15), p. 304.

[39] Louise Dauner, "The Pernicious Rib: E. A. Robinson's Concept of Feminine Character," *American Literature*, XV, 148 (May, 1943).

[40] When Esther Bates asked him, while he was writing *Roman Bartholow*, "if he had it in for women as much in this book as in the others . . . he said he didn't think he had it in for women any more than the world had it in for

women" (Bates, p. 12). He once wrote to Miss Peabody, concerning the unhappy situation of a married couple among their friends: "Sometimes it looks to me like one of those cases where the woman is fated to pay for the man's salvation" (unpublished letter, dated March 28, 1901, in Houghton Library).

[41] Mr. Neff supplies a note for which many readers will be grateful: "Palissy, the sixteenth century French potter whom Robinson encountered in Longfellow's 'Keramos' as a symbol of 'the prophet's vision,' has told in his autobiography of his sixteen-year search for the secret of white enamel, ــ which he sacrificed everything, even feeding his kiln with his household furniture as a last resort" (p. 120).

[42] Compare his comment to Mrs. Richards that "sex is important, the Lord knows, but even Solomon didn't think of it all the time" (unpublished letter, undated but postmarked Aug. 28, 1927, in Houghton Library).

[43] *Letters*, p. 97.

[44] A different interpretation of Robinson's treatment of love in the Arthurian poems (but arriving at a similar *general* conclusion) is given by Frederic I. Carpenter, "Tristram the Transcendent," *New England Quarterly*, XI, 501-523 (Sept., 1938).

[45] The last point is suggested by Mr. Fussell, p. 535.

[46] And, of course, woman's love for man. Merlin assumes that it is a man's world; and perhaps Robinson also feels that it is men who *do* things. Yet in his poems there is always "Partnership" between the sexes; and it is not as passive objects of desire, but as beings possessed of passion and will, that women influence men's acts.

[47] Robinson commented to Hagedorn that "the torch of women [sic] is to be taken literally" (*Letters*, p. 113). For a further discussion of the philosophy of *Merlin*, see pp. 118-119. I am not certain that I have correctly interpreted Robinson's views as to just *how* "woman . . . is yet to light the world." But I do not know that a more plausible view has been suggested. I can find nothing, for instance, to support Mr. Neff's suggestion that Robinson is thinking of "the instinct of women to abhor war" (p. 194). He himself abhorred war, but he was not a pacifist. On one occasion he wrote to Miss Peabody about "the most ferocious young person I have ever met. . . . She likes war and she thinks killing is a good thing; and she may be right. That depends largely on who is killed, and why. . . . Killing, to me, is a nasty business that must now and then be done" (unpublished letter, dated Oct. 8, 1900, in Houghton Library).

[48] Floyd Stovall (VII, 49) comments that Zoë is "the woman of Merlin's Vision who is to save the world, for she combines the beauty of the chivalric ideal with the truth which the Grail revealed" (p. 22).

[49] *Letters*, p. 17. Compare the following comment to Betts in regard to the potion in the Tristram legend: "Surely Fate can make trouble enough without the aid of so crude a symbol as an impossible drink that turns the two who drink it into Mr. and Mrs. Thomas Cat, with no further human responsibilities" (unpublished letter, dated Aug. 17, 1926, in Houghton Library).

[50] *Letters*, p. 137.

[51] Hagedorn, p. 332.

[52] *Ibid.*, pp. 332-333.

[53] *Letters*, p. 121.

[54] *Ibid.*, p. 140.

[55] *Untriangulated Stars*, p. 251.

[56] *Ibid.*, pp. 265-266. In the letter to Miss Peabody quoted in Note 47 above,

Robinson expresses abhorrence of "the atmosphere and miserable tyranny of military life."

[57] *Untriangulated Stars*, p. 296.
[58] *Letters*, p. 115.
[59] *Untriangulated Stars*, p. 216.
[60] *Letters*, p. 29.
[61] *Ibid.*, p. 128.
[62] *Ibid.*, p. 134.
[63] *Ibid.*, p. 112.
[64] *Ibid.*, p. 134. Perhaps a few more words should be said about the political allegory in *Merlin* and *Lancelot*, concerning which the critics have not always agreed. Perhaps Mr. Neff goes farthest, saying that "Arthur, who adumbrates the tradition-bound British Empire, and the light-minded, materialistic Gawaine, who corresponds to the America of 'Cassandra,' perish" (p. 194). My own view is that we are not justified in going beyond what the poet himself said, in the letters to Hagedorn (*Letters*, pp. 112–113) and Miss Helen Grace Adams (*ibid.*, p. 160) already referred to, and in the interview with Nancy Evans. When Miss Evans asked him "whether the Arthurian poems were allegories . . . intended to parallel the great War," he replied that "they tell of the breaking up of the old order." More specific than this he refused to be, saying, "It is all there—it is all quite clear" (p. 677).
[65] *Letters*, p. 175. But Carl Van Doren (IV, 7) records: "He distrusted Soviet Russia: this was the only political opinion I ever heard him express" (p. 164).
[66] *Letters*, p. 175. Such comments were common in Robinson's last years.
[67] Mr. Winters, who calls this "perhaps the greatest" of Robinson's short rhymed poems, has a somewhat different interpretation (pp. 38–39).
[68] Compare his comment on William Jennings Bryan after the 1896 election (in which he voted for McKinley): "I was hoping, though, that Bryan would get a larger vote, as I am coming more and more to look upon him as the greatest political figure in America since Lincoln" (*Untriangulated Stars*, p. 261). In 1900, however, he wrote an editorial urging McKinley's election, which appeared in the New York *Tribune* on Oct. 7. This editorial (apparently the only one ever published of several that he wrote in an attempt at a journalistic career urged upon him by E. C. Stedman) was tentatively identified by Alice Meacham Williams in her article "Edwin Arlington Robinson, Journalist," *New England Quarterly*, XV, 715–724 (Dec., 1942). The identification is confirmed by a reference in an unpublished letter to Mrs. Marks, dated Nov. 10, 1921, in Houghton Library.
[69] *Letters*, p. 51.
[70] *Ibid.*, p. 158.
[71] *Untriangulated Stars*, p. 251.
[72] *Edwin Arlington Robinson: A Collection of His Works from the Library of Bacon Collamore* (Hartford, Conn., 1936), pp. 9–10.
[73] *Untriangulated Stars*, p. 296.
[74] *Letters*, p. 176.
[75] *Ibid.*, p. 115.
[76] *Ibid.*, p. 175.
[77] Hagedorn, p. 370.
[78] *Ibid.*, p. 91.

General Index

Absalom and Achitophel (Dryden),
283
Adams, Helen Grace, letter from
Robinson to, 44, 190–191, 200
Aeneid (Virgil), 14
Allegory. See Symbolism
America, Robinson's attitude toward,
22, 32, 61, 112–113, 191, 235, 260, 261,
262, 269, 270
American Tragedy, An (Dreiser), 180
Andrea del Sarto (Browning), 199
Appearance and Reality (Bradley),
192
Arabella (Crabbe), 291
Arnold, Matthew, 3, 4, 193, 211, 296.
See also Culture and Anarchy;
Dover Beach; To Marguerite

Bates, Esther Willard, quoted, 15, 28,
278, 283–284, 291, 302–303; comments by Robinson to, 23, 151, 169,
196, 199, 245, 274, 275, 290, 292, 301;
letters from Robinson to, 15, 298
Beatty, Frederika, quoted, 276, 289
Benét, William Rose, 290
Betsky, Seymour, 277
Betts, Craven Langstroth, 245, 280;
letters from Robinson to, 219, 273,
275, 298, 302, 303
Biblical subjects and allusions in Robinson's poetry, 22, 33–34, 278–279.
See also Christianity; Job, Book of
Biographia Literaria (Coleridge), 88

Biographical and autobiographical in-
terpretation of Robinson's poems,
280–281, 289, 291, 298
Blair, Arthur, 281
Blank verse (Robinson's), effects
achieved in, 81–87; increasing use
of, 15, 63; earlier and later styles
compared, 81–83
Boswell, James, 240
Bradley, Francis Herbert, quoted, 54,
130. See also Appearance and Real-
ity
Braithwaite, William Stanley, 275;
comments by Robinson to, 1, 20
Brooke, Rupert, 65
Brooks, Van Wyck, 297
Brothers, The (Crabbe), 293–294
Brown, David, quoted, 288
Brown, Rollo Walter, 275, 298;
quoted, 24, 198, 292; comments by
Robinson to, 52, 196, 275–276, 293,
296
Browning, Robert, 219, 274, 279. See
also Andrea del Sarto; Rabbi ben
Ezra; Ring and the Book, The
Bryan, William Jennings, 258, 304
Burnham, George, 245, 279, 280
Butler, William E., 245
Bynner, Witter, letter from Robinson
to, 261

Caldwell, Erskine, 252
Carlyle, Thomas, 118. See also Sartor
Resartus

Redman, Ben Ray, 290; quoted, 101, 279, 287, 292
Richards, Mrs. Laura E., 213, 245, 275, 280; quoted, 198, 244, 290, 297; letters from Robinson to, 26–27, 54, 138, 151, 164, 210, 211, 214, 215, 216, 220, 257, 258, 264, 265, 270, 274, 275, 277, 282, 294, 297, 298, 300, 303
Ring and the Book, The (Browning), 177, 199
Robbins, Linville, 281
Robinson, Dean, 133, 214, 236
Robinson, Edwin Arlington, compulsion to write poetry, 9–13; practice and theory of poetic composition, 13–18; conception of the function of poetry, 18–23
 Obscurity of poetry: statement of the problem, 24–28, sources of obscurity: compression of style, 28–34, apparent diffuseness and use of negative or indirect statements, 34–40, insufficient data in narrative and dramatic poems, 40–43, symbolism and allegory, 43–45, dramatic method, 45–48, conviction of elusiveness and indeterminateness of human experience, 48–50
 Indifference of public to early poetry, 51–52; use of plain language, 53–55; use of traditional poetic devices, 55–56; adaptation of language to subject matter, 57–62; adaptation of form to subject matter: in sonnets, 62–68, in rhymed dramatic or emotional lyrics other than sonnets, 68–74, in rhymed reflective poems, 74–79, in unrhymed poetic forms, including blank verse, 79–87
 Definition of "organic form" as an approach to his poetry, 88–89; organic form achieved in poems by means of: repetition of words or symbols, 89–94, unity of material in narrative and dramatic poems, 94–98, narrative or dramatic structure, 98–106, character development in long narratives, 106–110, logical structure in reflective poems, 110–115, reciprocal effect of story and theme, 115–120
 Interest in individual human be-

ings, 121–122; classes of characters portrayed: apparent failures who achieve inward triumph, 122–126, apparent successes who are inward failures, 126–130, apparent total failures, 130–134, victims of loneliness, especially disappointed or bereaved lovers, 134–139, possessors of apparently unqualified happiness, 139–143; difficulty of hard and fast classification, 144–148
 Concern with inward experience rather than external behavior, 149–156; refusal to distinguish between physical and mental phenomena, 156–159; methods of character portrayal: physical appearance, 159–163, actions and thoughts, 163–169, monologue and dialogue, 169–176; attitude toward characters, 176–181; humor in characterization, 181–188
 Dislike of being called a philosopher, 189–190; "antimaterialism," 190–196; alleged pessimism: refuted by direct statements, 196–203, refuted by general tenor of work, 203–207, considered in relation to traditional systems, 208–216; belief in spiritual growth through struggle, 217–220; views on freedom versus determinism, 220–227; conception of character as fate, 227–230; acceptance of doctrine of Grace, 231–232
 Conception of the good life for the individual by himself: as involving the right calling and moral fortitude, 233–239, as involving appreciation of beauty, 239–242; conception of ideal human relations: between individuals in general, 242–249, between individuals of different sex, 249–256; conception of ideal society: in relation to American democracy in practice, 256–259, in relation to nationalism and capitalism, 259–265, in relation to the future of America and the world, 265–272
Robinson, Emma (Mrs. Herman Robinson), 10
Robinson, Henry Morton, quoted, 249
Robinson, Herman, 133, 279
Roosevelt, Franklin D., 266

Index to Robinson's Works and Characters

(Reference to the title of a poem may include
reference to a character named in the title.)